THE ANCIENT CITY

Y0-BCI-327

Greece and Rome were quintessentially urban societies. Ancient culture, politics and society arose and developed in the context of the polis and the civitas. In modern scholarship, the ancient city has been the subject of intense debates due to the strong association in Western thought between urbanism, capitalism and modernity. In this book, Arjan Zuiderhoek provides a survey of the main issues at stake in these debates, as well as a sketch of the chief characteristics of Greek and Roman cities. He argues that the ancient Greco-Roman city was indeed a highly specific form of urbanism but that this does not imply that the ancient city was somehow 'superior' or 'inferior' to forms of urbanism in other societies, just (interestingly) different. The book is aimed primarily at students of ancient history and general readers, but also at scholars working on urbanism in other periods and places.

ARJAN ZUIDERHOEK is Associate Professor of Ancient History at the Department of History, Ghent University. He is author of *The Politics of Munificence in the Roman Empire: Citizens, Elites and Benefactors in Asia Minor* (Cambridge University Press, 2009) and editor, with Paul Erdkamp and Koenraad Verboven, of *Ownership and Exploitation of Land and Natural Resources in the Roman World* (2015).

KEY THEMES IN ANCIENT HISTORY

EDITORS

P. A. Cartledge
Clare College, Cambridge

P. D. A. Garnsey
Jesus College, Cambridge

Key Themes in Ancient History aims to provide readable, informed and original studies of various basic topics, designed in the first instance for students and teachers of Classics and Ancient History, but also for those engaged in related disciplines. Each volume is devoted to a general theme in Greek, Roman, or where appropriate, Graeco-Roman history, or to some salient aspect or aspects of it. Besides indicating the state of current research in the relevant area, authors seek to show how the theme is significant for our own as well as ancient culture and society. By providing books for courses that are oriented around themes it is hoped to encourage and stimulate promising new developments in teaching and research in ancient history.

Other Books in the Series

Death-ritual and social structure in classical antiquity, by Ian Morris 978 0 521 37465 1 (hardback) 978 0 521 37611 2 (paperback)

Literacy and orality in ancient Greece, by Rosalind Thomas 978 0 521 37346 3 (hardback) 978 0 521 37742 3 (paperback)

Slavery and Society at Rome, by Keith Bradley 978 0 521 37287 9 (hardback) 978 0 521 37887 1 (paperback)

Law, violence, and community in classical Athens, by David Cohen 978 0 521 38167 3 (hardback) 978 0 521 38837 5 (paperback)

Public order in ancient Rome, by Wilfried Nippel 978 0 521 38327 1 (hardback) 978 0 521 38749 1 (paperback)

Friendship in the classical world, by David Konstan 978 0 521 45402 5 (hardback) 978 0 521 45998 3 (paperback)

Sport and society in ancient Greece, by Mark Golden 978 0 521 49698 8 (hardback) 978 0 521 49790 9 (paperback)

Food and society in classical antiquity, by Peter Garnsey 978 0 521 64182 1 (hardback) 978 0 521 64588 1 (paperback)

Banking and business in the Roman world, by Jean Andreau 978 0 521 38031 7 (hardback) 978 0 521 38932 7 (paperback)

Roman law in context, by David Johnston 978 0 521 63046 7 (hardback) 978 0 521 63961 3 (paperback)

Religions of the ancient Greeks, by Simon Price 978 0 521 38201 4 (hardback) 978 0 521 38867 2 (paperback)

Christianity and Roman society, by Gillian Clark 978 0 521 63310 9 (hardback) 978 0 521 63386 4 (paperback)

Trade in classical antiquity, by Neville Morley 978 0 521 63279 9 (hardback) 978 0 521 63416 8 (paperback)

Technology and culture in Greek and Roman antiquity, by Serafina Cuomo 978 0 521 81073 9 (hardback) 978 0 521 00903 4 (paperback)

Law and crime in the Roman world, by Jill Harries 978 0 521 82820 8 (hardback) 978 0 521 53532 8 (paperback)

The social history of Roman art, by Peter Stewart 978 0 521 81632 8 (hardback) 978 0 52101659 9 (paperback)

Ancient Greek political thought in practice, by Paul Cartledge 978 0 521 45455 1 (hardback) 978 0 521 45595 4 (paperback)

Asceticism in the Graeco-Roman world, by Richard Finn OP 978 0 521 86281 3 (hardback) 978 0 521 68154 4 (paperback)

Domestic space and social organisation in classical antiquity, by Lisa C. Nevett 978 0 521 78336 1 (hardback) 978 0 521 78945 5 (paperback)

Money in classical antiquity, by Sitta von Reden 978 0 521 45337 0 (hardback) 978 0 521 45952 5 (paperback)

Geography in classical antiquity, by Daniela Dueck and Kai Brodersen 978 0 521 19788 5 (hardback) 978 0 521 12025 8 (paperback)

Space and society in the Greek and Roman worlds, by Michael Scott 978 1 107 00915 8 (hardback) 978 1 107 40150 1 (paperback)

Studying gender in classical antiquity, by Lin Foxhall 978 0 521 55318 6 (hardback) 978 0 521 55739 9 (paperback)

The ancient Jews from Alexander to Muhammad, by Seth Schwartz 978 1 107 04127 1 (hardback) 978 1 107 66929 1 (paperback)

Language and society in the Greek and Roman worlds, by James Clackson 978 0 521 19235 4 (hardback) 978 0 521 14066 9 (paperback)

THE ANCIENT CITY

ARJAN ZUIDERHOEK

Universiteit Gent, Belgium

CAMBRIDGE
UNIVERSITY PRESS

University Printing House, Cambridge CB2 8BS, United Kingdom

One Liberty Plaza, 20th Floor, New York, NY 10006, USA

477 Williamstown Road, Port Melbourne, VIC 3207, Australia

4843/24, 2nd Floor, Ansari Road, Daryaganj, Delhi - 110002, India

79 Anson Road, #06-04/06, Singapore 079906

Cambridge University Press is part of the University of Cambridge.

It furthers the University's mission by disseminating knowledge in the pursuit of education, learning and research at the highest international levels of excellence.

www.cambridge.org
Information on this title: www.cambridge.org/9780521166010

© Arjan Zuiderhoek 2017

This publication is in copyright. Subject to statutory exception and to the provisions of relevant collective licensing agreements, no reproduction of any part may take place without the written permission of Cambridge University Press.

First published 2017

A catalogue record for this publication is available from the British Library

Library of Congress Cataloging in Publication data
Names: Zuiderhoek, Arjan, 1976- author.
Title: The ancient city / Arjan Zuiderhoek.
Description: Cambridge, United Kingdom : Cambridge University Press, 2016. |
Series: Key themes in ancient history
Identifiers: LCCN 2016011203 | ISBN 9780521198356 (Hardback)
Subjects: LCSH: Cities and towns–Rome. | Cities and towns–Greece. |
Civilization, Classical. | Greece–History–146 B.C.-323 A.D. | Rome–History–Empire,
30 B.C.-476 A.D. | BISAC: HISTORY / Ancient / General.
Classification: LCC DE86 .Z85 2016 | DDC 307.760938–dc23 LC record available at
https://lccn.loc.gov/2016011203

ISBN 978-0-521-19835-6 Hardback
ISBN 978-0-521-16601-0 Paperback

Cambridge University Press has no responsibility for the persistence or accuracy of URLs for external or third-party internet websites referred to in this publication, and does not guarantee that any content on such websites is, or will remain, accurate or appropriate.

For Irene, Maarten and Yrsa

Contents

List of Figures   *page* x
Acknowledgements   xi
List of Abbreviations   xii

1   Introduction: The Ancient City as Concept and Reality   1

2   Origins, Development and the Spread of Cities in the
     Ancient World   20

3   City and Country   37

4   Urban Landscape and Environment   56

5   Politics and Political Institutions   78

6   Civic Ritual and Civic Identity   94

7   Urban Society: Stratification and Mobility   106

8   The Urban Economy   131

9   City-States and Cities and States   149

10   The End of the Ancient City?   167

Bibliographical Essay   186
Bibliography   191
Index   221

Figures

4.1 Plan of Miletus (after 479 BCE)
  Source: A. von Gerkan, *Griechische Städteanlagen. Untersuchungen
  zur Entwicklung des Städtebaues im Altertum* © 1924 Walter de
  Gruyter, Abb. 6. Reprinted with permission of Walter de
  Gruyter GmbH   *page* 60

4.2 Plan of Priene (later fourth century BCE)
  Source: A. von Gerkan, *Griechische Städteanlagen. Untersuchungen
  zur Entwicklung des Städtebaues im Altertum* © 1924 Walter
  De Gruyter, Abb. 9. Reprinted with permission of Walter de
  Gruyter GmbH   61

4.3 Plan of Cosa (third and second century BCE)
  *Source: Ancient Cities: the Archaeology of Urban Life in the Ancient
  Near East and Egypt, Greece, and Rome*, 2nd edn, Charles Gates,
  © 2011 Routledge, 336, fig. 20.4. Reproduced by permission of
  Taylor & Francis Books UK   62

4.4 Diagram of a Roman legionary fort (*castrum*), Novaesium,
  Lower Germany
  *Source: Ancient Cities: the Archaeology of Urban Life in the Ancient
  Near East and Egypt, Greece, and Rome*, 2nd edn, Charles Gates,
  © 2011 Routledge, 334, fig. 20.3. Reproduced by permission of
  Taylor & Francis Books UK   63

4.5 Five blocks, Olynthus
  Source: Robinson, David Moore and Paul Augustus Clement.
  *Excavations at Olynthus: Part XII: Domestic and Public Architecture
  (with Excursus L on Pebble Mosaics with Colored Plates, Excursus II
  on Oecus Unit, Testimonia, List of Greek Words, Etc.).* Plate I.
  © 1946 Johns Hopkins University Press. Reprinted with permission
  of Johns Hopkins University Press.   64

Acknowledgements

This is a short book on a gigantic subject. As is inevitable with books like this, it is based on the detailed research of a great number of scholars past and present. Many colleagues have displayed an interest and have offered a word of advice. I would like to thank a number of people in particular. At Ghent, my fellow ancient historians Koen Verboven, Wim Broekaert, Peter Van Nuffelen, Marloes Deene, Lindsey Vandevoorde and Wouter Vanacker have been a constant source of support and encouragement throughout the period that I was working on this book. I would also like to thank my department colleagues Anne-Laure Van Bruaene, Jelle De Rock, Toon Vrints and Marc Boone, with whom I have now for several years been teaching an MA seminar on comparative urban history. This has been (and continues to be) intellectually very stimulating, as well as good fun, and it has provided me with much food for thought for this book. Paul Erdkamp and Henrik Mouritsen have been so kind as to make some of their work available to me in advance of publication. Above all, however, I am grateful to Peter Garnsey and Paul Cartledge, who not only invited me to contribute a volume to their series, but who also both read through the entire manuscript several times and provided me with numerous insightful comments and suggestions. As a result, this is a much better book than it would otherwise have been. Of course, it should not be presumed that they agree with everything that follows, and I alone am responsible for any errors that remain. Michael Sharp, Elizabeth Hanlon and Chloe Harries at Cambridge University Press have been a great pleasure to work with and were a constant source of support throughout the production process. Joris Angenon kindly helped with the illustrations. Last but by no means least, and on a more personal note, I am grateful to Irene, Maarten and Yrsa for their constant love and support. This one is for the three of you!

Syll.[3]	W. Dittenberger, *Sylloge Inscriptionum Graecarum*. 3rd edn. Leipzig (1924)
TAPA	*Transactions of the American Philological Association*
ZPE	*Zeitschrift für Papyrologie und Epigraphik*

CHAPTER I

Introduction: The Ancient City as Concept and Reality

Urbanism has many faces, as the following two descriptions – of indigenous New World and West African Islamic cities respectively – make clear:

> Indigenous urban centers in central Mexico were arranged according to astronomical bearings dictated by cosmological criteria ... They were focused on great squares that served ceremonial, as well as commercial, needs or functions, close to prominent temples and palaces to project a particular social order and proclaim dynastic power. As the visible markers of wealth and status dissipated with increasing distance from the city center, crowded residential quarters for commoners were organized around more modest, sacred places. At the urban perimeter, the landscape dissolved into less structured villages and hamlets surrounded by market gardens.[1]

> Traditional Hausa cities have a clearly identifiable focal center, a bounding wall, and building of fairly uniform character occupying most of the land between. There is usually a triple focus, for in addition to the Emir's palace and the main city market there is the Grand Mosque, often an imposing building rising above the generally even skyline ... The city is divided into wards or quarters, and further sub-divided into compounds, in each of which rights of occupation are passed down within a family. All compounds once included some cultivated land, though most families also had fields within and outside the city wall: but as the population has grown, ever more dwellings have been built within each compound. Narrow winding paths run between the compound walls, which often remain intact, broken only by a single doorway ... Minor markets and small mosques are spread through the various wards, and craft industries are also widely scattered, so that for many people residence and workplace are the same.[2]

This book is about one particular, historical type of urbanism: the ancient Greek and Roman city. It is not a comprehensive treatment of its topic, that is, it neither deals with all of the different aspects and features of ancient Greek and Roman cities, nor with all of the modern scholarly

---

[1] Butzer (2008) 89–90.   [2] O'Connor (1983) 196–7, cited in Kusimba (2008) 232–3.

discussions and debates concerning Greco-Roman urbanism. Rather, my aim has been to outline what I consider to be the most distinctive features of Greek and Roman cities – features which single them out as one particular manifestation of the global, world-historical phenomenon of urbanism – and to deal with some of the modern discussion regarding these features.

The book is bracketed by two broadly 'historical' chapters (Chapter 2 'Origins, development and the spread of cities in the ancient world' and Chapter 10 'The end of the ancient city?'), in which I explicitly discuss some aspects of the development of ancient urbanism over time. The chapters in between have broad thematic titles, e.g. 'City and country', 'Urban landscape and environment', 'Politics and political institutions', 'Civic ritual and civic identity', and so on. Here, the stress is on continuities and similarities rather than on change and diversity (although these two aspects are not entirely ignored) so as to delineate most clearly the specific characteristics of ancient urbanism. In each of these chapters, I focus on those aspects of, say, Greco-Roman urban landscapes or civic politics that I consider most typical. I am well aware that the choices that I have made, both of inclusion and of omission, can be questioned. Also, it might be argued that I generalise too much and am not sensitive enough to the particularities of time and place. However, besides providing students and other interested readers with a brief introduction into some of the major aspects of the topic, my main purpose in writing this book has been to provide scholars interested in the comparative study of urbanism (whether they are historians and archaeologists working on other periods or social scientists and others active in urban studies) with a useful 'working definition' or 'model' of ancient Greco-Roman urbanism, based on a fairly wide range of existing research. Models are always provocative since for the sake of analytical clarity they highlight some aspects of the phenomenon under study while ignoring or diminishing others. That, however, is partly the point: if this book succeeds in provoking people to pursue their own research and to come to their own conclusions regarding the various aspects of ancient civic life, or to include the ancient city in comparative analyses of (pre-modern) urbanism, then it has well served a main part of its purpose.

Although I deal with aspects of the ancient city broadly from Homeric times (eighth/seventh centuries BCE) until late antiquity and draw on material and discussions relating to cities throughout the regions that eventually came to constitute the Roman Empire (though with an unavoidable emphasis on Greece/Athens and Italy/Rome, given the bias of both ancient sources and much modern debate), there is one important thematic demarcation: this book is about the ancient city and civic life, that is, about aspects of ancient urbanism, but not about *urbanisation*. Even though there is some brief discussion of urban networks in Chapter 3 on 'City and country', the data and literature on pre-modern urbanisation are sufficiently complex and wide-ranging for a comparative study of ancient urbanisation processes to require a volume of its own. To some extent, it is a different topic, and though I touch upon it from time to time, it is not systematically dealt with here.[3]

Reading through the vignettes of New World and West African urbanism cited above, it is possible to discern both differences and similarities between these two descriptions, on the one hand, and differences and similarities between these descriptions and Greco-Roman urbanism, on the other. Central squares with temples around them, for instance, sound familiar to classical scholars, as do workshops doubling as residences, but city plans dictated by astronomy and narrow winding paths (instead of straight paved roads) have a less familiar ring to them. The similarities we perceive between manifestations of urbanism widely scattered in time and space would suggest that it is indeed justifiable to speak of 'the city' as a phenomenon shared by different cultures and societies. Yet at the same time, the idiosyncrasies displayed by the urban traditions of different societies would seem to lend credence to particular culture-bound categories such as 'the Maya city', 'the medieval European city' and 'the (pre-modern) Chinese city'. Even within particular societies or cultures, moreover, the diversity of urban experience can be breathtaking: one need only compare a small Archaic Greek polis or a modest Roman provincial town with the sprawling urban mass of the imperial capital of Rome or other imperial urban giants, such as Alexandria in Egypt or Syrian Antioch.

In the remainder of this chapter, I shall discuss some of the answers that scholars have given to the question 'What is a city?' and also to the question of whether it is justifiable to speak of 'the ancient city' as a specific analytical category. Since some of the answers that have been given to this latter question were influenced by several long-lasting debates in western scholarship on the nature of Greek, Roman and later European urbanism, we shall pay attention to these debates as well, and also explain why, in spite of some recent scholarly trends, the study of ancient cities still remains highly relevant.

---

[3] For discussions of ancient urbanisation, see Woolf (1997); Osborne and Cunliffe (2005); Bowman and Wilson (2011).

What is an (Ancient) City?

'It will not have escaped notice that I have so far avoided defining what I mean by a city', Moses Finley wrote, a few pages into his famous essay on the ancient city. 'Neither geographers nor sociologists nor historians have succeeded in agreeing on a definition', he continued, '[y]et we all know sufficiently what we mean by the label, in general terms'.[4] This, as the archaeologist George Cowgill has noted in a different context, is a bit like saying that cities are like pornography – we cannot define it but we know it when we see it.[5] Yet as usual Finley was onto something: as a (historical) topic of study, the city has proved particularly intractable. Scholars have variously tried to come up with some sort of trans-cultural and trans-historical definition of the city, but none of these attempts has been entirely successful, at least not 'without excluding whole periods of history in which we all know cities existed', in Finley's words.[6]

Most familiar is probably the demographic approach, which comes in two varieties: a focus on population size and density (population magnitude) and a focus on the characteristic (demographic) features of an urban population (population makeup).[7] How large does a settlement have to be to count as a city? Historians of early modern Europe have often used 10,000 inhabitants as a yardstick.[8] Clearly this would disqualify the majority of Greek poleis and Roman civitates which, on the basis of other criteria, are generally thought of as cities, as well as many cities in later periods.[9] Throughout Greco-Roman antiquity, the majority of urban residents would have lived in towns of 5,000 inhabitants or fewer. Moreover, the socio-political fusion of urban core and rural territory typical of Greco-Roman cities complicates the use of population numbers attested in ancient sources for purposes of cross-cultural comparison (e.g. with medieval Europe, where a strict administrative separation between town and country was often observed).[10]

An alternative is not to look at overall population size as such but at population *density*, or nucleation. As Spiro Kostof has observed: 'Cities are places where a certain energized crowding of people takes place. This has nothing to do with absolute size or with absolute numbers: it has to do with settlement density. The vast majority of towns in the pre-industrial

---

[4] Finley (1981a) 5.   [5] Cowgill (2003a) 1.   [6] Finley (1981a) 5.
[7] The distinction and the terms used derive from Storey (2006a) 2.   [8] See De Vries (1984).
[9] Clark (2009) 7 defines small towns (meaning, *c.* 1500 CE, a place with 2,000 inhabitants or less) as 'a prominent feature of the European urban network (unlike elsewhere in the world)'.
[10] Scheidel (2007) 79–80.

world were small: a population of 2,000 or less was not uncommon, and one of 10,000 would be noteworthy'.[11] Recently, Robin Osborne has advocated a similar population density approach to urbanisation in Archaic Greece.[12] From a cross-cultural perspective, however, the density approach gets us into trouble too, for it cannot really accommodate the so-called dispersed cities one finds in parts of pre-colonial Africa, Asia and the New World, which somewhat counter-intuitively combine relatively low population densities spread out over vast areas with other, clearly urban features.[13]

Instead of focussing on population magnitude (size and density), one might also inquire into the specific makeup of an urban population, that is, in terms of its particular demographic features (fertility, mortality, morbidity, age structure and sex ratio). Here we can point, for instance, to the much-debated 'urban graveyard' theory, according to which in larger preindustrial cities, the number of deaths always outstripped the number of births, necessitating a continuous inflow of migrants to stop the urban population from dwindling over time.[14] Or, one might concentrate on the specific socioeconomic makeup of an urban population. The populations of places we tend to call cities are generally characterised by differentiation according to occupation, status and wealth, resulting in social heterogeneity and hierarchy.[15] Occupational specialisation and occupational diversity are often singled out as particularly distinctive criteria: the city population and the surrounding countryside constitute a market of sufficient size to make specialised production of goods and services economically possible.[16] These criteria create some problems for small Archaic and Classical Greek poleis, where a majority of citizens would have been farmers; but even in such settlements, artisanal specialisation was probably greater than in a village. Moreover, these poleis are often considered to be cities on the basis of yet other criteria, such as density of settlement or having a clearly defined urban centre, which was true of almost every polis.[17]

This brings us to yet another way one might define cities, that is, by means of layout and the structure of the built environment (urban landscape): the presence of central squares or plazas, paved streets, defensive

[11] Kostof (1991) 37, cited in Marcus and Sabloff (2008b) 12.   [12] Osborne (2005).
[13] Kusimba, Barut Kusimba and Agbaje-Williams (2006) with reference to Yoruba cities; Hansen (2008) 75–6 with many references to specialist literature.
[14] See Chapter 4 for discussion.   [15] Kostof (1991) 37–8.
[16] Mumford (1961) 103–9 for a classic analysis.
[17] As the research by the Copenhagen Polis Centre has made clear, see Hansen (2003) 266–7, 237–76; (2006) 98–100.

walls and gates, public architecture for religious, political or ceremonial/ entertainment purposes and some element of town planning. It is perhaps in this sphere that the intuitive understanding of a settlement as 'urban' (we know it when we see it) is strongest. Thus Cortés and his Conquistadores, upon entering Tenochtitlan, the capital of the Aztec empire of Mexico, immediately recognised the place as urban, as 'a great city', despite the fact that it was the product of a civilisation entirely alien to them, a culture that had developed independently on another continent.[18]

As if taking their cue from this famous encounter, in a tradition stretching back to V. Gordon Childe's famous 1950 paper on 'The Urban Revolution', archaeologists working on 'early cities' in Egypt, Mesopotamia, Asia, Africa and the Americas have increasingly engaged in wide-ranging comparative studies of urbanism. They have observed striking similarities between cities across space and time, particularly in terms of layout and the general structure of urban landscapes, for instance between New World and Old World urbanism, or, to mention just one particular example, between the city of Amarna in New Kingdom Egypt and late medieval London.[19] Structural similarities between pre-modern cities have also been noted by historians and sociologists, most prominently by Gideon Sjöberg, who argued that the pre-eminent distinction in urban development throughout time was that between the preindustrial and the industrial city.[20] Even this long-accepted distinction is now being questioned. As Monica Smith has argued, pre-modern and modern cities share such features as fluid urban-rural boundaries (i.e. it is often impossible to mark clearly the point where the city ends and the countryside begins as urban features might continue well beyond official 'city limits' or city walls; in other words, there is nothing specifically modern about 'suburban sprawl'). Pre-modern and modern cities might also share characteristics such as links with distant hinterlands through exchange and the use of luxury goods as social markers. What all these similarities through time and space suggest is 'that the capacities for human interaction in concentrated locations are exercised within a limited set of parameters'.[21] This, in turn, prompts the observation (in Glenn Storey's words) that '[h]uman nucleation behaviour into cities might be a form of [evolutionary] group selection strategy that has proved eminently adaptable for humans and has fostered strong interspecific ties of cooperation'.[22]

---

[18] Renfrew (2008) 45, citing Díaz del Castillo (1956) 216.
[19] Renfrew (2008) 44–9; on Amarna and London, see Carl et al. (2000) 344–5.   [20] Sjöberg (1960).
[21] M.L. Smith (2003b) 3–8 (quote from p. 6).   [22] Storey (2006a) 23.

Along such broad interdisciplinary lines, combining insights from human geography, ecology and evolutionary biology, we may eventually be able to arrive at some universal understanding of urbanism. However, the attempt requires analysis at a very high level of generality, which might at first sight seem unhelpful to historians and archaeologists interested in specific urban cultures. Yet the broad comparative study of world urbanism does supply us with a rough cross-cultural template that can be used to sketch the outlines of a particular type of urbanism, in order to bring out, as sharply as possible, its cultural specificities.

To do this properly, however, we need, in addition to the mostly 'etic', outside analytical perspectives mentioned so far, to try also for a more 'emic' approach that looks at the ways in which people in the past themselves defined and thought about those settlements in their society that we would call 'urban'. One way to do this is to look at the legal and political terms and criteria used to define cities within the society one studies, a strategy often employed by historians. Thus, for instance, historians of medieval Europe have focussed on civic charters and the legal and political terminology used to describe and acknowledge civic status.[23] In the ancient world, particularly under Roman rule, cities often had clearly defined legal statuses, being, for instance, *municipia, coloniae* or *civitates peregrinae* (see Chapter 5). In looser terms, ancient texts from Homer to Constantine recognise as essential elements required of a polis or civitas (i) the presence of a political community, a citizenry and (ii) the presence of a particular set of public buildings and civic amenities.[24] Although often somewhat tautological, such statements and descriptions allow us some insight into the criteria by which Greeks and Romans distinguished their poleis and civitates from other types of settlement. On occasion, the emic approach can seem misleading: the Greek travel writer Pausanias, writing during the Roman imperial period, noted that even an insignificant place like Panopeus in Phocis, Greece, which had no

---

[23] See Boone (2013) for an overview.

[24] Note e.g. Homer, *Il.* 1.1–305, 2.1–282 (the Greek army before Troy behaves like the popular assembly of a polis); *Od.* 2.1–259 (popular assembly on Ithaca); 9.105–115; Alcaeus fr. 28, fr. 112; Thuc. 7.77.4; Plato, *Leg.* 778a–779d (men make the polis); Homer *Od.* 6.262–8 (a description of the urban landscape of Scheria, polis of the Phaeacians), Lycurgus, *Leoc.* 150; Pausanias 10.4.1 (territory, buildings and amenities make the polis); Vergil, *Aen.* 1. 419–29, 441, 446–9, 505–9 (Roman vision of the city as consisting of public buildings, elective political institutions and laws and statutes projected on the mythical foundation of Carthage; see Edmondson (2006) 250); Dio Chrys., *Or.* 7 (vivid descriptions of civic buildings and an account of a lively popular assembly, with even poor herdsmen holding citizenship and participating); *CIL* 3.7000 (letter of the emperor Constantine to the town of Orcistus, stressing its civic character by referring to its large citizen population and splendid buildings and amenities).

public buildings at all, was in his day thought of as a polis (10.4.1), while a large and powerful polis like Classical Sparta arguably had no clearly defined urban centre (Thucydides 1.10.2).[25] On the whole, however, Greek and Roman sources do refer to either one, and often to both, of the two elements just mentioned (citizenry and urban core with public buildings and amenities) when describing poleis and civitates.[26]

What, then, is a city? Given that, through application of a few very strict criteria to define urbanism, we often lose more, in cross-cultural terms, than we gain, and since a clear scientific definition of urbanism as a type of human nucleation behaviour still lies in the future (if indeed it will ever be forthcoming), it is probably best to work with concepts of urbanism, whether general or culture-specific (e.g. Greco-Roman urbanism), that are a bit fuzzy around the edges. One relatively useful strategy has already been mentioned, which was also successfully employed by Mogens Herman Hansen and his colleagues at the Copenhagen Polis Centre in their massive research project on the Archaic and Classical Greek polis, namely to focus on those settlements that the Greeks (and, for this book, Romans) themselves considered to be poleis (or *civitates, municipia,* or *coloniae*...).[27] Another, compatible approach is suggested by Glenn R. Storey in his introduction to a recent collection of papers on *Urbanism in the Preindustrial World,* namely to regard as cities those places which are considered to be cities by the majority of specialist scholars who study them, even if such sites 'may not look like a city according to our modern standards'.[28] Though not ideal, these two strategies, when combined, in practice mostly suffice for the purpose of comparative research, and they also underlie my approach in this book.

What, though, was 'the ancient city'? Can we actually, with any intellectual justification, speak of 'Greco-Roman urbanism', as I have done so far? My argument, in this book, is that we can, and the book itself is an attempt to provide a sketch of this particular type of urbanism. There were some essential differences between Greek and Roman cities, of course, and to some extent these will become apparent in subsequent chapters. Concepts of citizenship differed somewhat, for instance, with the Romans developing a far more legalistic notion (citizenship as a clear, legally defined set of duties and privileges), making it much easier for them to

---

[25] See Hansen (1997) 34–5 for a different view of Sparta.

[26] Hansen (2006) 56–65 on 'the polis as city [i.e. with a clear urban core] and state', though, contrary to Hansen, the fact that poleis (and civitates) were political communities does not necessarily make them 'states', see Chapter 9 for discussion.

[27] Hansen (2006) 56.   [28] Storey (2006a) 2.

admit foreigners and even freed slaves to the citizen body.[29] To mention some other differences, Roman centuriation practices arguably imply a far greater desire to control and administer the shape and division of civic territory than we can find among the Greeks[30], and Roman cities from the earliest days of imperialist expansion in Italy had been part of a hierarchy of strictly defined civic statuses, with each status implying a specific legal relationship with the city of Rome itself.[31] On the whole, however, the similarities outweighed the differences, as I hope this book will make clear. Since this argument is essentially contained in the chapters that follow, I shall limit myself here to discussing briefly several famous earlier attempts to formulate a general 'model' of the ancient Greco-Roman city.

'Roman cities were just like Greek cities', Nicholas Purcell has recently written, referring to strong similarities in the manner of exploitation of territories, social structure, expressions of communal identity and urban landscapes. Purcell's essay is mildly polemical, for, as he notes, 'the idea that ancient urbanism should be taken as a single phenomenon ... has not been popular among ancient historians' even though '[i]t is familiar to archaeologists'. He justifiably singles out Frank Kolb's major study of *Die Stadt im Altertum* as one important exception among more recent scholarship.[32] However, for several important nineteenth- and twentieth-century thinkers, 'the ancient city', comprising both the Greek polis and the Roman civitas, was an analytical category of crucial significance. Here I refer primarily to Fustel de Coulanges, Max Weber and Moses Finley. For all three, delineating the contours of 'the ancient city' as an ideal type served to stress the essential *differences* between antiquity and modernity, and for each of them, emphasising these differences served a broader political and intellectual agenda.

The French historian Numa Denis Fustel de Coulanges was provoked to write his *La Cité antique*, published in 1864, by the use Jacobin revolutionaries had made of ancient Greco-Roman examples to justify radically egalitarian policies.[33] In this he was a late representative of the *Idéologues,* a group of liberal intellectuals who in the decades around 1800 had already sharply criticised the Jacobin use of antiquity as inspiration for the (violent) reform of French society.[34] Greek and Roman mentality and institutions, Fustel argued, were irremediably different from

---

[29] E.g. Gauthier (1981).　　　[30] Though note Boyd and Jameson (1981).
[31] Cornell (1995), esp. 345–52.　　　[32] Purcell (2010) 579, 590; Kolb (1984).
[33] Fustel de Coulanges (2001) 5; Momigliano (1994) 169; Vlassopoulos (2007a) 30–1.
[34] Vlassopoulos (2007a) 30–1, 45–7.

those of later Europe. The ancient polis or civitas, according to Fustel, found its origin in a primordial, Indo-European notion of private property (which at a stroke also ruled out 'primitive communism' as mankind's pristine state, another revolutionary favourite).[35] Early Greeks and Romans worshipped their ancestors, who were spiritually located in the hearth of the household. Ancestor worship was therefore closely linked with the cult of Hestia or Vesta, the hearth-goddess. Given that this religion was centred on the family house and the family tomb, possession by the family of the house and its tomb and the land on which these stood was sacred and inalienable. Over time, the unification of families (*gentes*) into phratries, tribes and, ultimately, cities transferred these notions to the level of the community, exemplified by the cult of the civic hearth. Ancient cities, Fustel aimed to show, thus came into being in a way fundamentally alien to the medieval and early modern European urban experience.

The great German sociologist Max Weber was similarly preoccupied with the differences between Greco-Roman and medieval European cities, but in his case the preoccupation stemmed from his desire to explain the origins of European capitalist modernity. Although he would famously stress the role played by the Protestant Reformation in stimulating 'the spirit of capitalism' in northwestern Europe, the origin of European commercialism lay for Weber in the specific structures of the medieval city and the collective mentality of its burghers. In this he stood in a tradition going back, via Werner Sombart, Karl Bücher, Karl Marx and others, to Adam Smith.[36] Like the economist Bücher, who in 1893 had aroused the ire of contemporary ancient historians, above all Eduard Meyer, by contrasting the medieval 'city economy' (*Stadtwirtschaft*) and modern national economy (*Volkswirtschaft*) with what he called the ancient 'household economy' (*Hauswirtschaft*), Weber employed an ideal type of the ancient city to bring out, by contrast, the unique characteristics of the medieval city. Ancient cities, according to Weber, were in origin clubs of warrior-farmers, whose membership (citizenship) and political participation were predicated on their ownership of land in the community's territory, and who supplied their own armoury.[37] The ancient polis or civitas thus represented a union of town and country, and even when the cities became more 'democratic', admitting the landless to their citizen bodies, agrarian interests continued to reign supreme, as exemplified by

---

[35] Momigliano (1994) 169.   [36] Finley (1981a).
[37] Weber (1972) 809; see Martin (1994) 97–9 for a good short discussion of Weber's view of the ancient city.

the *thetes'* and proletarians' eternal call to redistribute the land and abolish debts.[38] Citizens might engage in some trade and manufacture on the side, but, especially among the elite, agriculture remained the most important source of income. Since this income was derived from the countryside as rent, without providing a stream of manufactured products in return (as the medieval producer city did), the ancient city was a consumer city, a concept Weber borrowed from Sombart.[39] The presence of slaves, moreover, restricted free labour and blocked the formation of a true and prosperous trading and manufacturing class organised in guilds. The ancient city was, first and foremost, a political association of citizens, and ancient man a *homo politicus*, unlike the medieval European *homo economicus*.[40]

The most famous model of the ancient city, and one that has played a dominant role in ancient historical debates over the past forty years, was however developed by the Cambridge ancient historian Moses Finley. Finley was strongly influenced by Weber, and took over his notion of the ancient city as a consumer city, yet developed it more fully in a highly specific way, so that it came to form the analytical core of a much broader model of 'the ancient economy'.[41] According to Finley, the strong link that existed in antiquity between citizenship and agriculture bred a mentality, particularly among the citizen-elites of the poleis and civitates, which was fiercely anti-commercial and acquisitive, not productive, discouraging productivity-enhancing investments. This mentality, along with the prevalence of the ideal of the free, self-supporting citizen-farmer, led to an offloading of commercial and manufacturing work onto marginal groups, mainly slaves, freedmen and resident foreigners, which obstructed the formation of a commercial middle class. The same ideal, moreover, prevented the development of proper markets in land (real property could be owned only by citizens), labour (working for a wage was considered slave-like) and capital (lending at interest between citizens was morally suspect, and most borrowing was for non-productive purposes).[42] Thus, the social structure of the ancient city, and the mentality and ideals associated with it, directly blocked the development of a commercial and industrial capitalism along later European lines.

Two of the most distinctive characteristics of the ancient Greco-Roman world, slavery and democracy, were also direct products of the ancient city

---

[38] Weber (1972) 797; Martin (1994) 97.
[39] Weber (1972) 797, 803; Finley (1981a) 12–17; Martin (1994) 97.
[40] Weber (1972) 798, 805; Finley (1981a) 15; Martin (1994) 98.   [41] Finley (1999 [1973]).
[42] For good discussion of Finley's views on the ancient economy see Morris (1994) and (1999).

and its particular citizenship structure. Finley linked the rise of slavery to the abolition of debt-bondage and the development of citizenship in Archaic Greece and Rome, which generated a direct need for an alternative source of exploitable labour. When, in the later Roman Empire, citizenship lost its socio-political value, the statuses of slaves and ordinary citizens gradually converged, since the free poor could now be exploited again as easily as their distant debt-bound ancestors in early Archaic times.[43] Even if slavery was a distinct element of the ancient city, however, the notion of the basic political equality of all adult male citizens also created the conditions for a historically unique level of political participation, particularly during the Greek Classical period and in Republican Rome.[44]

These models of the ancient city, particularly the one developed by Finley, were to exert an enormous influence on subsequent scholarship, an influence which continues to this day. Much of the reception has been (highly) critical, and has led not just to a questioning of whether one could justifiably employ a model of ancient urbanism that encompasses both Greek and Roman cities, but also, in the case of the post-Finley debates, to a devaluation of the phenomenon of urbanism itself as a variable in broader analyses of ancient economic and socio-political development. Fustel, Weber and Finley have all been praised for their comparative approach. Yet it will not have escaped notice that, in stressing the otherness of antiquity, all three were engaged in a much broader discourse concerning the nature and causes of western exceptionalism, that is, the unique development towards capitalism, the Industrial Revolution and modern liberal society in which western European medieval cities were thought to have played a crucial part. It is to these issues, and the impact they have had on recent research concerning the ancient city, that we shall now turn.

Grand Debates, New Directions

In Finley's model of the ancient economy, his conceptualisation of the ancient city as a consumer city served as an explanation for the ancient world's relative economic underdevelopment (compared to medieval and early modern Europe). As we saw, Finley's strong emphasis on the ideological link between agriculture and citizenship that comes to the fore

---

[43] Finley (1998 [1980]), see in particular Shaw's introduction (pp. 38–9) for a good summary of Finley's views. For the most recent discussion of late Roman slavery, see Harper (2011), who criticises the notion of a 'merger' of slaves and the free poor in the later Roman world.

[44] Finley (1983), (1985).

particularly in elite texts such as Xenophon's *Oeconomicus* and Cicero's *De Officiis* led him to conclude that in the ancient city, trade and manufacture were driven to the social margins, carried out by relatively poor, low status individuals (slaves, freedmen, resident foreigners). Hence, unlike their medieval counterparts, ancient cities did not produce a bourgeois class that could initiate a commercial take-off which would lead, ultimately, to capitalism and industrialisation (here Finley differed slightly from Weber, who had identified, in some periods of antiquity, notably the late Republic, a 'political capitalism' based on imperialist exploitation[45]).

Responses to Finley's views of the ancient city and its role in the ancient economy can be divided into two broad categories. First, there were those who (with some justification) argued that Finley had ignored whole swathes of mainly documentary evidence (e.g. inscriptions, papyri, and coins) and archaeological data that showed that the ancient urban trading and manufacturing sectors had been considerably more sophisticated and important in social and economic terms than his model allowed for. Scholars who took this line strongly questioned Finley's identification of ancient cities as consumer cities and often argued for the existence in antiquity of a variety of city types, while some created their own ideal types, such as 'the service city' (as we shall see in Chapter 3, however, despite the arguments of Finley *and* those of most of his critics, there is no *a priori* reason why the presence of consumer cities should imply a commercially underdeveloped, static economy).[46]

A second broad response to the Finley model, which developed partly out of weariness over the stalemate that the debate on the nature of the ancient economy had reached by the late 1990s, was to question the validity of the city as an explanatory variable as such. Thus, scholars have increasingly drawn attention to institutions and notions of community that transcended or existed alongside or within the civic community, such as *ethnos* (nation, people, ethnic group) or clubs and associations (*phylai*, phratries, *hetaireiai, collegia*) of all kinds, their studies suggesting a more complex and multifaceted model of ancient social relations in which 'the polis' was not people's sole frame of reference.[47]

Similarly, economic historians have questioned whether it is justified to speak of a single 'ancient economy' with a 'Greco-Roman city' as its nucleus, as Finley did.[48] It has been felt that the difference in scale between

---

[45] Love (1991).   [46] Engels (1990).
[47] Morgan (2003); Cohen (2002); Hall (2002); Verboven (2007); N. F. Jones (1999); Van Nijf (1997).
[48] See Mattingly and Salmon (2001b) 8–9.

Archaic and Classical Greece, on the one hand, and the Hellenistic kingdoms and Rome, on the other, in terms both of the territorial extent of states and of the size and number of cities, slides into a difference of quality, making, say, pre-modern China or Mogul India a better comparison to the Roman Empire than the Greek societies that preceded it.[49] Analysis of larger structures (urban systems, kingdoms, the empire) is becoming the norm: one is hard put to find in the recent *Cambridge Economic History of the Greco-Roman World* much analysis of the possible effects of the city, civic structures and civic ideology on economic performance.[50] In addition, the incorporation of archaeological survey data into ancient history has focussed historians' attention on rural society and the peasantry, on life 'beyond the Acropolis' as actually lived by the majority of the ancient world's inhabitants.[51] Finally, in recent ecologically inspired accounts of ancient Mediterranean history, the city recedes into the background completely, becoming, in the words of Horden and Purcell, '"epiphenomenal" to larger ecological processes'.[52]

These ancient historical arguments 'against the city' are in many ways in line with a general development within pre-modern European and world economic history away from the city as an important category of explanation. Some ancient historians questioned the stark contrast Finley, following Weber, had drawn between ancient consumer cities and medieval and early modern producer cities, arguing that in pre-modern Europe, only a handful of cities could really be characterised as the sort of (proto-) capitalist commercial powerhouses Weber and particularly Finley had in mind.[53] In this they were following the lead of their colleagues specialising in later periods: R. J. Holton called the theory that the medieval European cities and their commercial bourgeoisies were the most important factor in 'the Rise of Capitalism/the West' an 'ex post facto folk myth of the modern western bourgeoisie and its urbanist intellectuals'.[54] Robert Brenner argued that agrarian class relations rather than commercial cities provided the best explanation for western European exceptionalism while E. A. Wrigley demonstrated that the sustained economic growth of the Industrial Revolution resulted from the adoption of fossil fuels as sources

---

[49] See Bang (2008) for a comparison between the Roman and Moghul empires; Scheidel (2009) and (2015) on Rome and China.

[50] Scheidel, Morris and Saller (2007), though see now Erdkamp (2012).

[51] See Potter (1979); Van Andel and Runnels (1987); Cartledge (1993b), (1995); Garnsey (1998a) and the papers in part III of De Ligt and Northwood (2008).

[52] Horden and Purcell (2000) 90.   [53] This is the *Leitmotiv* of Pleket (1990).

[54] Holton (1986) 11.

of energy rather than from a centuries-long development of capitalism with a distant origin in medieval urban communities.[55] All of this, of course, prompts a question: if medieval and early modern European cities were not, after all, that important to the 'Rise of the West', are ancient historians not also wasting their time when they study Greco-Roman cities as a means to explaining ancient economy and society?[56] Do cities actually matter?

The problem with framing the question in this way, of course, is that despite all of the arguments *pro* and *contra* the importance of cities we still remain locked in a rather narrowly Eurocentric discourse, in which we allow the intellectual value of the attempt to study cities in other periods and parts of the world to be determined by the relative value accorded to cities as an explanatory variable in European history. This is, to say the least, an arbitrary and parochial point of view. By this I do not mean to argue that medieval and early modern European urbanism cannot be used as a comparative example when studying ancient cities, just as one would refer to urbanism in other parts of the world (indeed, in the chapters that follow references to later Europe are often made); the argument is rather that to privilege the European urban experience *at the expense of the rest of the world* may in the end not be very helpful if we want to come to a better understanding of Greek and Roman cities.

Here we touch upon another argument that has recently been made against allocating a central position to the ancient city in our accounts of ancient history. The ancient city has exerted a powerful influence in modern political thought, for instance in the work of thinkers such as Karl Popper and Hannah Arendt, while a tendency to use the ancient world to formulate theories on how to change contemporary politics and society, which Fustel so deplored among the Jacobins, can be traced back at least to Machiavelli. Yet, as Kostas Vlassopoulos has recently shown, accounts of Greek history that settle on the polis as the primary form of political, social and economic organisation in the ancient Greek world start appearing only from the mid-nineteenth century onwards, following in the footsteps of an earlier, Romantic-era conceptualisation of the ancient Greeks as a 'nation'.[57] Behind this relentless focus on the polis, which continued to characterise scholarship well into the late 1990s and beyond, Vlassopoulos

---

[55] Jongman (2002). See Brenner (1976); Wrigley (1990) and Pomeranz (2000) for a world-historical adaptation of Wrigley's thesis, comparing eighteenth-century Europe and China and adding colonies to coal as another contingent western advantage.
[56] Jongman (1991), (2002) for good discussions of this topic.   [57] Vlassopoulos (2007a).

detects a Eurocentric master narrative in which the Greek polis is separated from its wider Mediterranean and Near Eastern context and presented as 'the first stage' in the history of the West. This, Vlassopoulos argues, has been to the detriment of ancient historical scholarship: other ancient Greek forms of socio-political organisation besides the polis (e.g. *ethnos* and *koinon*) were largely ignored, as was diversity among the Greek poleis themselves, and ancient historians lost their connection with developments in scholarship on the ancient Near East.

Vlassopoulos certainly has a point, and his concerns have been felt to some extent by other scholars. As he himself acknowledges, recent studies have in various ways attempted to break free from the dominant polis perspective. Catherine Morgan has done important research on *ethne*, while, paradoxically perhaps given their exclusive focus on the polis, the highly empirical work of the Copenhagen Polis Centre has dispelled a number of historiographical myths concerning 'the polis' (e.g. that political autonomy was a key characteristic of the polis).[58] Most revolutionary perhaps has been the ecologically inspired account of Mediterranean history by Peregrine Horden and Nicholas Purcell, in which they, as we saw, reduce cities, in ecological terms, to epiphenomena and focus on the fragmentation of the Mediterranean region into diverse micro-ecologies and the interaction (connectivity) between these.[59] Vlassopoulos himself argues that we should aim to study Greek poleis as part of a *système-monde* (a concept he borrows from Fernand Braudel), a larger system of interacting entities (communities, groups and regions) that is, in a sense, a world unto itself.[60]

What are the implications of these views for a book such as this? Is writing a book on 'the ancient city' an intrinsically Eurocentric affair? Are we engaged in the study of a mere epiphenomenon? I would disagree. Vlassopoulos actually points to the way forward, by highlighting a number of important similarities between Greek poleis and Near Eastern cities in terms of political organisation and deliberation: the close study of urbanism in different cultures is important precisely for comparative purposes (as is also evident from the comparative volumes on 'city-state cultures' produced by the Copenhagen Polis Centre).[61]

But what if cities are indeed as unimportant to the grand sweep of (Mediterranean) history as Horden and Purcell claim? Horden and

---

[58] Hansen (2003), (2006); Morgan (2003).   [59] Horden and Purcell (2000).
[60] Vlassopoulos (2007a) 143–5 and *passim*.
[61] Vlassopoulos (2007a) 101–22; Hansen (2000), (2002a). It may be doubted, however, whether it is analytically useful to apply the term 'city-state' to the ancient polis or civitas, see Chapter 9 for discussion.

Purcell's polemic *contre villes* is partly a consequence of the fact that they are so strongly focussed on combating Finley and his model of the ancient economy, in which cities assume primary importance, that they feel compelled to marginalise the role of cities. Yet, for instance, precisely the excess mortality characteristic of pre-modern cities, necessitating, according to many scholars, a constant flow of migrants from country to city to keep urban populations numerically intact, would have contributed significantly to the mobility of people which Horden and Purcell rightly place at the centre of their analysis. Also, the local and regional ecological impact of cities (as relatively large and dense concentrations of human beings) in terms of requirements of food, water, fuel, clothing and building materials, as well as waste disposal, will have been pronounced, which again makes it hard to understand why, especially in an ecological history, they should have been sidelined as epiphenomena.[62] Then there is the fact, emphasised by Purcell himself in a different context (that is, the essay quoted at the beginning of this section), of the strong similarities in many respects between Greek and Roman cities spread across the Mediterranean region and beyond, in widely different micro-ecological contexts, which suggests that ecology explains much but certainly not all. Finally, in response to both Vlassopoulos and Horden and Purcell, we should point again to the world-historical importance of urbanism as a near-universal form of human settlement behaviour in complex societies. Close study of cities in particular societies produced with the aim of easing future comparative research are of crucial importance if we want to achieve a better understanding of urbanism in this broadest, world-historical sense. Cities matter not just because we happen to find them in Greece, Rome or medieval Europe, but because we find them almost *everywhere*.

In addition to such arguments, there are also a number of recent scholarly developments 'closer to home', as it were, which suggest that the intensive study of polis and civitas remains paramount. For reasons of space, I will only very briefly mention those I find most promising. To begin with, the recent wave of studies devoted to non-polis and sub-polis/civitas forms of organisation mentioned above, instead of signalling the analytical dead-end of city-based approaches, might actually have the potential to take our understanding of the ancient city to a new level. For instance, research by the Copenhagen Polis Centre has exploded the old distinction between *ethnos* and polis in the Greek world, noting that areas dominated by a regional *ethnos* did in fact often contain many

---

[62] See e.g. Morley (1996) on Rome.

communities organised as poleis.[63] Then again *koina*, or leagues of cities, often had their own magistrates and assemblies, mimicking the structures of their component parts. In similar vein, the study of civic subgroups, such as clubs and associations (*collegia*) and of sub-polis settlements and villages, has demonstrated that such bodies almost without exception organised themselves as mini-poleis or mini-civitates, with their own elected magistrates, assemblies, 'laws', cults, festivities and public buildings.[64] What this suggests is that 'the civic model' was and remained *the* crucial template for socio-political organisation in antiquity, even at the supra- and sub-city level, providing some substance to an idealised vision of society in which even the Roman Empire could be viewed as one big city (Aelius Aristides, *Roman Oration* 36). This is a topic that would bear further study.

Another theme, already alluded to above, is the ecological impact of cities and the specific ecology of the pre-modern urban milieu. Scholars have studied the extraordinary economic, agricultural and demographic impact of the imperial city of Rome with its one million inhabitants on the Italian countryside and the wider empire, but the analysis can be extended to include other, more 'normal' cities in the ancient world. Recently, for instance, Andrew Wilson has drawn attention to the massive fuel requirements of Roman cities generated by the presence of heated public baths, which might well have caused a certain degree of deforestation over the centuries, while a considerable amount of scholarly attention has been paid in recent years to the complexities of the urban food supply, particularly of larger cities.[65] Ongoing research into the urban disease environment and the health and nutritional status of urban inhabitants, particularly through the study of skeletal remains, despite many methodological problems increasingly provides us with glimpses of what life actually may have been like, at a very basic level, in ancient cities.[66]

A similar sense of how ancient urban lives may actually have been lived emerges from recent studies into movement and the use of space in urban environments.[67] The study of urban landscapes has increasingly shifted from the static analysis of buildings and monuments to a consideration of how buildings, streets, squares and so forth were actually used and experienced by ancient urban inhabitants. How did people, animals and goods flow through the city, on ordinary days and nights, but also, for instance,

---

[63] Hansen (2003) 280 with references.
[64] See Mackil (2013) on *koina*; Van Nijf (1997); Harland (2003) on *collegia* and Schuler (1998) on villages in the Hellenistic and Roman East.
[65] Wilson (2012) 149–50; Garnsey (1988), (1998a); Erdkamp (2005); Moreno (2007); Oliver (2007).
[66] See Chapter 4 for discussion of these issues.   [67] Scott (2012).

during religious festivals and public events? Sophisticated analysis of architectural remains, artefacts and textual sources, with the aid of novel methodologies and software applications, increasingly homes in on these lived urban experiences, 'repopulating' the urban landscapes that often seem so desolate and artificial in many 3-D digital reconstructions.[68] This focus on space and movement is a highly important new current that increasingly allows us to bridge the analytical gap between the city as a material entity and the city as community, integrating archaeological, historical and social scientific approaches.

Finally, I signal the recent work, primarily among social scientists, economists and historians of early modern Europe, on the possible links between participatory, inclusive political systems and socio-political stability, institutional performance and economic development. Inspired by political science studies – such as those of Robert Putnam on civic engagement as expressed in a strong associative life (civil society) and its effects on democratic participation, public trust and economic prosperity – early modernists have increasingly engaged in research on guilds and associations and the effects of such participatory institutions in early modern cities.[69] Economic historians and economists have similarly stressed the importance of urban citizenship and what has been termed inclusive political institutions for the rational use of public goods, the discouragement of elite predation, the lowering of transaction cost and the securing of property rights, all of which are beneficial to economic growth.[70] The analytical relevance of all of this for ancient urban history requires no special pleading; Greek and Roman cities were thoroughly participatory at all levels (even if they were by no means all radical Athenian democracies), especially when we also take into account their strong traditions of voluntary associations.

These issues, and many others, will be addressed in the chapters that follow, with the intention of providing food for thought and in order to stimulate discussion and productive disagreement. As the foregoing will have shown, 'the ancient city' has always been a highly contentious topic, and, if the vehemence of its current detractors is anything to go by, it will probably continue to be just that. This book aims to contribute to these ongoing debates, but will also, I hope, succeed in pointing out some possible routes that we might follow to move beyond them.

---

[68] See the many innovative contributions in Laurence and Newsome (2011), esp. the chapter by Claire Holleran for a critique of digital reconstructions. See also Kaiser (2011a).
[69] Putnam (1993), (2000); Epstein and Prak (2008); Prak (2010).
[70] See Acemoglu and Robinson (2012); Prak and Van Zanden (2006).

CHAPTER 2

Origins, Development and the Spread of Cities in the Ancient World

What were the origins of the ancient city? When and how did cities rise, and how did they spread throughout the ancient world? These are the questions that will be addressed in the present chapter. I start with a section on the origins and early development of the polis and civitas in Greece and central Italy. Then we move on to the mechanisms by which cities of this type spread throughout the ancient world.

Origins

What does it mean to ask for 'the origins of the ancient city'? After all, the search for origins begs the question of definitions. Here I propose that we interpret the question as an inquiry into the historical formation of the two central defining features of the ancient city, i.e. the peer group of citizens who together ruled, owned land in the territory of, worshipped in, and fought for, the polis or civitas, and the urban landscape of monumental public and religious architecture and lay-out characteristic of the Greek and Roman city.[1]

Ever since the publication of V. Gordon Childe's famous paper on 'The Urban Revolution' in 1950, archaeological and anthropological studies of the origins of cities have often been dominated, implicitly or explicitly, by two overriding concerns.[2] The first is a search for structural features of environment or society that, almost as if by natural force, brought about the rise of urban communities in certain periods and regions. This is so because in Childe's cultural evolutionary model, as, with varying degrees, in those of scholars inspired by him, the rise of cities is only a part, and a symptom, of a far broader process of increasing societal complexity and state formation. Thus sedentary agriculture (the Neolithic Revolution) gave rise to population growth and an increasingly stratified society.

---

[1] See Chapter 1.   [2] Childe (1950); Cowgill (2004) and M.E. Smith (2009) survey the debates.

Subsequently, governmental and religious elites successfully managed to centralise political and economic power and to spend the results of surplus extraction on monumental structures (e.g. temples and palaces). Around this core, the non-elite population clustered to serve the needs of the elite. Craft specialisation, infrastructure and so forth followed in due course, and, largely as an unintended consequence of political, socioeconomic and religious developments, the first cities were born.[3]

The second concern referred to, already implicit in the first one, is the persistent connection that is drawn in many studies between urbanisation and state formation. For Childe and the neo-evolutionist archaeologists and anthropologists of the 1960s and 1970s, city formation was a symptom of state formation.[4] In fact, however, there is no reason to assume an organic connection between the rise of cities and the formation of (territorial) states.[5] There have been cities without states, and states without cities.[6] Indeed, the early poleis and civitates in Greece and central Italy are prime examples of cities that arose without a pre-existing or simultaneously developing overarching state structure.[7]

As regards the evolutionism of Childe and those inspired by his work (the city as a natural, if unintentional, consequence of larger social, economic, political or other developments), it should be noted that recent research into city origins increasingly stresses agency (cities as deliberate creations by powerful groups/individuals) and historical contingency.[8] Work on the world's earliest cities in Mesopotamia during the Middle and Late Uruk periods, c. 3800–3100 BCE, for instance suggests that '[s]ettlement in the first cities may have been prompted by an environmental accident – changes in the Tigris and Euphrates watercourses – and the resulting concentration of people around Uruk – or perhaps by exceptional control exercised by an early ruler'.[9] Greco-Roman history of course abounds in examples of cities deliberately created, whether by kings and emperors or as 'colonies' by individual poleis or Republican Rome,

---

[3] Cowgill (2004) 528; M. E. Smith (2009) 6–8.
[4] M. L. Smith (2003b) 12. See Childe (1950); Adams (1966), esp. 90; Fox (1977) 24 ('cities are found only in societies that are organized as states'); Trigger (1972) 592. Among more recent studies, see Zeder (1991); Storey (1992) 28.
[5] Cowgill (2004) 528; M. L. Smith (2003b) 12–16; M. E. Smith (2009) 7; Osborne (2005) 2–3.
[6] States without cities: see e.g. Wisseman Christie (1991) for state formation conspicuously lacking an urban component on early Java. Cities without states: e.g. M. L. Smith (2003c) on the rise of independent cities in the Ganges valley from the sixth century BCE onwards.
[7] For discussion of the issue whether poleis and civitates should themselves be considered (city-)states, see especially Chapter 9.
[8] Cowgill (2004) 534–5   [9] Emberling (2003) 258–60, quote from 259.

with Alexandria in Egypt as the paradigmatic case. Hence the 'city as a deliberate creation' is a useful model for classical scholars, almost to the point of being a truism. However, even if cities can be ordered into existence, they cannot be forced to prosper.[10] Comparative research into urban origins has revealed several instances of 'created cities' that subsequently declined, presumably because the broader social, political, economic or ecological context did not provide a secure enough 'base' to guarantee their longevity much beyond the political lifespan of their creators.[11] This implies that a workable model of urban origins needs to pay attention to structural factors as well as to agency. Archaeological and historical research into the rise of the Greek polis and the origins of Rome and urban communities in central Italy of the past several decades does arguably allow us to sketch just such a model.

After the collapse of the Mycenaean Bronze Age societies in the late second millennium BCE, a long 'Dark Age' ensued in Greece, during which both population and material culture declined and Greek society regressed towards less complex social and political formations (albeit with notable regional variation). Even writing was lost, and this is where our troubles begin. For by the time alphabetic writing was introduced in the eighth century, and, some time later, our first written sources for Greek history proper, the orally transmitted epic poems of Homer, were committed to script, we seem already to have missed much of the story of early Greek city formation. It used to be thought that the society reflected in Homer was either a confused unhistorical amalgam of elements stretching back to Mycenaean times (some scholars still think this), or represented the pre-polis society of Dark Age Greece in the tenth and ninth centuries BCE.[12] Close textual analysis, however, has in recent decades increasingly led scholars to the belief that the polis and most of the elements associated with it are indeed present in the Homeric epics, albeit at an early stage of development during the (later) eighth and early seventh centuries BCE.[13] Thus Homer's heroes, aristocratic chiefs (*basileis*) of their communities, are

---

[10] M. L. Smith (2003b) 2.

[11] Note e.g. Joffe's (1998) survey of so-called disembedded capitals, cities created 'de novo by an elite or group of elites seeking to found a new power base' (549), which were often 'disconnected from the local economic matrix (550)' and existing social and administrative networks and therefore lacked long-term viability. He discusses examples from pharaonic Egypt (Tell el-Amarna), ancient Mesopotamia and the 'Abbasid Caliphate (Samarra). Early Archaic Greece also counted a number of 'failed poleis', see Snodgrass (1991) 7–10; Osborne (2005) 11–13 and below.

[12] Snodgrass (1974) and Finley (1978) for the classic statements.

[13] Scully (1981), (1990); Bowden (1993); Raaflaub (1993), (1997); Crielaard (2009). Skepticism: Finley (1978) 155–6; Starr (1986); Osborne (2009).

represented as taking every important decision, whether at war or at home, in the context of a popular assembly, where the people, even if, as a body, they do not take actual decisons (that is still the aristocrats' prerogative), at least collectively express their dislike or approval of the proposals brought forward. The Greeks encamped in the plain before Troy in the *Iliad*, for example, are depicted as a temporary polis, with its own assembly meetings.[14] Also, despite Homer's focus on the exploits of his individual heroes, mass fighting, foreshadowing the hoplite phalanx of later centuries, is clearly present in the *Iliad*.[15] Hence the epics clearly depict the people acting collectively politically and militarily in a manner we tend to associate with a Greek citizen community. Moreover, when Homer describes the physical aspect of his communities, it is often clear that what we get is an early version of the typical urban landscape of a Greek polis.[16] Although it is still recognised that the epics contain many references to earlier periods, many scholars now think that the social and political context of the world Homer describes, including the Homeric version of the polis, belongs to the later eighth century BCE.

The 'discovery' of the polis in Homer, coupled with the dating down of Homeric society to the later eighth century, has several important consequences for our analysis of the rise of the polis. One of these is that we cannot relate polis formation *solely* to a 'hoplite revolution' in the seventh century BCE (given that mass fighting is already depicted in Homer), or to the actions of Archaic tyrants and lawgivers. The roots of the polis must be located much earlier, well before c. 750 BCE. Another consequence, crucially, is that for this early process of polis formation, we do not have any contemporary written sources.[17] Nonetheless, archaeology, analysis of political and kinship terminology in Homer (containing many survivals from earlier periods) and anthropologically informed speculation in a number of analyses from recent decades allow a rough outline.[18]

The formation of the polis, then, seems to have occurred in two phases, 'crystallisation', roughly during the ninth and eighth centuries BCE, and 'formalisation/integration', in the seventh and sixth.[19] During the first

---

[14] See e.g. *Il.* 2.35–282 and 9.9–79; *Od.* 2.1–259 and 8.4–45; Raaflaub (1993) 54–5 and Raaflaub and Wallace (2007) for careful discussion.

[15] Raaflaub (1993) 53–4; Bowden (1993); Krentz (2007).

[16] Raaflaub (1993) 47–53; Crielaard (2009) and see below.   [17] Raaflaub (1993) 77.

[18] E.g. Snodgrass (1977), (1980), (1991); Donlan (1980), (1985), (1989); de Polignac (1995); Morris (1987), (1991), (2000), (2009); Raaflaub (1993). See Mitchell and Rhodes (1997); Shapiro (2007) and Raaflaub and van Wees (2009) for stimulating contributions and surveys of the main debates.

[19] Raaflaub (1993) 75–82.

phase, the small, scattered chiefdom-communities of the Dark Age
developed into the clearly recognisable, but still loosely structured and
un-formalised poleis we find in Homer. The prime mover of this process
seems to have been population growth.[20] Highly optimistic claims from
the 1970s, based on grave counts at Athens and Argos, have since been
tempered, but settlement excavations and surface surveys do indicate that
population in the Greek world (Aegean Greece and the overseas settlements) did start to increase slowly from the tenth century BCE.[21] Demographic growth accelerated during the eighth century, when population
may have doubled.[22] What caused it? Climate change has been suggested,
with a change to a cooler and wetter Subatlantic regime c. 850–750 BCE
that benefitted agricultural productivity and somewhat reduced disease-
related mortality in the Mediterranean.[23] More important, however, were
its effects. A growing population made land scarcer. Good arable land that
had been unoccupied during the Dark Age was brought into cultivation in
the eighth and seventh centuries. Thus, scattered villages ruled by *primus
inter pares* chiefs (*basileis*) became more integrated, and limited political
centralisation ensued as the *basileis* agreed to cooperate, perhaps designat-
ing one among them as a new overall *primus inter pares* chief, as Odysseus
seems to have been on Ithaca (this process arguably may be what lies
behind stories of synoecism in early Greek history as told by later Greeks,
e.g. Thucydides 2.15.1–2 regarding Athens).[24] It is important to realise that
this development need not necessarily imply physical integration (though
it frequently did); a political unification of regionally scattered settlements
was certainly a possibility, as the example of Sparta, which remained a
cluster of separate villages into the Classical period, illustrates. Population
growth also led to the development of a notion of 'territoriality' as border
disputes arose between various communities-in-the-making in what was
now a more densely populated world.[25] It has been argued that in eighth-
century Greece, rural sanctuaries were used to mark and formalise such
community borders, which of course would further have reinforced collective identity by creating powerful symbolic ties between territory and
inhabitants.[26]

---

[20] Raaflaub (1993) 78; Morris (2009) 66–8. Some scholars remain skeptical, e.g. Osborne (2009)
68–75.
[21] Snodgrass (1977), (1980); Morris (1987), (1991); Scheidel (2003b).   [22] Morris (2009) 66–8.
[23] Morris (2009) 66–7; see Manning (2013) 112–15 for discussion.
[24] Raaflaub (1993) 77–80; Morris (2009) 70–2.   [25] Snodgrass (1993) 37–9; Morris (2009) 70–2.
[26] De Polignac (1995); Hall (2007) 86–7 for some criticism.

It is not unrealistic to assume that the population growth postulated for the eighth-century Greek world was in fact a Mediterranean-wide phenomenon.[27] It is at least archaeologically attested for central Italy (Old Latium) as well.[28] Why should such demographic change necessarily have led to the rise of polities of the polis and civitas-type, with their emphasis on the political peer group of male citizens? After all, other types of polities did develop in early Greece, varying from *ethne* to territorial monarchies, and elsewhere in the Mediterranean region.[29] This is a difficult question, and more than one plausible answer is possible. In the regions where poleis and civitates developed, several interrelated factors seem to have been crucial. First, population growth is likely to have led not just to the (political) integration and territorial definition of communities, but also to internal social unrest created by land scarcity, with peasants and the landless encroaching on the estates of the rich. Sending away part of the population to found a new community elsewhere, i.e. colonisation (about which more will be discussed in the next section), no doubt eased the strain somewhat, but not wholly. Second, the process of 'territorialisation' and the many, no doubt violent, boundary conflicts between communities this involved would have required a (gradual?) militarisation of (a part of) the non-elite population. In other words, elites lost their monopoly on armed combat, if they ever had it (remember, hoplite-like mass fighting in close formations already figures in Homer). Third, and perhaps most importantly, the elites of Dark Age and Archaic Greece and Archaic central Italy were *comparatively* weak.[30]

This last point requires some elaboration. It is important to stress the word 'comparatively' here, as I have done. The Homeric poems are full of references to the wealth of the *basileis*, their treasure rooms stocked with riches, their large flocks of sheep and herds of cattle, while the many precious metal objects and examples of imported luxury ceramics recovered from the so-called princely tombs of Archaic Latium convey a similar impression of richness. It has been pointed out, however, that compared to what we know of the wealth of, say, the roughly

[27] Tentative comparisons of regional archaeological surface surveys seem to indicate this, see Morris (2009) 66.
[28] Cornell (1995) 55, 81, referring to Latial phase IIB (c. 830–770 BCE) and Latial phase III (c. 770–730/20 BCE).
[29] Davies (1997) 27 for this reason proposes to place polis, *ethnos* and the like in the general category of 'microstates'. *Ethne* could however contain poleis, see Hall (2007) 88–91. I do not think, however, that it is analytically useful to call the polis or civitas a state, whichever way one chooses to qualify the term, see Chapter 9 for discussion.
[30] Snodgrass (1993) 39; Raaflaub (1993) 79; Morris (2009) 74–5.

contemporaneous nobilities of Lydia, Persia, Assyria or Egypt, the riches of Dark Age and Archaic Greek elites look decidedly unimpressive.[31] The same would be true *mutatis mutandis* of elites in Archaic Rome and Latium, especially if, as one expert has pointed out, when 'searching for a social context to explain the princely tombs of central Italy, we need look no further than the world of Odysseus'.[32] Relatively weak aristocrats, confronted by a growing demand for land (re)distribution from a restive populace in a context of continuous aggressive pressure from neighbouring communities, could in fact do little but yield some power and possessions, especially since the military mobilisation of the larger population was desperately needed to defend the community, and given the fact that, to be able to acquire costly arms and armour, the common man needed sufficient landed property.

Here, in this blending together of military and political participation and (modest) landownership for (a part of the) non-elite population, it can be argued, lies the origin of the Greek and Roman notions of citizenship. The true members of the community were those who owned land in its territory, defended it on the battlefield, and participated in its public assemblies.[33] Archaeologically, this broadening and institutionalisation of the sociopolitical community might be visible in increased access to burial rights and the development of common cult places.[34]

Yet if the nascent institution of citizenship provided a potential basis for social and political consensus, it did not immediately do so. Later Classical sources tell of fierce conflicts within the elite (*eupatridai* and the richest non-*eupatridai*) of seventh- and early sixth-century BCE Attica, and of ruthless exploitation by such elites of the common people (*demos*), hoplites or not, through serfdom-like institutions and debt bondage. Similar stories are told about later sixth- and fifth-century BCE Rome where an aristocracy of patricians exploited the so-called plebeians or non-elite citizens. In some poleis, such conflicts led to the rise of tyrants, aristocrats who via a coup, sometimes with the support of the *demos*, acquired sole rule. In others, continuing social conflicts, fuelled by ongoing population growth

---

[31] Odysseus' goatherd Eumaeus describes his master as one of the wealthiest men of his day, but, as Morris (2009) 74 points out, the fifty-nine flocks of cows, sheep, goats and pigs in addition to one treasure room would not have impressed contemporary eastern nobles (*Od.* 14.98–99; 2.337–347; 14.96–104).

[32] Cornell (1995) 86–92, quote from 88; C. Smith (2005) 102–4 argues for comparability between eighth- and seventh-century BCE Greek poleis and Rome on precisely this point. See also C. Smith (1997) on structural similarities between the societies of early Rome and Latium and the Archaic Greek poleis.

[33] Raaflaub (2000) 29.   [34] Morris (1987), (1991); Snodgrass (1991).

and consequent scarcity of resources, nearly tore the social fabric to shreds. It is clear that, in a situation of continuous border warfare and territorial conflicts that characterised relations between communities in Dark Age and early Archaic Greece and Archaic central Italy, such violent internal discord represented a grave threat to the survival of any polis or civitas. Solutions had to be found, and were, in the formalisation of political institutions.

Attempts to write down and codify laws (sometimes through the appointment of specific mediators, such as Solon at Athens in 594 BCE) led to reform and to more transparent definitions of institutions, rights and duties. Early Greek laws suggest a proliferation of formal offices, implying a dismantling of the previously existing informal executive and judicial monopoly of the Homeric *basileis*. It has been plausibly argued that these laws, obsessed as they seem to be with determining which office holder may do what, and for precisely how long a term, are evidence of a self-regulating aristocracy, intent on sharing power by dividing it up among formally defined and rotating offices, thus curbing intra-elite dissent and the risk of tyranny.[35] However, by tying power to formally defined offices rather than to the person of the office holder, such reforms also opened the way for the sharing of power across a wider social spectrum, not an illogical development in citizen-communities where most members already had some say in politics via public assemblies. It seems therefore not unreasonable to assume that, as in Athens after Solon's reforms, in many poleis political elites increasingly came to be defined by wealth rather than birth (the Bacchiadae at Corinth constitute one important exception).[36] At the same time, the authority of the citizen-assembly (often simply, but significantly, referred to as the *demos/damos* or polis), already an important political force in the Homeric epics, was formalised and reinforced.[37] Examples of this development are, among others, the Spartan constitutional reform called the Great Rhetra, c. 650 BCE, which assigned final decision-making powers to the demos (Tyrtaeus fr. 4 W; Plut., *Lyc.* 6.2, 8) and the constitutional law from Cretan Dreros, c. 650–600 BCE, which

---

[35] Raaflaub (1993) 74–5; Osborne (1997), (2009) 175–6; Hall (2007) 134–5.
[36] Thus the Archaic lyric poet Theognis complains about intermarriage between *esthloi/agathoi*, the traditional aristocracy, and newly rich *kakoi*, i.e. nouveaux riches from among the ordinary citizens (183–92, 53-60). Alcaeus (fr. 348) states that Pittacus, tyrant of Mytilene, was of low birth (*kakopatridas*), and (fr. 70) owed his prominence to marriage into the aristocratic house of the Penthilidai. See also Solon fr. 15 (Plutarch, *Solon* 3.2): in early sixth-century Athens, many *agathoi* had become poor while many *kakoi* were now rich.
[37] Raaflaub (1993) 64–75; Gehrke (2009) 399–400.

opened with 'So decided the polis' (*had' ewade poli*. Meiggs/Lewis no. 2 = Fornara no. 11). In Athens, Solon's reforms strengthened the powers of the *demos* through his (admittedly controversial) institution of election by lot and a non-aristocratic council of four hundred (*Ath. Pol.* 8).

At Rome, a popular assembly organised by tribes and *curiae*, the *comitia curiata*, had long since existed alongside the kings and the (proto-) senatorial aristocracy. Reforms ascribed to King Servius Tullius led, in the late sixth century, to the creation of another popular assembly, the *comitia centuriata*, structured according to property ownership (census classes) and army units (*centuriae*), thereby explicitly defining what it meant to be a Roman citizen (ownership of land and military and political participation) in a way very similar to the contemporaneous Greek notion. Then, towards the end of the century, the Roman aristocracy drove out the last 'tyrannical' King Tarquin and his clan, and, perhaps following a trend started in the Greek world, where few tyrannies survived into the fifth century, or among other Latin civitates, which seem to have been ruled by aristocracies in the Archaic period, they installed a Republican regime of dual annual magistrates, the consuls.[38] Thus the Roman patrician aristocracy also opted for power sharing through rotation. Further formalisation and integration would follow in the succeeding centuries, first with the plebeian agitation which led to the creation of yet another assembly, the *concilium plebis*, and plebeian magistrates, then a codification of the laws, the Twelve Tables, around 450 BCE, and finally, through a long series of piecemeal reforms, to the creation of a patrician-plebeian elite of wealth and office, the *nobilitas*, towards the end of the fourth century BCE.

It is interesting to note that the political formalisation of the polis and civitas just described largely coincides with and, especially in the case of the development of the notions of citizen community and citizenship, is clearly mirrored in the formation of the urban landscape of Greek and Roman cities, the second crucial aspect of the ancient city. Homeric audiences around the turn of the eighth century BCE were clearly already familiar with cities sporting 'a mighty wall, and a fine harbour on either side' with 'a place of assembly (*agore*), constructed with quarried stone, and built around a beautiful temple of Poseidon', which is the way Scheria, the admittedly idealised polis of the Phaeacians, is described in the *Odyssey*

---

[38] Cornell (1995) 230–2, who also argues that the Etruscan cities, Rome's neighbours to the north, remained firmly monarchical throughout the fifth century BCE, despite the existence of an apparently complex hierarchy of magistracies below the kings. Evidence for republican forms of government among other Italic peoples (e.g. Umbrians and Oscans) is attested from the third century BCE onwards.

6.262–8. Note the explicitly mentioned agora or assembly place, the presence of which neatly matches Homer's descriptions of public assemblies in both epic poems. This was clearly what Greeks in the early Archaic period thought a polis should look like.[39] I shall be brief here because a separate chapter of this book is devoted to the ancient urban landscape. I shall take Homer's description of Scheria as my cue and discuss the appearance of walls, agoras/fora and temples/public buildings as signs of growing political formalisation and integration, with a special focus on the archaeological visibility of the emerging citizen community.

Surrounding walls are often viewed as an essential aspect of the urban quality of a settlement. A little over 40 per cent of known Archaic settlements appear to have had some form of fortification walls.[40] Dating them precisely is often difficult, however, as is determining their exact circuit. Settlements that were walled in the eighth century include Old Smyrna, Zagora and Hypsele on Andros, Koukounaries on Paros, Agios Andreas on Siphnos, Xobourgo on Tenos, Ionian Melie, Minoa on Amorgos, Emborio on Chios and Asine in the Argolid. Early seventh-century Eretria followed suit. It has been pointed out, however, that a number of these sites did not survive as proper settlements beyond c. 700 BCE, e.g. Zagora, Hypsele, Koukounaries, Agios Andreas and Xobourgo. The relative remoteness of these 'failed poleis', a consequence of a rather single-minded focus on defensibility, which also produced their early fortification circuits, made them unsuitable to function in the Mediterranean-wide network of poleis that sprang up around 700 BCE, in which accessibility to overseas trade and communication was vital.[41] The construction of walls encircling the entire urban area rather than just, say, the central citadel or acropolis might be taken to imply the sort of communal consciousness and level of organisation associated with a civic community proper.[42] Yet many early Archaic sites that clearly were poleis did not have walls, nor did early Rome (if we exclude an early earthen rampart or *agger* and the recently discovered 'Palatine wall' which seems to have been a 'ritual circumference', i.e. a symbolic wall[43]) until the fourth century BCE, long after the formation of the city.[44] A number of important Greek poleis, such as Argos and Athens, acquired walls only in the later sixth and early fifth centuries, and Sparta never did so before

[39] Crielaard (2009) 351–2. [40] Hall (2007) 72. [41] Snodgrass (1991) 7–11; Osborne (2005) 11–13.
[42] Snodgrass (1991) 7.
[43] C. Smith (2005) 93–4: 'a ritual circuit, connected with the [ritual of the] ploughing of the circumference of the city, which we know was common practice for colonial foundation'.
[44] Cornell (1995) 198–202, with a summary of the debate and many references.

the late fourth.[45] Fortification walls might be a hindrance as well as a benefit to a developing polis or civitas, as the example of the 'failed poleis' suggests, and anyhow, their construction might be as indicative of a strong centralising power as of a developing and self-conscious citizen community.

We arguably stand a better chance of 'locating' the developing citizen community archaeologically with another primary topographical/architectural feature of the ancient city, namely the agora or forum. Homer, as we saw, already has his people's assemblies meet in agorai, open, public spaces in the city, for public, communal decision-making.[46] The clearing from the central part of the site of the agora at Athens of burials around c. 700 BCE and the paving of the Roman forum around 625 BCE, can be seen as decisive moments in the city formation (*Stadtwerdung*) of both communities, signifying a new communal political self-consciousness.[47] The formal delineation of the Athenian agora with boundary stones (*horoi*) and its embellishment with temples, altars, a stoa, a fountain house and a row of shops to the north would have to wait until the (later) sixth century, however.[48] The polis of Dreros had an agora around 700 BCE while monumentalised agorai with temples and public buildings were created during the later seventh and early sixth centuries BCE at the colonial settlements of Megara Hyblaea and Metapontum. The agora of the latter town even contained an assembly building with a capacity of 7,000–8,000 people in the shape of an amphitheatre, constructed during the sixth century.[49]

As these last examples indicate, there was often a close association between agorai/fora and public buildings and particularly temples. Agorai or fora were often laid out close to the main sanctuaries, either with the temples on a separate but nearby acropolis, such as at Athens, Megara or Cyrene, or at Rome, where the temples of Jupiter Optimus Maximus and Juno Moneta were built on the Capitoline hill above the forum, or just alongside or on the edge of the agora, as with the temples of Apollo at Dreros and Argos.[50] In spatial terms, it is in fact possible to visualise the original development of the Greco-Roman city as an increasing territorial separation, over time, between three distinct 'public spaces': a) the agora/forum, for the political meetings of the (adult male) citizens, b) the sanctuaries for the gods of the polis/civitas, and c) the cemeteries, the

---

[45] Hall (2007) 72–3.   [46] Raaflaub (1993) 55.
[47] Athens: Snodgrass (1991) 11; Rome: Cornell (1995) 93–4, 100–3.   [48] Crielaard (2009) 365–6.
[49] Morris (1991) 40; Crielaard (2009) 365–6.   [50] Hölscher (2007) 168.

territory of the dead ancestors.[51] In a first step, cemeteries were relocated, from the central area of habitation to the outskirts of the town, as, for example, at Athens, Argos, Corinth and Rome between 750–700 BCE.[52] Next, the temples for the main polis divinities became clearly separated from the agora/forum. This is not to suggest that the agora lacked religious elements and associations; on the contrary, it often contained sanctuaries, altars and the like, and its boundaries were sacred. Yet the temples for the most important deities were often clearly separated from the political space of the agora.[53] To be sure, this model does not work for each and every individual ancient town, but as a broad analysis of the spatial effects of polis/civitas formation, it is certainly very useful.

One conclusion from this tentative reconstruction of the sociopolitical and urban-architectural processes of ancient city formation is that it becomes rather difficult to accommodate the early polis or civitas within the Childean and later (neo-)evolutionist models of urban origins, still much in favour among archaeologists and anthropologists. Often based on Mesopotamian, Asian or Mesoamerican evidence, such models, with many variations, tend to place great stress on intense social stratification and the needs of powerful elites or kings to legitimate their rule (and surplus extraction), something which they achieved through the construction of monumental architecture, both sacred and profane, around which (dependent) populations clustered, thus forming cities.[54] Whatever the impact on urban life of state or imperial elites in later periods of antiquity (see briefly below and Chapter 9), it seems clear that the polis/civitas *in its earliest formation* was ultimately grounded on a compact between social elites and the large group of 'middling' peasant-landowners (*mesoi*) who were neither *thetes/proletarii* nor (eventually) dependent tenants, resulting in the 'invention' and gradual institutional formalisation of the notion of the citizen community.[55] The developments involved took time, displayed many (violent) twists and turns, and were subject to considerable local and

---

[51] Hölscher (2007) 167–72, esp. 168.
[52] Morris (1987) 62–9, 183–96; C. Smith (2005) 96–9; Hölscher (2007) 166.
[53] Hölscher (1998) 43–5, 49–62; (2007) 168–9.
[54] Readers should be aware that this is but a crude summary for the sake of argument of an extremely rich, subtle and varied literature. We may, however, wonder whether such models in fact even fit all aspects of the urban cultures on which they are in practice mostly based. Mesopotamian cities, for instance, knew citizen 'assemblies' of some form in addition to kings, though citizenship was restricted to a small subset of the population, see Jacobsen (1943); Emberling (2003) 260. In the New World, furthermore, Inca cities contained enormous plazas, 'areas designed to be experienced by thousands of people', which, however, primarily served cultic needs, Moore (2003) 97.
[55] Donlan (1997) sees the *mesoi* as the independent variable in the formation of the polis.

regional variation. Nonetheless, I do think we have here a valid generalisa-
tion about the origins of the ancient city, exemplified, in a way, by the
pristine centrality of agorai or a forum in the Archaic urban landscapes of
the Greek poleis and Rome. At the heart of the ancient city we do not find
a temple or a palace but a public meeting place.

Spread

The spread of cities of the polis and civitas-type throughout the geographical space that would come to constitute the ancient Greco-Roman world
occurred in three broad waves.[56] The first of these, with vaguely defined
historical contours, consisted of a scattering of Greek settlements far
beyond 'Old Greece', more or less contemporaneous with the later,
formalising phase of polis formation in Greece itself. Greek poleis were
founded around much of the Mediterranean and along the coasts of
the Black Sea. Traditionally, this process is referred to among historians
as the 'Archaic Colonisation', dated roughly 750–550 BCE, with the caveat
that 'colonisation', though ultimately derived from the ancient Latin term
colonia, is an inappropriate label since it envokes anachronistic images of
later European colonial rule and economic exploitation. Greek 'colonies'
were independent new settlements, not economic dependencies of their
mother cities.

Scholars used to draw a sharp distinction between the so-called Ionian
migration of the tenth and ninth centuries BCE during which Greeks
spread out over the Aegean and the islands and west coast of Asia Minor,
resulting in the foundation of famous poleis, such as Ephesus and Miletus,
and the planned colonial movements of the Archaic age. In recent
work, however, a more sceptical attitude towards the (mostly Classical,
therefore late) written sources for early migrations and colonisation, and an
increasing appreciation of the archaeological evidence, has resulted in a
picture of a long-term trend towards Greek settlement abroad, starting
somewhere around 1000 BCE and lasting well into the Classical period,
which should be seen as only one aspect of the overall high mobility of
people, goods and ideas in later Dark Age and Archaic Greece. Greek
settlement overseas should moreover not be viewed in terms of singular,
planned acts of polis foundation. Rather, foundation implied a process

---

[56] Roughly equivalent to the Roman Empire at its widest territorial extent, but also including parts of
modern-day Afghanistan (Bactria), Uzbekistan (Sogdiana) and India (Indus valley), where Greek
cities flourished in the period after Alexander's conquests.

lasting perhaps several generations, involving an initial small group of settlers, to whose number other migrants later added themselves, resulting, eventually, in a development towards urbanisation.[57] Irad Malkin has, however, convincingly argued that we should take seriously our sources' focus on a relatively short foundation period, lasting from the initial arrival of the settlers to the death of the founder (*oikistes*), during which the new community, forced by an often hostile environment, quickly had to develop the sociopolitical and material structures of a polis. An important corollary of this argument is that the colonial foundations' freedom to experiment led to the development of a more general model of what a polis should be like, in terms of urban planning (e.g. the 'Hippodamian' orthogonal street plan adopted by Megara Hyblaea on Sicily) and sociopolitical organisation. This had important feedback effects on the settlers' home communities ('mother-cities'), stimulating the urbanisation process in Greece itself. Thus, 'colonisation' should be viewed as an organic part of the overall process of polis formation, rather than as a separate phenomenon.[58]

The second and third waves of urban spread in the ancient world involved the founding of many new cities by Alexander the Great and the Hellenistic monarchs who succeeded him, on the one hand, and by the Roman Republican and imperial governments, on the other. Lacking professional armies and administrative bureaucracies, ancient poleis and civitates were notoriously bad at territorial expansion. Possible solutions to this conundrum were either hegemonial domination of other existing poleis by means of rapidly-to-be-mobilised hoplite armies or a fleet (e.g. Archaic and Classical Sparta in the Peloponnese and the fifth-century BCE Athenian sea-borne 'empire' in the Aegean) or the creation of new, formally independent but loyal poleis/civitates in newly conquered territory. These poleis/civitates then served as local political and administrative centres and military outposts, leading to the development of a network of power and influence for the hegemonial city, without the need for full administrative and military integration of the conquered territory into its own political structure. 'Creation' should here be taken to mean either the creation of new cities *ex nihilo*, or (more often) the refashioning of an existing settlement into a polis or *colonia*, adding a contingent of Greeks or

---

[57] Hall (2007) 93–118 and Osborne (2009) 110–21 are in this vein, with good surveys of recent debates. The list of Greek foundations in Osborne (table 5, 114–18) gives insight into the long-term nature of the phenomenon.

[58] Malkin (2009).

Romans to the native population. Republican Rome employed the technique with great success in its conquest of the Italian peninsula, founding a string of citizen-colonies, awarding (versions of) its citizenship to other existing communities, and enlisting yet others as *socii*, allies (of varying status).

For those ancient rulers confronted with the challenge of governing far-flung and ethnically and geographically highly diverse territories, such as the Hellenistic kings or the early Roman emperors, familiarity with a world full of poleis or civitates made a similar strategy seem eminently rational. Philip of Macedon, father of Alexander the Great, had already founded or re-founded cities as colonies of Macedonian and other Greek settlers to pacify Thrace, and in this as in so many other respects, Alexander followed in his father's footsteps when attempting to bring his own, newly conquered and huge empire under control. Thus numerous Alexandrias were founded, from Egypt to Bactria, all in the form of Greek poleis, with councils, magistrates and assemblies, and settled by Macedonian Greek immigrants and veterans of Alexander's army. Alexander's Successor Kings, especially the Seleucids, followed suit, founding a great many poleis. Motives were mostly military and administrative, sometimes crudely economical (e.g. protection of trade routes and exploitation of natural resources), and, in all cases, ideological.[59] Founding and benefitting Greek cities named after their dynasties, cities in which their ruler cult was woven into the civic and religious fabric, enabled the kings to put an indelible stamp on their foreign 'spear-won' possessions. Moreover, the sophisticated 'gifts-for-honours' diplomacy that developed between the kings and the poleis allowed political reciprocity to replace the naked exercise of power, legitimating monarchical rule while allowing the cities enough room for manoeuvre to take care of day-to-day local administration.[60]

Imperial Rome to some extent continued Hellenistic settlement policies, founding several poleis, yet most Roman city-founding took place in the largely non-urbanised western provinces, many of which were soon thriving with civitates, *municipia* and *coloniae*. Thereafter, relations

---

[59] Tscherikower (1927); Jones (1940) 1–50; Cohen (1978) on the Seleucids, and (1995) for an overview of Hellenistic settlement in Europe, the Aegean and Asia Minor, see esp. 63–71 on motives. See also Cohen (2006), (2013) on settlements in North Africa and the rest of the East; Billows (1990) on Macedonian foundations and Fraser (1996) on cities founded by Alexander. The Ptolemies were something of an exception, founding only a few Greek poleis but numerous cities according to the Egyptian model of town planning, see Mueller (2006); Tacoma (2006) on cities in Roman Egypt.

[60] See Ma (1999) for this aspect of the relationship between kings and cities. See Chapter 9 for a more detailed discussion of relations between cities and Hellenistic and Roman territorial states.

between emperors and provincial cities largely followed the Hellenistic template: emperors were fathers and benefactors of the cities, which honoured and worshipped them, in a ritualised process of diplomatic exchange that largely veiled the actual distribution of powers.

The most significant conclusion to emerge from these brief remarks is that, barring those poleis and civitates that originally developed in Old Greece and Archaic central Italy, and their (overseas) 'colonies', most cities in the ancient world were in fact creations of large territorial powers, kings and emperors. In this context, it is interesting to note that cities with over 100,000 inhabitants living within the city walls are not attested in the ancient world until the late fourth and third centuries BCE.[61] Their rise thus roughly coincided with that of the Hellenistic kingdoms and Carthage and Rome as Mediterranean superpowers. 'Top-heavy' urban networks, characterised by a few very large cities next to numerous much smaller ones, are in fact characteristic of pre-modern territorial empires, in which the spending power of rent-seeking political elites encouraged large concentrations of people and resources, leading to the formation of administrative urban giants.[62] Ptolemaic, Seleucid and Roman imperial urban networks do seem to fit this pattern. Hence, it is interesting to note that recent research comparing medieval and early modern European and Arab urbanisation has suggested that the comparative decline of Arab urban networks during the early modern period was precisely due to the fact that these were top-heavy, 'sovereign-oriented', as part of successive imperial structures (caliphates). The European networks, so the theory goes, were not only less top-heavy, but, due to European interstate warfare and political fragmentation, were also characterised by cities with robust local participatory institutions.[63]

What might be the implications of this argument, if we choose to believe it, for the cities of the ancient world? I would suggest that Hellenistic and Roman imperial urban networks were certainly 'sovereign-oriented', yet at the same time also not completely determined by the presence of empires. Greek and Roman cities arose long before Greek and Roman territorial states. Like those of medieval European cities, the institutions of the Greek polis and Roman civitas originally developed in an anarchic context of intercommunity warfare, which arguably made them similarly robust. When, in later centuries, kings and emperors started founding cities, they used the existing, tried-and-tested institutional

---

[61] Morris (2006); Scheidel (2007) 77–8.   [62] Ades and Glaeser (1995).
[63] Bosker, Buringh and van Zanden (2008); see also (2013) for a more concise version of the argument.

models of polis and civitas for their creations, thus ensuring, whether consciously or not, that these cities could cope with the demands of local administration required of them in the strongly decentralised structures of kingdoms and empire. Thus, ancient cities had it both ways, benefitting from the institutional robustness derived from their anarchic original context as well as from the presence of larger territorial powers later on.[64] Here is one possible explanation for the remarkable institutional longevity, encompassing the better part of 1,500 years, of the ancient city.

[64] This is based on the assumption that the benefits of empire outweighed the costs of tribute, taxes and occasional exactions to which cities belonging to the Hellenistic and Roman imperial states were subjected. Given the growth in numbers and the evident flourishing of cities in many parts of the Hellenistic world and the Roman Empire during its early centuries, this seems indeed to have been the case.

CHAPTER 3

City and Country

How did city and countryside relate to each other in the ancient world? In what follows, we shall discuss various dimensions of the urban-rural relationship, administrative, economic and cultural. Then, we move on to a short discussion of urban networks. As stated in Chapter 1, this is primarily a book about the general characteristics of the Greek and Roman, or ancient, city as such, and not so much about urbanisation. However, if only to place what is said about individual cities and their territories in a broader context, we need to engage briefly with the important debates about urban systems and their economic significance.

Cities, Villages and Settlements

In ancient cities, the urban core (*asty* or *urbs*) and surrounding territory (*chora* or *ager/territorium*) of the settlement were regarded as a single administrative and sociopolitical unit. Administratively and politically, therefore, there *was* no distinction between city and countryside. Citizens of the polis or civitas could live either in the urban core or in the surrounding territory, and unity might be emphasised by the use of the same administrative/geographical divisions for both the urban and rural parts of the city (e.g. demes or tribes). Inhabitants of the *chora* or *territorium*, whether citizens or non-citizens, could live dispersed in individual farmsteads, or on large estates, but, especially in cities with relatively large territories, might also reside in smaller towns and villages (e.g. *komai*, *demoi*, or *vici*) that fell under the administrative and political control of the polis or civitas. The many (139 or 140) deme-villages of Attica are of course a case in point, but Athens was not unique in this respect. Many poleis of the Hellenistic and Roman East had large territories full of villages inhabited sometimes by citizens but mostly by native groups living in (partial) subjection to the civic community (e.g. *paroikoi*, *katoikoi*, *kometai*, *laoi*). In the western provinces of the Roman Empire, large civitates united numerous smaller settlements within a single political-administrative unit. Thus a Greek-speaking eastern Roman city like Celaenae-Apamea in Phrygia held many towns and villages 'in submission' (*hypekooi*) to it (Dio Chrys., *Or.* 35.14–15). In the West, the territory of Nemausus (Nîmes) contained twenty-four dependent villages (Strabo 4.1.12), while Oenoanda, in Lycia, again in the East, had a *chora* numbering no fewer than thirty-five such settlements.[1]

The precise nature of the relationship between poleis/civitates and the communities in their territories is debated.[2] It has been suggested that villages might pay tribute to the polis or civitas centre; for most cities, we should probably assume some form of centralised control over the alloca-tion of village agricultural surpluses. Generally, the centres functioned as political and administrative cores, collecting contributions from their territories for payment to the central government (royal or imperial), and as seats of local jurisdiction. It might, however, sometimes be difficult for the civic political centre to cut through existing ties between local landowners and village communities: the Athenian tyrant Pisistratus famously instituted local judges in Attica outside Athens, which are often thought to have been intended as a substitute for the assumed legal powers of local aristocrats (*Ath. Pol.* 16.5). In later times, powerful land-lords continued to serve as arbiters in peasant disputes, as did Pliny the Younger at Tifernum (*Ep.* 7.30). Villagers, disaffected with the city courts, might also turn to soldiers, governors and even the emperor. In the later empire, powerful systems of rural patronage arose that largely by-passed the city.[3]

The ancient written sources offer only sparse and scattered information on the nature of the rural hinterland of Greek and Roman cities. We have in recent decades, however, learnt much from archaeological exploration of urban territories, even if the data thus gathered are rarely unambigu-ous. Variation, both geographical and over time, seems the key element in the picture that has emerged from this research.[4] For instance, detailed archaeological surface surveys in the territories of Classical Greek cities have led to the conclusion that the majority of polis inhabit-ants (70–80 per cent) commonly lived in the urban core, while the remainder lived in villages and farms throughout the *chora* – to which it should immediately be added that many of those urban core-dwellers

---

[1] Mitchell (1990) 188.   [2] Corbier (1991).   [3] MacMullen (1974) 39–40.
[4] See e.g. Witcher (2008) who stresses regionality as the most important common theme emerging from survey research in Roman Italy.

will in fact have been landowners or urban-based farmers who commuted to their fields.[5]

In parts of Roman Republican and early imperial South Etruria, by contrast, urban territories seem to have been dominated by a dense clutter of small settlements, presumably mostly smaller and middle-sized farmsteads, suggesting that a sizeable section of inhabitants lived dispersed in the countryside.[6] Surveys in Roman Spain (*ager Tarraconensis*) and Britain revealed similarly dense patterns of villas and settlements around urban sites, which became denser with proximity to the city.[7] In mountainous Samnium, back in Roman Italy, however, the number of rural sites seems to have contracted with the establishment of Roman cities there between the late first century BCE and the early second century CE, with the amalgamation of smaller farmsteads into large estates.[8] In fact, Roman imperial Italy as such, being one of the most intensively surveyed parts of the ancient world, is emblematic of the great variation in rural settlement patterns uncovered by archaeological surface survey. In some areas, for instance, site numbers seem to remain constant for centuries from the Augustan period onwards (e.g. in the *ager Faliscus* in southern Etruria), sometimes well into the third century CE. In others, site numbers even increased during the second century CE (e.g. in parts of Lucania). The predominant pattern, however, seems to be a decline in the number of rural sites during the first and second centuries CE (e.g. in the *ager Cosanus*, along the Etruscan coast, in northern Campania and in Apulia).[9]

A very similar pattern has been reconstructed for Roman Greece (Achaea), where smaller and middling sites gave way to large estates or villages in cities' rural hinterlands with the incorporation of the region into the empire.[10] The root cause of the observed variation should probably be sought mostly in the interaction of specific local and regional conditions and wider historical developments. For imperial Italy, for instance, John Patterson has stressed migration from the countryside to the cities, and, particularly, the accumulation of estates in the hands of the elite, as crucial factors responsible for reducing the number of (smaller) sites in

---

[5] See Bintliff (2008) 21, who summarises the results of research on Keos in the Cyclades, in the Southern Argolid and in Boeotia. Hansen (2006) 70–2 notes that this settlement pattern was typical of the majority of small and middle-sized poleis. In very large poleis, such as Athens and Sparta, however, most inhabitants lived in the countryside, as Thucydides states expressly for Athens (2.14.1–2).

[6] Potter (1979) 120–5 and (1991) 197–202. [7] M. Millett (1991). [8] Patterson (1991).

[9] See Patterson (2006) 5–9 and the 'survey of surveys' in the appendix to his first chapter.

[10] Alcock (1993).

many regions.[11] The variegated nature of settlement structures throughout the ancient world should be borne in mind, and we may note that it fits in well with the emphasis in recent ecologically inspired work on the effects and consequences of micro-ecological fragmentation in the ancient Mediterranean region.[12]

Villages and cities, particularly in the Greek East, have been described as 'worlds apart' on the basis of differences in '[l]anguage and nomenclature, diet and lifestyle, cults and patterns of authority'.[13] Many villages, however, had some political institutions modelled on the city: assemblies, councils of elders (*gerousiai*) and magistrates, as well as some public buildings. Councils (*boulai, curiae*), characteristic of cities, are often absent, though some are attested in Roman Italy and North Africa.[14] Some large villages did not differ much from small cities, and, as imperial rescripts attest, it was regarded as the pinnacle of achievement for a large town to acquire polis or civitas status of its own, and thus become independent.[15] Also, while villages had their own cults and feasts, they were often clearly integrated into the larger festive and cultic life of the polis/civitas: at Lycian Oenoanda, all thirty-plus villages sent sacrificial animals to a large quadrennial musical festival in the city, and representatives of the village communities participated in the procession that was part of the festivities.[16]

Finally, we should note that, just as large villages in the territories of poleis or civitates often shared some 'urban' characteristics with the urban core or centre, so within or very close to the urban core it was not unusual to find some 'rural' activity (see also briefly Chapter 8). The urban area generally included some cultivated land – meadows for grazing or orchards –and kitchen gardens, which Pliny the Elder described as 'the poor [city] man's *ager*' (*NH* 19.51–2), while in the suburban areas of cities, various forms of horticulture and arboriculture were commonly found. In many respects, therefore, the boundary between village/territory and urban core within the polis or civitas was exceedingly diffuse.[17]

---

[11] Patterson (2006).   [12] Horden and Purcell (2000).   [13] Mitchell (1993) 1:195.
[14] MacMullen (1974) 1–27; Mitchell (1993) 1:176–97; Patterson (2006) 44–7.
[15] Mitchell (1993) 1:179–81 for references.   [16] Mitchell (1990).
[17] Morley (1996) 83–107 on the city of Rome; Goodman (2007) on the 'periurban' or peripheral areas of Roman cities. Many poleis/civitates of course had city walls surrounding the *asty/urbs* which constituted, on the face of it, a very real and physical barrier between the urban core and rural territory. Yet such walls were not meant to keep the rural population out of the polis/civitas centre – this would make no sense, as the rural population often included a good many citizens – but to provide a 'citadel-like' place of refuge for the entire (citizen) population, urban or rural.

Imagining the Country from the City and Vice Versa ...

Given the administrative, political and, as we shall see, economic integration of city (in the sense of urban core) and country (in the sense of *choral territorium*) in the Greco-Roman world, it comes as something of a surprise that in many ancient literary representations of city and country both are pictured as very different, even divided, worlds. In many texts, a sharp contrast is drawn between the *asteios/urbanus*, or city-dweller, and the *agroikos/rusticus*, the countryman, in which the latter is often, from the urban perspective, regarded as a simple fool or a boor, as in Theophrastus' description of the *agroikos* in his *Characters* (4), who 'is the kind of person who will take a potion before going to the Assembly, declares that no perfume smells sweeter than thyme, wears sandals too big for his feet, and talks in a loud voice ... He is neither surprised nor frightened by anything he sees on the street, but when he spots an ox, an ass or a goat, he will stand still and gape at it'. The implied comparison with the smart man-about-town is evident throughout.

Alongside this, however, there exists a whole tradition in both Greek and Roman literature in which the contrast between city and country serves rather to emphasise the negative aspects of urban living, stretching from Hesiod's comments on the city as the seat of corrupt elites (*Works and Days* 213–69) to Aristophanes' *Acharnians* (34–5), in which an Athenian farmer, forced to live inside the city-walls during the Peloponnesian War, is made to long for the sights and sounds of his rural *deme* 'where no-one shouted: "buy charcoal, buy vinegar, buy oil", where the word "buy" is unknown', to the Roman satirists Martial (*Epigrams* 12.57) and Juvenal (*Satires* 3.160–80) who contrast the filth, noise and horrors of city life with the peace and quiet of the country. The rural or pastoral idyll, quite detached from agricultural realities, became a literary *topos* which made its influence felt even in supposedly more 'factual' texts such as Pliny the Younger's epistolary descriptions of his Tuscan and Laurentine villas (*Ep.* 5.6; 2.17). A particularly Roman type of agrarian utopia is represented by the morality tales of the rustic, village-like Rome of early Republican times, home to sturdy peasant-warriors whose leaders still ploughed their own fields (e.g. Livy 3.26), which was contrasted with the debauched and corrupt imperial metropolis of the (Augustan) present.

How real was the supposed attitudinal gap between city and country? According to the orator Libanius, the territory of fourth-century CE Antioch was filled with thriving villages that constituted a world unto themselves without much need for the city (*Or.* 11.230). A few centuries

earlier, a different orator, Dio Chrysostom, had described the bewilder-
ment of an Euboean peasant when confronted with the goings-on in the
public assembly of the city in whose territory he lived (*Or.* 7.21–26). Some
recent scholarship on Classical Athens has indeed stressed the deep social
and cultural divide separating urban and rural Athenians.[18]

However, the contrast can be overdrawn. Note that Theophrastus'
agroikos, despite all his rural boorishness, does participate in the popular
assembly, and even likes to do so, telling his farm labourers all about it
after his return home (*Characters* 4.3–4). The Athenian assembly contained
many peasants as well as shopkeepers, craftsmen and traders, as the curse
on assemblymen voting for bad officials ('neither shall their cattle produce
offspring, nor their soil bear crops') makes clear, and the same was
probably true for most Greek and Roman cities, particularly smaller ones.[19]
Indeed, countrymen and city-dwellers consistently participated in the same
civic political institutions and processes as fellow-citizens, and this must
have gone some way towards homogenising attitudes among them. What
we are dealing with here, among citizens at least, is therefore to some
extent an exaggeration of minor differences. It is however typical of such
differences that they can acquire huge significance in a political context, as
Publius Scipio Nasica, canvassing for election to the curule aedileship in
second century BCE Rome, found out to his cost: grasping the horny hand
of a rural voter, he asked in jest whether the man liked to walk on his
hands. The citizens in the rural tribes failed to appreciate the joke, and
Scipio lost the election (Valerius Maximus 7.5.2). The anecdote can also be
read, however, as a comment on a type of differentiation among the
citizens which was of far greater consequence than that between urban
and rural dwellers: the divisions of wealth and social class, between those
who had to work for a living, and those who did not have to do so.

To be sure, the cultural rift between an inhabitant of the teeming
metropolis that Rome was to become and an Italian country villager could
be wide, as was of course the social distance between urban citizens and
low-status, non-citizen rural workers, whether they were Spartan helots or
the farming populations still speaking their native languages who lived in
the territories of Roman provincial cities. What is important to realise is
that many if not most of the images of the country, its people and their
relation to the city that we find in our literary sources (technical manuals
on farm management and so forth excluded, of course) were urban in
origin. This does not make them *a priori* inaccurate, since some knowledge

[18] E.g. N. F. Jones (2004).   [19] Ehrenberg (1962) 84 for references and discussion.

from observation or experience may well have been involved from time to time, yet it does suggest that the images will often be highly politically charged. Idealisations of the rural past, for instance, had a significant part to play in intra-elite debates and struggles during the late Roman Republic, and became a stock accessory of the Augustan conservative revival. The peasant and his world rarely speak to us in unmediated form, apart from, arguably, in Hesiod's *Works and Days*, and in some inscriptions and papyri. The images of the rural world that we find in our literary sources (technical authors again excluded) are therefore, in many respects, shadow images of the city, and they reflect its concerns and values far more than those of the countryside.

Economic Relations between City and Country

Greece and Rome were certainly not the only cultures whose terms for 'city' encompassed both urban core and rural territory (including the people living in both, the civic community). Such a conflation is in fact quite common. For instance, the term *ilú* among the Yoruba people of West Africa referred to the city and the farmland surrounding it. The same was true of the Maya term *cacab*, while the Aztec *altepetl* referred simultaneously to the city and the political territory belonging to it.[20] What this signifies is that for many pre-modern societies, a conceptual unit encompassing the urban core (what we would call the city) as well as the people associated with it and the territory controlled by this people or its ruler was an idea that came naturally. It also underlined an important economic reality: a city could not exist without the agricultural surplus produced by the countryside surrounding it. Viewed from this perspective, the medieval European idea (not always realised in practice and concealing much actual regional and chronological variation) of a fairly strict legal and sociopolitical separation between city and country seems an interesting anomaly.

It was precisely this separation between town and country in Europe that was assigned great economic significance by the fathers of modern social science (e.g. Smith, Marx and Weber) and by historians (e.g. Pirenne) looking for the origins of European industrial capitalism.[21] The medieval (Northern) European city, in this 'town-based model', became the realm of merchants and manufacturers who engaged in a reciprocal relationship with peasants and landlords, exchanging manufactured goods

---

[20] Marcus and Sabloff (2008b) 22.   [21] See Finley (1982) for discussion and references.

for agricultural surpluses, which allowed for increasing specialisation and technological innovation on both sides, growing efficiency and expansion of markets. The numerous cities of antiquity, however, could not be assigned such a pivotal role because the ancient world did not industrialise, it disappeared. Hence, as we saw in Chapter 1, ancient cities were dubbed consumer cities and contrasted with the dynamic producer cities of later Europe. In the model championed by Weber and Finley, the consumer cities of antiquity were 'republics' of landowning citizens, who drew in agricultural surplus from the countryside in the form of rents and taxes without offering any manufactured goods in return, and who left whatever commerce and manufacture they needed to satisfy their own demands to landless citizens or low-status groups, such as slaves, freedmen and resident foreigners (*metoikoi, incolae*). The low status, and thus assumed poverty, of these commercial groups, combined with the disinclination of the land-owning citizen-elite to invest in trade and manufacture, led Finley to conclude that the ancient world, however complex, stratified and urban-ised, did not harbour the potential for market expansion and *per capita* economic growth.[22] Thus, in Finley's model, the consumer city was linked to the notion of a *comparatively* static, *comparatively* under-commercialised economy, dubbed 'primitive' by his scholarly adversaries though not by Finley himself.[23]

Criticism was (and is) rife. Scholars have pointed to the wealth freedmen and foreigners could amass in trade, to citizens active as manufacturers or merchants, to elite investment in commerce, mostly via middle men (slaves and freedmen again), and to specialised production for the market on the estates of the wealthy.[24] Alternative city types were introduced, such as the service city, the organiser city (*cité organisatrice*, i.e. the city as 'organiser' of the countryside and rural production) or even the producer city (though with regard to the latter it should be noted that neither Weber nor Finley had ever denied that a few such cities might be present in the ancient world. No sociological or historical model can cover all known instances; what matters is that it covers most).[25] Others, as we saw in Chapter 1, pointed out

---

[22] Finley (1999).

[23] It should in fairness be noted that Finley presented a nuanced account, allowing for some development, if not growth, see Saller (2002) 253–5. These nuances were, however, lost in the heat of subsequent debate, see for instance Hopkins' characterisation of Finley as a 'static minimalist', Hopkins (2002) 217.

[24] See the papers collected in Scheidel and Von Reden (2002) for some classic contributions to this (huge) debate. Their 'Guide to Further Reading' (272–8) offers a convenient starting point for novices.

[25] E.g. Engels (1990); Leveau (1983); Mattingly et al. (2001).

that cities or urbanism might not necessarily constitute the only or the crucial variable for understanding the totality of economic, social or political structures in the ancient world, or any society, for that matter.

If our focus is the city, however, and its economic relationship with the countryside surrounding it, there is nonetheless still a good case to be made for the consumer city model, even if some of the criticism of Finley's particular interpretation of it was justified. To begin with, what has been lost sight of somewhat amidst the furore about the relative importance of trade and markets, is that the model actually very accurately describes the specific city-country economic relations characteristic of the majority of Greek and Roman cities. It is clear, for instance, that from one end of antiquity to the other, the bulk of the income of Greek and Roman urban elites, the wealthiest stratum of society, was derived from the exploitation of agrarian property. This is perhaps the most important fact about the ancient economy, and one that any good economic model of city-country relations in antiquity should take as its starting point, as the consumer city model indeed does.

To elucidate further how the consumer city model encapsulates the essence of ancient city-country relations, we might best construct a very crude typology based on city-size. Extensive research has confirmed that most Archaic and Classical Greek poleis, especially the majority that had fewer than 5,000 inhabitants, mostly consisted of urban-based citizen-farmers who commuted to their fields.[26] These so-called *Normalpoleis*, *Dorfstaaten* or 'agro-towns' (*Ackerbürgerstädte*) have sometimes been contrasted with the consumer city model but in fact represent just a lower-level or small-town version of it, the only difference being that the majority of citizens worked their own land instead of drawing income from it in the form of rents (though the wealthier among them did). The market for manufactured goods would be fairly small because elites were not numerous nor very rich and there was comparatively little surplus to spend. Hence, there would be relatively few traders and manufacturers present, yet those that were there mainly catered to citizens spending their agricultural incomes. Thus, the comparatively small size of many Archaic and Classical Greek poleis and the fact that many of their urban-based citizens farmed their own land do not preclude these cities from being consumer cities.[27] The crucial issue is not population size or the relative abundance of

---

[26] See section 'Cities, Villages and Settlements' above. Kirsten (1956); Ruschenbusch (1985).

[27] *Contra* Hansen (2004) who has based his criticism of the consumer city model as applied to the Greek polis primarily on the presence of urban-based citizens cultivating their own fields, so-called *Ackerbürger*. See Morris (2006) 31–2 for a brief critique of Hansen's position.

Ackerbürger but the presence or absence of a non-reciprocal economic relationship between city and countryside (see below).

On the next level, we then find larger cities with a more clearly demarcated citizen-elite of large landowners, who had large urban households of slaves and dependents and exercised a much greater demand for (luxury) manufactured goods and commercial services, which they paid for with the rents they drew from their rural holdings. So, there would be a larger trading and manufacturing sector, which however does not preclude the continuing presence of large numbers of ordinary citizen-farmers and/or agricultural labourers; even large poleis and civitates could and did retain certain *Dorfstaat* characteristics.

A third level would then be represented by cities such as fifth-century BCE Athens, the Hellenistic capitals or imperial Rome, cities that headed, or were supported by, military empires, and whose elites thus drew in agricultural surplus in the form of rents and taxes from far beyond their own cities' territories. On all three levels, despite the many differences between the cities concerned, what matters is that the relationship between city and country was non-reciprocal, that is, agricultural produce was taken to the city as direct income (in the case of citizen-farmers), elite rent income or government tax income, in short, as a consequence of legal and political entitlements, and not in exchange for manufactured products and services provided to the countryside.[28]

The non-reciprocal nature of city-country relations in antiquity has been the focus of a recent thoughtful re-evaluation of the consumer city model by Paul Erdkamp.[29] His arguments (developed initially for cities under the Roman Empire but arguably equally applicable to ancient cities in other periods of antiquity) provide what is perhaps the most important reason to retain the model: not only does it accurately define the essence of the economic relationship between city and country in the ancient world, but, as Erdkamp shows, the model is by no means incompatible with the notion of a complex, dynamic urban economy, with a flourishing commercial sector, a developed market economy, and even economic growth. Thus there is no self-evident causative link between the consumer city model and a comparatively static, relatively under-commercialised economy. A pre-modern society with mostly consumer cities was not *necessarily*

---

[28] For a division of Greek poleis into five broad bands on the basis of size of territory, see Hansen and Nielsen (2004) 71.

[29] Erdkamp (2001), (2012). See also Scheidel (2007) 82; Morris (2006) on Greek poleis as consumer cities.

any less complex or dynamic economically than one with primarily producer cities. The crux of the matter is that non-agricultural economic activity in ancient cities was in fact a function of elite rent income (or citizen-farmer income) from rural property. In any Greek or Roman city, but especially larger ones, landowning urban elites with their large households would exercise a considerable demand for manufactured goods and services, including those that could not be manufactured locally, which gave rise to interregional trade. Consumer cities could thus be part of larger commercial systems.[30]

The merchants, artisans, shopkeepers and others who provided these goods and services would in turn spend the income they thus earned, which was essentially derivative of elite agricultural rents or citizen-farmer income, again on goods and services they themselves required. With increasing levels of urbanisation and growing overall elite wealth, such spin-offs gave rise to competitive local and regional market economies, in which there were incentives for organisational and technological innovation, and modest to impressive levels of wealth might be achieved by merchants and manufacturers. Add to this the stimulus to trade and manufacture created by central (fifth-century BCE Athenian, Hellenistic and Roman) governments' demand for tribute or taxes and their spending of tax monies in the imperial centre or in provincial cities and it is clear that a consumer city economy could be very dynamic indeed. Much original criticism of the consumer city model in terms of its incompatibility with the evidence for flourishing trade and markets is therefore beside the point, as the model is in fact compatible with this.

Nor is the model disproved by evidence for elite involvement in trade or manufacture, as this simply represents a more direct injection of non-reciprocally acquired agrarian surplus into the urban commercial economy.[31] Another objection to the consumer city model, or to any city-based model of economic development generally, should give us some pause, however. This is the argument, associated with C. R. Whittaker and others, that productive activity we think of as urban did not necessarily take place in a city-context.[32] Peasant families, for instance, probably produced much of what they needed themselves. Given that there were large parts of the year, in between the peak periods of sowing and

---

[30] Of course, Greek and Roman cities were also connected through trade in basic commodities such as building materials or, especially, staple foods (e.g. grain, wine and olive oil), since some of them were too large to be able to feed their entire population from their own territory, whereas others periodically needed to import foodstuffs due to harvest failures, see Chapter 8.
[31] Erdkamp (2001) 339–40; also Bang (2008) 26–8.   [32] E.g. Whittaker (1990).

harvesting, when there was not that much to do on the farm, it was often cheaper for peasants to produce their own clothing, pots and so forth than to buy them on the urban market. The same was true *mutatis mutandis* for the estates of the wealthy. Housing, clothes and food for workers were often produced on the estate, as were transport ceramics and other pots, farming implements and so on. Self-sufficiency, though in practice unattainable in its complete form, was an important aim for the estate owner, as the Greek and Roman agricultural writers make clear. Military forts and camps were similarly foci of 'urban' manufacture, and we should also note that (temporary) rural fairs and village markets served as nodal points of exchange.[33]

Erdkamp however argues that extra-urban non-agricultural activities do not provide a strong argument against the consumer city, as these activities too were spin-offs of non-reciprocally acquired agrarian surplus.[34] We might add that in a world dominated by consumer cities, whose manufacturing and trading sectors after all mainly served the urban market, widespread low-level rural manufacture on peasant holdings and elite estates and a prevalence of small rural fairs actually made perfect economic sense. They do beg an important question, however, namely why still *most* if not all trade and manufacture remained in fact focussed on, and located in, cities, as is clear from the archaeological and documentary record. One answer is of course that this is where demand was highest, as Greco-Roman elites and their extensive households needed to congregate and live together in cities for the elites to be able to fulfil their political, administrative and religious roles. Another answer might be the role of cities in lowering the typically high transaction costs characteristic of pre-modern economies by establishing new institutions or 'rules of the game' that facilitated commerce and manufacture and created economies of scale and lower transport costs through concentrating production, demand and services (though the continued existence of rural markets does indicate that the co-ordinating role of cities was certainly not perfect). We shall explore this argument on the internal organisation of the urban economy further in Chapter 8.

Once the consumer city model of non-reciprocal economic relations between city and country[35] is disconnected from the notion of a relatively static, under-commercialised economy, with which it has no *a priori*

---

[33] De Ligt (1993).   [34] Erdkamp (2001) 342.
[35] Or, to be more precise, non-reciprocal relations between non-food producing sectors, which were *mostly but not exclusively* urban, and a food-producing sector, which was *mostly but not exclusively* rural.

relationship anyhow, it becomes clear that the model represents just one route via which a pre-modern agrarian society might achieve a level of economic complexity and development, just as the producer city model, with its emphasis on town-country reciprocity, represents another. Consumer cities were not exclusive to Classical Antiquity; examples can be found in many pre-modern societies, including medieval and early modern Europe, just as the ancient world might well have contained some producer cities, and perhaps yet some other city types. It should thus be clear that, reformulated in this way, the consumer city model, as an analytical tool, is no longer necessarily connected to a Eurocentric narrative in which a 'primitive' antiquity is contrasted with a 'modern' (that is, highly commercialised) medieval Europe.[36] The observation that economic relations between city and country throughout the ancient world seem mostly to have conformed to the consumer city model is nonetheless highly important from a comparative point of view. It offers us a clear methodological point of departure for cross-cultural and comparative analysis of pre-modern cities and their relations with their hinterlands. This then is a final argument for the retention of the consumer city model in ancient economic history.

Hinterlands and Urban Networks

The economic hinterland of an ancient city did not necessarily overlap with the territory under its administrative control (its *chora* or *territorium*). Demand, especially in larger cities (but also in smaller cities in times of need) was often such that the resources of regions (much) further afield needed to be mobilised to satisfy it. Classical Athens, for instance, in a normal year could feed about half of its inhabitants from its Attic territory, depending on imported grain to feed the rest.[37] Peasants from Boeotia immediately north of Attica are recorded as bringing food to Athens, and other regions in mainland Greece, in the Aegean and in the western Mediterranean may have contributed too, but it is clear from the sources that the bulk of Athenian foreign grain imports came from the northern shore of the Black Sea (according to the fourth-century orator Demosthenes, Athens annually imported 400,000 *medimnoi* of wheat from the Cimmerian Bosporus alone, a figure which may not be too wide off the

---

[36] Vlassopoulos (2007a) 123–41 criticises Finley for using the consumer city model to argue for such a dichotomous view.
[37] Garnsey (1988) 105.

mark, as recent research has suggested).[38] The imperial city of Rome, many times larger than the city of Athens in its heyday, depended on continuous large-scale imports of food (primarily grain, oil and wine) from mainland Italy itself and the provinces in Spain, Gaul, Sicily, Sardinia, North Africa, Egypt and elsewhere to feed its hungry masses.

What these observations make clear is that 'economic hinterland' is in fact a pretty vague notion: a large city's 'hinterland' might well encompass a wide network of settlements and regions, stretching across seas, oceans and even continents (does India belong to imperial Rome's hinterland because spices from there reached the capital?). It might be dispersed and fragmented. Also, the boundaries of such a 'hinterland' might be continuously shifting.[39] It makes more sense, therefore, to think in terms of 'systems' or 'networks' of cities that served as the nodal points linking diverse local and regional economies.[40] Geographers have developed a range of such 'network approaches'. These models mostly aim to discover and explain the patterns according to which larger and smaller settlements are distributed throughout the landscape. Many start from a notion of settlement or urban hierarchy. I shall briefly discuss a few examples that have found application in the work of ancient historians and classical archaeologists.

One such approach is Von Thünen's model of agricultural location.[41] This model explains the clustering of settlements (e.g. towns, villages and farms) engaged in different types of agricultural activities around an urban market by focussing on the distance between settlements and the central market. Crucial variables are transport costs and the relative rate at which produce perishes. Thus horticulture, which produces soft fruit, and dairy farming will take place close to the market, while bulky crops such as wheat, expensive to move yet not so perishable, will be grown at a further distance. Furthest out are pastoralism and livestock breeding, which makes sense: sheep and cattle can walk to the market. In Von Thünen's ideal landscape, settlements specialising in different branches of agriculture are clustered around the urban market in neat concentric rings. In reality, of course, many factors distort this pattern, e.g. differences in climate and soil fertility between regions, the presence of waterways (absent in the model), the level of commercialisation of agriculture (the model assumes all farmers produce for the market), the existence of other (local) markets and so on. Still, it has been found through application of the model that relative ease

[38] Bintliff (2008) 24–6; Demosthenes, *Or.* 20.32; Bissa (2009) 169–77.
[39] Horden and Purcell (2000) 115–22.   [40] De Vries (1984).   [41] Von Thünen (1930).

of access to the central urban market exerted a determining influence on settlement structures and the location of agricultural activities in Roman Italy and beyond (in the case of imperial Rome), in Classical Attica and in the hinterland of Syrian Antioch during the Roman period.[42]

Another type of 'urban hierarchy' approach is Central Place theory. Models developed in this tradition try to discover and explain the regular spatial patterning across the landscape of settlements of different sizes (Central Places, i.e. cities, villages and hamlets) by reference either to the provision of different types of goods and services (small villages provide mainly day-to-day services for a small area, cities more specialised ones for a large region), or to the way smaller and larger settlements function as nodal points in transport and communication networks, or to the relations of political control between them or to a combination of such factors.

Arguably, processes of nucleation and the development of Central Place hierarchies in antiquity were initially driven primarily by the forces of political centralisation and the establishment of administrative control.[43] In the Mediterranean heartlands of classical civilisation, Greece and central Italy, poleis and civitates that emerged as larger settlements acquired dominance over smaller rural population foci, developing into the urban core plus *chora/territorium*-with-villages model outlined above (see also Chapter 2). Greek 'colonial' foundations often developed into politically dominant settlements in their regional setting while Hellenistic kings, the Roman Republic and the emperors used city foundations as a means to control newly conquered landscapes, creating settlement hierarchies based on administrative centralisation and control. Over time, however, such administrative hierarchies were reinforced by, and adapted to, the circulation of goods, people and information, a process which was often stimulated by the establishment of road networks connecting the various nodes. Villages and cities became concentration points of agricultural surpluses and providers of lower-order and higher-order specialised goods and services respectively for their localities and (sometimes large) regions.

Comparative study using Central Place models has shown, however, that the urban hierarchies of antiquity did not achieve the level of competitive commercial integration characteristic of those in some late medieval European regions, such as England. Even in what was presumably one of the most commercialised regions of the ancient world, for which we have good evidence in the shape of epigraphically preserved calendars of

---

[42] Rome and Italy: Morley (1996); Attica: Bintliff (2002), (2008); Antioch: De Giorgi (2008).
[43] Bintliff (2002) synthesises a great deal of research.

weekly town-based markets (*nundinae*), early imperial Campania, close to the huge Roman market, the central place system remained one 'where the vast bulk of rural surplus is consumed within the region, if not the nearest, small market town'. Furthermore, Campania lacked 'a dense series of overlapping access catchments for rural producers' stimulating commercial competition in the marketing of surplus as reconstructed for late medieval England. Moreover, the timing of the town markets (as reconstructed from the calendars) does not suggest that they were 'organized in the kind of systematic cycles' favouring 'urban-based merchants "bulking-up" local surplus for major export to regional centres and foreign clients'.[44]

A third type of urban hierarchy approach, closely related to Central Place theory, is the rank-size model. Here, the crucial variable is the size of the urban population. The model is based on the empirical observation that in any given region, small settlements (far) outnumber larger ones. The rank-size rule states that 'when ranks of cities, arranged in descending order, are plotted against their populations (rank 1 being given to the largest, and so on) in a doubly logarithmic graph, a rank-size distribution results'.[45] If the result is a log-normal distribution then the urban system might be regarded as well integrated in economic terms.[46] Tentatively calculated rank-size distributions for cities in Roman Spain, Britain and Asia Minor, using city area as a proxy for population size given the absence of reliable population figures, however, reveal convex distributions rather than straight ones (i.e. the largest settlement is smaller, or the smaller settlements are larger, than the rank-size rule would predict), which have been observed to go together with low *per capita* trade volumes and hence low levels of urban system integration. A convex distribution might imply that the region under examination contains only a peripheral part of a larger dendritic ('outward-branching') settlement system, and that the regional system is focussed on a large core outside the study area. Convexity is often associated with primate dendritic urban systems (such as the one reconstructed by Neville Morley for imperial Campania), that is, urban systems containing one or more 'primate centres', settlements (cities) which are much larger than most other settlements within the system.[47] Such 'top-heavy' urban networks are thought to be typical of empires (as well as of colonial urbanism and the urban systems of modern

---

[44] Bintliff (2002) 229–30.   [45] Marzano (2011) 201, citing Das and Dutt (1993) 125.
[46] Johnson (1980) 234–40.
[47] Morley (1996), (1997); Johnson (1980); Marzano (2011) on Roman Britain and Spain (but note the exception of Lusitania, where the distribution is almost log-linear, 218–22); Hanson (2011) on Roman Asia Minor. See Tacoma (2006) on Roman Egypt.

Third World countries).[48] The Ptolemaic, Seleucid and Roman Empires are indeed prime examples; the size of cities such as Alexandria, Antioch and Rome was way beyond that of most other cities within their systems. A comparison with urban systems in early modern Western Europe is revealing.

The early Roman Empire had between six and twelve cities with 100,000 inhabitants or more. By 1500 CE, only four European cities had exceeded this number of inhabitants. By 1600, eight had done so, by 1700, eleven, and by 1800, sixteen. However, no continental European city by 1800 equalled the 1 million plus inhabitants of the city of Rome. Furthermore, only Paris and London had half a million inhabitants or more by that time, the probable size of Alexandria, Carthage and Antioch in early imperial times, and only three other European cities had over 200,000 inhabitants. What Europe by 1800 *did* have, however, were 300 to 400 cities of 10,000 inhabitants or more, a middle category of which the Roman Empire had far fewer (though there may have been more cities of this size in some regions, notably Asia Minor or Egypt, than in others, notably the Roman West).[49] There are many caveats to be issued here, given our uncertainties about population numbers in the ancient world, and notably the difficulties of intercultural comparison of urban population figures, but the plausible suggestion is, as Greg Woolf has argued, that a rank-size curve for the Roman Empire (and probably for the Ptolemaic and Seleucid Empires, too) would be much steeper than for early modern Europe. In other words, the urban systems of the empires of Classical Antiquity were dominated by some very large cities the size of which was inflated because they were home to courts and imperial or high provincial elites. These cities attracted a large and continuous stream of migrants because of the economic opportunities they offered and drew in extremely large quantities of agricultural surplus in the form of rents and taxes, 'distorting' patterns of trade and migration by acting as black holes swallowing up people and goods from all over their empires, thus leaving comparatively little room for the development of a layer of middle-range centres with a more regional focus, such as existed in the politically far more fragmented world of early modern Europe.[50]

Should we then conclude that the urban systems of antiquity were generally driven by political and administrative demands, mostly those of

---

[48] Woolf (1997) 7.
[49] Pleket (2003) 91. Woolf (1997) 6–7, citing De Vries (1984) for data from early modern Europe.
[50] See Ades and Glaeser (1995) on 'urban giants'.

empires, as the sociologist Gilbert Rozman argued for the Roman Empire?[51] That is too much of a simplification, I would argue, and for several reasons. First, as we saw in Chapter 2, the formation of poleis and civitates in the Archaic Greek world and Archaic central Italy preceded the rise of territorial states. Thus, Mediterranean Greek and central Italian urban networks already existed and functioned for several centuries before powerful poleis, such as Athens, Sparta or Rome, established their hegemonial proto-states or the Macedonian kingdom began its expansion. Similarly, and second, as Woolf has argued, in the pre-Roman, Hellenistic East there already existed an urban network based as much on commercial and cultural interaction as on Hellenistic imperial power, including the old Aegean centres that were never central to the Hellenistic administrative structures. This might account for the presence of more 'middle ranking' cities with over 10,000 people in the Roman East than in the West; in the East, a flourishing urban network preceded Roman rule and was modified by it, in the West, such a network was practically created *de novo* (although often along existing tribal lines).[52] Third, as Morley has shown for early imperial Campania, urban networks involving a fair degree of commercial integration certainly could and did exist under direct imperial rule and in the (close) presence of 'primate cities', even if such integration did not necessarily reach the level achieved in some of the most commercialised regions of late medieval and early modern Europe.[53] In fact, 'parasitical' primate cities or megalopoleis, absorbing huge flows of people and resources from wide areas, could themselves have strong positive effects on their hinterland(s), stimulating agricultural and manufacturing productivity and the development of marketing systems, as has been demonstrated for imperial Rome or early modern London.[54] Thus, administrative primate urban hierarchies do not necessarily preclude a level of commercial integration; there may in fact be an indirect organic connection between the two, via the positive feedback on the surrounding territory of the centre's imperial demands.

While the urban systems approaches we have so far discussed concern themselves mainly with the economic effects of cities on their hinterlands and the nature of their linkages with other settlements and regions, the economic significance, for preindustrial economies, of a comparatively high level of urbanisation *per se* has not yet been touched upon. Urban network models are mainly concerned with structure (e.g. the character of linkages, commercial or administrative or other, between settlements), and

---

[51] Rozman (1978) 75.   [52] Woolf (1997); Pleket (2003).   [53] Morley (1997).
[54] Morley (1996); Wrigley (1967).

only secondarily with the performance, in terms of *per capita* growth, of the economies within which the urban systems are located. In line with the contemporary shift in ancient economic history towards performance, however, Elio Lo Cascio has argued that the level of urbanisation of the Roman Empire might well serve as a proxy for agricultural productivity, i.e. the growth potential, in *per capita* terms, of the economy.[55] Simply put, a high number of non-agriculturally active urban residents implies a productive agricultural sector, capable of producing a sizeable surplus. Thus, the comparatively high level of urbanisation posited by many scholars for the Roman world, especially for Roman Italy and Egypt, would then imply a comparatively high level of economic performance.

This sounds intuitively plausible, but there are problems with the argument. Even apart from the difficulty of empirically establishing rates of urbanisation for the ancient world, the argument assumes a significant degree of overlap between the urban and the non-agriculturally active population. Cities conforming to the 'agro-town' or *Dorfstaat* model, which proliferated in Archaic and Classical Greece, are obviously problematic for the argument, as are non-agriculturally active rural residents. Lo Cascio acknowledges this but downplays both phenomena for the Roman Empire.[56] However, the agriculturally active and the non-agriculturally active were not neatly separated groups. Pre-modern agriculture was characterised by much under-employment, which meant that peasant families had a low substitution threshold to take on other, non-agricultural work, at least outside the peak periods of the agricultural year because it was bound to bring in more income than any additional (i.e. marginal) work on the farm. The same was of course true for urban-based farmers.[57] Thus, in the Greco-Roman world as in other pre-modern societies, there were probably many people in the countryside devoting part of their labour to non-agricultural pursuits (manufacture, whether for the market or for home consumption, or trade), while most cities probably counted a sizeable number of people who were agriculturally active at least some of their time, i.e. who were urban-based farmers but who also engaged in manufacture, trade or other non-agricultural work. This does not completely invalidate arguments such as Lo Cascio's, but it does at least show that the relationship between urbanisation rates and agricultural productivity is not quite as straightforward as he would have us believe.[58]

---

[55] Lo Cascio (2009).   [56] Lo Cascio (2009) 89–91.   [57] Erdkamp (2005) 83–87.
[58] Scheidel (2008) 35–7 for trenchant criticism along similar lines. Wilson (2011) again takes up Lo Cascio's argument and supplies guesstimates for urban population figures and rates of urbanisation in various parts of the Roman Empire. See Morley (2011) in the same volume for cautionary remarks.

CHAPTER 4

Urban Landscape and Environment

The city is a social and political community as well as a sphere of heightened cultural and economic interaction. But most emphatically perhaps for those visiting them or living in them, cities are material entities, artificial landscapes of buildings, streets, squares and monuments that contrast sharply with the surrounding countryside. Even in our modern urbanised world, great cities never fail to impress the first-time visitor, but especially in a pre-modern agrarian society, where most people lived in the country, entering a large city for the first time could be an unforgettable experience, even for an emperor:

> So then [in 357 CE] he [Constantius II] entered Rome, the home of empire and of every virtue, and when he had come to the Rostra, the most renowned forum of ancient dominion, he stood amazed; and on every side on which his eyes rested he was dazzled by the array of marvellous sights ... Then, as he surveyed the sections of the city and its suburbs, lying within the summits of the seven hills, along their slopes, or on level ground, he thought that whatever first met his gaze towered above all the rest: the sanctuaries of Tarpeian Jove so far surpassing as things divine excel those of earth; the baths built up to the measure of provinces; the huge bulk of the amphitheatre, strengthened by its framework of Tiburtine stone, to whose top human eyesight barely ascends; the Pantheon like a rounded city-district, vaulted over in lofty beauty; and the exalted heights which rise with platforms to which one may mount, and bear the likenesses of former emperors; the Temple of the City, the Forum of Peace, the Theatre of Pompey, the Odeum, the Stadium, and amongst these the other adornments of the Eternal City (Ammianus Marcellinus 16.10.13–14).[1]

Yet this was Rome, the megalopolis, the largest city of the empire, so Constantius' amazement was both natural and justified. A small Greek city on Euboea, however, could still greatly impress the poor country-dwelling

---

[1] Tr. J. C. Rolfe, Loeb Classical Library.

citizen who seldom came to town, and lead them to marvel at its thick walls, its large houses and its theatre 'hollow like a ravine' (Dio Chrys., *Or.* 7.22–25). Cities, and especially their monumental centres, often overawe the visitor and are a source of pride for the citizen. 'In our own daily lives', Paul Zanker writes, 'we are aware of the symbolic value of public and private architecture, of streets and public squares, and we know that their effect on us cannot be overestimated. In any historical context the shape of a city presents a coherent system of visual communication that may affect its inhabitants even at the subconscious level by its constant presence'.[2] Yet there was a darker side to the pre-modern urban landscape as well, hinted at by Juvenal (*Satires* 3) and Martial (*Epigrams* 10.5) when they speak of the noise, the overcrowding, the omnipresent filth in Rome, and of beggars dying in the streets: the dismal sanitary conditions, from a modern point of view, in which the majority of urban inhabitants had to spend their lives. In this chapter, we shall explore the material side of ancient cities, their buildings, streets, squares and monuments, and what these might have meant to the people who created them and lived in and among them, as well as the broader urban environment and its demographic and sanitary characteristics: the two sides, as it were, of the ancient urban coin.

The Structure and Meaning of Ancient Urban Landscapes

Each city is, in a way, unique, especially when it comes to its layout and morphology, its urban landscape. Yet at the same time, most cities are part of recognisable urban traditions. How to do justice to both dimensions? Can we outline the 'typical' urban landscape of the Greco-Roman city and highlight the points where it differs from or rather shares characteristics with other urban cultures? Childe's ten-point descriptive model of what might constitute a city was one attempt to generalise across diverse urban traditions, based on observed archaeological and organisational commonalities between them. 'Truly monumental public buildings' do feature in his list, but apart from that Childe does not say much about layout or planning.[3] When analysing urban layout many scholars have employed a simple dichotomy of planned versus unplanned or 'organic', where planned usually refers to an orthogonal layout, characteristic of many Greek and Roman cities (see below) but also frequently encountered in other urban traditions. Dissatisfied with such a simplistic and ethnocentric approach (because based on essentially Western notions of planning) and

---

[2] Zanker (1990) 18.   [3] Childe (1950) 12; M. E. Smith (2009) 17–18.

convinced that all urban sites are at least to some extent planned, even if
only partly, the archaeologist Michael E. Smith devised a more sophisticated model that encompasses a number of dimensions of planning and
measures the degree to which they are present in individual urban sites and
urban traditions.[4] To structure my account of Greek and Roman urban
layout and morphology, I will base my discussion loosely on Smith's
model of urban planning.

Smith's model centres on two main dimensions of the urban structure:
coordination, as expressed in the arrangement of buildings, the formality and
monumentality of the urban landscape, the plan (orthogonal or other) and
standardisation, as expressed in urban architectural inventories and the
spatial layout.[5] When we apply this model to the urban landscape of Greek
and Roman cities, the structural similarities which are evidence of a single
urban tradition clearly shine through, as well as the areas of overlap with
other urban traditions. For instance (starting with the dimensions of coordination), typically, in most Greek and Roman cities, government buildings
(e.g. council houses, magistrates' offices and court buildings) and the
temples for the most important deities tend to be arranged loosely around
the agora or forum and/or to cluster in its close vicinity. The most important
streets, such as the Street of the Panathenaia at Athens, the grand colonnaded avenues that became popular in Hellenistic and Roman-era Greek
cities, or the *cardines* and *decumani maximi*, the central streets crossing each
other at right angles in the axially planned Roman cities of the West, all led
to (and often crossed at) the agora or forum, emphasising its literal centrality
to civic life. There is a clear formality to this pattern, which we find
throughout antiquity, in the art-historical sense of its organising principles
being immediately clear to observers: the most important streets lead to the
central square at the heart of the city where one finds the majority of the
most important civic and religious buildings.[6] Those buildings were also
generally monumental, in the sense of being (much) larger than necessary
for utilitarian purposes.[7] The greater a city's political importance, the more
monumental its central civic architecture, council houses, stoas and temples
became. Examples are Athens under Pericles, Hellenistic Alexandria and

---

[4] M. E. Smith (2007).
[5] I leave out access and visibility (under coordination) and orientation and metrology, i.e. standard
units of measurement (under standardisation) since these are more technical features of urban
planning analysis that would require quite extensive discussion, for which there is no place in a
short chapter on Greco-Roman urban landscapes.
[6] M. E. Smith (2007) 8 for this definition of formality.
[7] For this definition of architectural monumentality, see Trigger (1990) 119–20.

Pergamon, and of course imperial Rome. Monumentality generally increased in Hellenistic Greek cities, as it did in Roman provincial cities from the Augustan period onwards, imitating the splendour of the royal or imperial capitals. Yet arguably Greco-Roman monumentality never quite reached the terrifying grandeur of the pyramids, palaces and temple complexes in early urban cultures, such as pharaonic Egypt, pre-conquest Mesoamerica or pre-modern southeast Asia (with imperial Rome as a possible exception). The aim generally seems to have been to impress observers but perhaps not to overawe them entirely.

A concern for design on a human scale is also evident in the planning of many Greek and Roman cities. Whereas most of the cities of old Greece, Rome itself and the cities of Latium Vetus grew 'naturally' (though with clearly planned city centres), cities founded later, as Greek colonies or Hellenistic or Roman foundations, often followed an orthogonal plan or chess board pattern, also known as 'Hippodamian'. This refers to the fifth-century BCE city-planner Hippodamus of Miletus, supposed inventor or at least populariser of the orthogonal grid plan and designer of Athens' port city Piraeus (Aristotle, *Pol.* 1267b). Although (variations of) orthogonal planning were known in other pre-modern urban traditions (e.g. pharaonic Egypt, the Near East, China and the pre-Columbian Americas[8]), nowhere was it as pervasive as in Greek and Roman urbanism. It is attested from quite early on. Megara Hyblaea, a Greek colony on Sicily, had an orthogonal street grid already by the seventh century BCE (which may have been present from its foundation in the late eighth), as did Selinous.[9] In Ionia (Asia Minor), Miletus pioneered the Hippodamian plan when the city was rebuilt after its destruction by the Persians in 494 BCE (see Fig. 4.1), and we also find it in several eastern Greek colonies. Priene, built against a hillside overlooking the Maeander River in southwest Asia Minor, and Olynthus in Northern Greece provide splendid examples of Greek orthogonal planning (see Fig. 4.2).[10]

Hippodamian town planning was common in the poleis founded by Alexander and his successors in Asia Minor and the Near East, but it was the Romans who developed the orthogonal urban grid plan to perfection. We see it in Republican colonies, with Alba Fucens and Cosa as good examples (see Fig. 4.3), but it reaches its perfect form in the colonies and *municipia* of the western provinces, where the clear axiality of the urban

[8] M. E. Smith (2007) 12–21.   [9] Crielaard (2009) 362 for references.
[10] Wycherley (1949) 15–35.

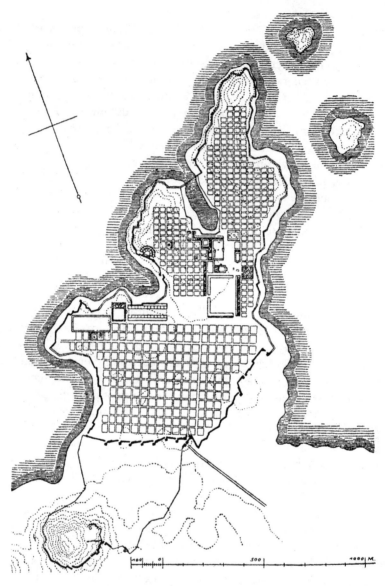

Fig. 4.1 Plan of Miletus (after 479 BCE)

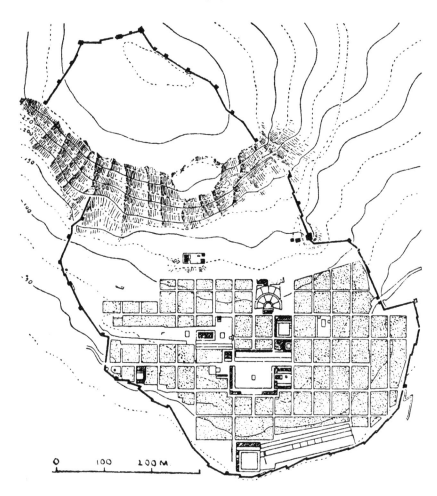

Fig. 4.2 Plan of Priene (later fourth century BCE)

plans betrays a close relation to the Roman permanent army camp (*castrum* –
see Fig. 4.4). Indeed some cities developed directly out of *castra*: examples
are Colonia Agrippina (Cologne) and Augusta Praetoria (Aosta).[11]

The smallest individual unit of the grid was commonly a block of houses
(what the Romans called an *insula*), sometimes bisected by small alleys, as

[11] Gates (2011) 334–5.

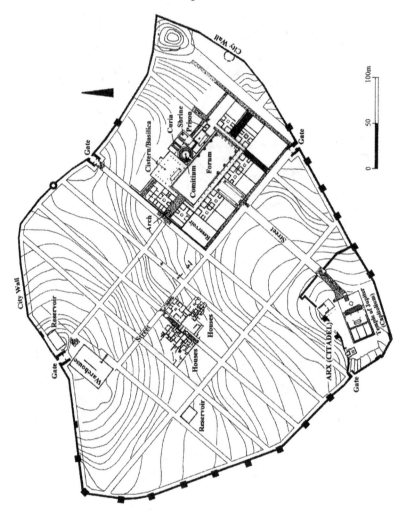

Fig. 4.3 Plan of Cosa (third and second century BCE)

at Olynthus (see Fig. 4.5).[12] Such a block might also include workshops (*ergasteria, tabernae*), as is clear, for instance, from well-preserved examples at Pompeii.[13]

If we move now from the dimensions of coordination to those of standardisation, it immediately becomes clear that the architectural inventories of Greek and Roman cities reflect a basic continuity in the ancient

---

[12] Gates (2011) 278–80.　　[13] Wallace-Hadrill (1994).

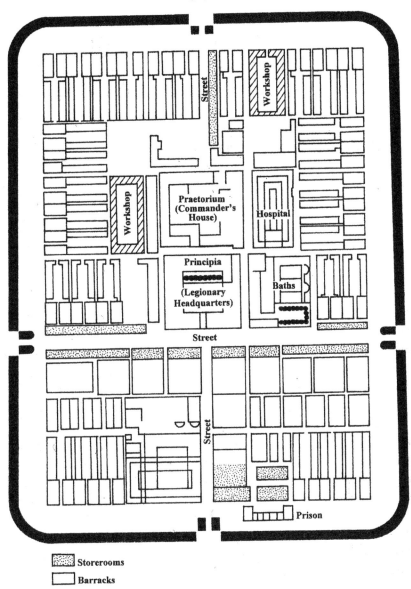

Fig. 4.4 Diagram of a Roman legionary fort (*castrum*), Novaesium, Lower Germany

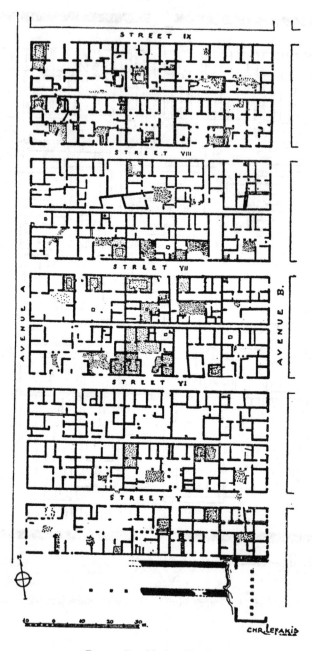

Fig. 4.5 Five blocks, Olynthus

urban landscape from the Archaic period to late antiquity. Naturally, there was much change over time. The increasing monumentalisation of post-Classical Greek cities, as well as of Roman cities from Augustus onwards, has already been mentioned, but this was in many cases a monumentalisation and elaboration of existing elements (e.g. the increasing architectural sophistication of the agora from late Classical times onwards, or the splendid fora of Roman imperial cities[14]). Also, Roman urban landscapes differed in some respects from Greek ones (although much creative synthesis took place under the empire, particularly in the East): think e.g. of the basilica and the amphitheatre, types of buildings unknown in the pre-Roman Greek world, while for instance the gymnasium was a typically Greek phenomenon. But the basic morphology of the Greco-Roman urban environment and its constituent elements betray a remarkable continuity over the centuries. These include the central square (agora/forum), surrounded by political/administrative buildings (council houses, magistrates' offices and basilicas), temples and sanctuaries and especially the prominence in the urban landscape of large-scale structures for collective religious, sporting, festive and entertainment purposes, such as the stadium/circus, the theatre/amphitheatre and the gymnasium/palaestra/bath house. What this basic inventory suggests above all is an urban landscape particularly geared towards an open, collectivist form of public life. Agora, forum and theatre were designed to accommodate political mass meetings; architectural amenities, such as the stadium, gymnasium and bath house, focussed on the collective enjoyment of leisure activities, while the typical open air altars in front of Greek or Roman temples were highly suited to religious traditions primarily organised around public cults and grand civic festivals.

Over time and across the ancient world there was of course much variation on this basic pattern, and some major trends in the character of the urban landscape have been directly linked to sociopolitical developments in the ancient city. For instance, a trend across fifth-century BCE Greece (of which Periclean Athens is only the most obvious, but by no means only, example), in which architectural sobriety and restraint in urban private housing and burial monuments went hand in hand with conspicuous architectural display in public building, has been tentatively linked to the level of control the ordinary citizens had over the behaviour of the rich, 'the most important cultural and sociological fact of

---

[14] See Dickenson (2012) on the post-Classical Greek agora.

the fifth century'.[15] By contrast, the growing architectural embellishment of the agora in Hellenistic and Roman-era Greek cities, and the clustering of temples, public buildings and monuments on and around it, have long been viewed as signifying the decline of popular participation in post-Classical civic politics, with the agora literally becoming less accessible and accommodating to mass popular meetings.[16] More recent research, stressing the continued importance of the popular assemblies (which, moreover, mostly met in theatres and not on the agora) in the post-Classical poleis, has increasingly questioned this view.[17] Some scholars have also assumed a strong link between the Hippodamian grid plan of many Greek cities and polis democracy, taking the grid plan as a spatial representation of political equality.[18]

Whatever might be said for and against such specific theories, it seems fairly clear that the public architecture of Greek and Roman cities lent itself particularly to a form of open air face-to-face politics, where political leaders were often confronted by, and came into close physical contact with, the mass of their ordinary fellow-citizens, whether officially assembled on the forum, in the theatre or some other location (such as the Pnyx hill in Classical Athens), or more informally, when the former were seeking support for proposals or were canvassing for elections (see Chapter 5). Fergus Millar has placed particular stress on this aspect of ancient civic politics, suggested to him by the physical layout of *curia*, *comitium* and forum, in his analysis of the role of the crowd in Republican Rome, but it remained to some extent true even in the Rome of the emperors.[19] However much Augustus and his successors turned the material appearance of Rome into a glorification of imperial power, the *princeps*, as his title also implied, was never physically that far removed from his fellow-citizens. There are various anecdotes in Suetonius' biographies and other sources of direct confrontations and contact between *plebs* and *princeps*, on the forum, in the streets and elsewhere.[20]

---

[15] Morris (1998a) 82–3.
[16] The contrast is of course with the spacious, relatively unadorned agora of Classical Athens, see Wycherley (1949); Martin (1951).
[17] Dickenson (2012) for criticism of the traditional view of the post-Classical agora; Rogers (1992); Ma (2000); Zuiderhoek (2008a) on post-Classical assemblies.
[18] See, for example, the contributions in Schuller, Hoepfner and Schwandner (1989) and Fleming (2002) on Thurii.
[19] Millar (1998).
[20] Suetonius, *Claudius* 18.2 is a classic example. See Millar (1967) for references and discussion, and in general Yavetz (1969).

The final aspect of the standardisation dimension of Smith's approach to ancient urban planning analysis is the spatial layout. This is a fairly loose term, encapsulating most of the earlier aspects of coordination (e.g. monumentality and city plans) and standardisation (architectural inventories). As by now will have become clear, throughout antiquity, Greek and Roman cities demonstrate clear similarities in basic spatial layout, which can easily be gauged by comparing a range of ancient city plans.[21] To summarise: most ancient cities would have had an urban centre structured around an agora or forum (or several of these), near to which many of the most important civic and religious buildings could be found, apart from those that required a lot of space (e.g. a circus) and/or a specific location (e.g. a hillside for a theatre). Several main streets would have led away from this urban centre, along blocks of residences intersected by smaller streets. There might have been a city wall with towers and several gates, and often, but certainly not always, the basic principles of orthogonal planning would have been adhered to. The spatial layout, in short, refers to the overall appearance of the city, integrating all of the various constitutive elements of the urban landscape, and it thus provides an important link to the fraught issue of meaning, to which we shall now turn.

How do urban landscapes communicate meaning, and can we decode this meaning? Scholars have suggested that it is possible to 'read' cities as one reads texts.[22] I have already briefly mentioned some attempts to link characteristics of the urban landscape to sociopolitical developments. Does there, however, exist a clear methodology for this kind of analysis? One influential model, referred to by Smith, is that of the architect Amos Rapoport, who identified three levels of meaning in urban landscapes: high-level (supernatural/cosmological symbolism), middle level (projections of power, status and identity) and low level (interaction between the built environment and people's daily behaviour and movements).[23]

Starting with Rapoport's high-level meanings, Greeks and Romans certainly seem to have regarded their cities as 'sacred spaces', as is demonstrated, for instance, by notions such as that of the *pomerium*, the sacred city boundary (symbolised by a furrow ploughed at the city's foundation, separating the city proper, the *urbs*, from the *ager*, the surrounding territory), by the banishment of those who had 'polluted' the community

[21] See, for example, Gates (2011) Parts II and III (Greek and Roman cities generally); Laurence, Esmonde Cleary and Sears (2011) on the Roman West; Parrish (2001) on the East (Asia Minor).
[22] E.g. Duncan (1990).
[23] Smith (2007) 30 for a good brief description of the model; Rapoport (1988), (1990).

through sacrilege and of scapegoats (*pharmakoi*) from the city's territory, and by the existence of city hearths with their perpetual flames guarded by the goddess Hestia/Vesta, which signified the sacred heart of the community.[24]

Such ancient notions and rituals have provoked some scholars to develop large-scale models of the religious and cosmological meaning of ancient cities. For Fustel de Coulanges, as we saw in Chapter 1, the religious origin of the Greek and Roman city lay in the Hestia/Vesta cult which provided a link between the household hearth and the civic hearth. More recently Joseph Rykwert has argued for the cosmological significance of the orthogonal grid plans of Roman cities, relating them to the city-foundation rituals the Romans took over from the Etruscans.[25] Such grand theories of origin, delving deeply into archaic religious notions, are often necessarily somewhat speculative. A more fruitful approach, I think, is to focus on the significance of civic ritual to contemporary observers and participants. This is what, for instance, Guy Rogers has done in his study of a religious festival in Roman Ephesus, demonstrating that religious processions, moving through the urban landscape, followed a distinct route past buildings and monuments related to different phases of the city's history, thus emphasising the community's identity as both the great old Greek city of Artemis and as a Roman provincial capital under the aegis of a deified emperor (see also Chapter 6).[26]

A good example of Rapoport's middle level meanings (projections of power, status and identity) in the urban landscape would be the extensive building programme of Periclean Athens, with its culmination in the Parthenon, reflecting and glorifying the city's power and identity as the head of an empire of subservient poleis. We might also think of the urban splendour of Hellenistic Pergamon, which exemplified the glory of the Attalid dynasty, and of course Augustan Rome, where the cityscape was transformed as a function of the new political order.[27] The representation of power, status and ideology in the urban landscape was not, however, the preserve of royal or imperial capitals; it was a feature of every type of city. To understand this, we need only look to Roman imperial Termessos, high up in the mountains of Pisidia, Asia Minor. This small city is exceptional chiefly because many of its preserved honorific inscriptions, which were

---

[24] Note also the practice of burying the dead outside the city walls to prevent sacred pollution (exemplified in Greek cities by the ritual of *ekphora*, carrying the dead outside the city for burying), and of requiring those associated with the pollution of death, such as public executioners, to live outside the city as well. See Marshall (2000); Bodel (2000) 144–8 in the same volume, on executioners.
[25] Fustel de Coulanges (2001); Rykwert (1976).   [26] Rogers (1991).   [27] Zanker (1990).

recorded on statue bases that would have carried an image of the honor-
and, were found still *in situ*. This has enabled Onno van Nijf to demonstrate how social hierarchy, status and power were spatially represented
throughout the urban landscape of Termessos.[28] Predictably, the distribution followed a hierarchical pattern: the statues of the most important
families, who held the highest magistracies and most prestigious priesthoods and were the city's largest public benefactors (and whose names
consequently appear most frequently in the city's epigraphic record),
are grouped around the most important public spaces of the city (near
the agora and near a stoa donated by King Attalos II of Pergamon, at the
temple of Zeus and near the council house). In this respect, Termessos was
typical *mutatis mutandis* of most late Hellenistic and Roman-era Greek
cities and of cities in the western provinces too.[29]

Rapoport's low level meanings (day-to-day interactions between people
and the built environment) are less easy to reconstruct for the ancient
world. How did people experience the urban landscape as they went about
their daily business? Some notion of this may be gathered from sources
such as Theophrastus' *Characters* or Juvenal's *Satires*. For instance, in the
Characters, a humorous description of the various personalities one might
encounter in Classical, fourth-century BCE Athens, the Athenian agora as
a public space plays a crucial role in the actions and behaviour of the types
of people portrayed. Thus the Flatterer is shown complimenting his patron
at the shoe shop in the agora, the Shameless Man cheats the butcher at his
stall in the market, the Stingy Man goes to the agora without buying
anything, the Man of Petty Ambition wants to be seen buying expensive
gifts for his friends in the agora, and so on.[30] As Paul Millett writes: '[t]he
behaviour of these and other Characters suggests that, for Athenians, the
crucial factor in defining status and regulating relationships, beyond relations and close friends, was interaction in civic space'.[31] Even people's sense
of time was determined by their sense of civic space: 'when the agora is full'
meant 'mid morning', while 'the breaking-up of the agora' indicated 'late
morning'.[32] Juvenal in his third *Satire*, by contrast, evokes the chaos and
dislocation of life in the teeming metropolis of imperial Rome, the throngs
of people, the influx of countless foreigners, the noise of rattling carts day
and night, the mud and filth in the streets, pots or their contents being

---

[28] Van Nijf (2000), (2011).
[29] See, for example, Laurence (1994) 33 on the clustering of inscriptions commemorating achievements
and benefactions by the local elite in and around the forum of Pompeii.
[30] Von Reden (2003) 106–7.   [31] Millett (1998) 211.   [32] Millett (1998) 212 with references.

thrown out of high apartment windows, the lack of safety on streets at night . . . Here anonymity and alienation are the main themes, rather than intimacy and close identification with the urban landscape.[33]

Other evidence might be employed as well to evoke something of an ancient experience of the urban landscape. Ray Laurence, for instance, has used the number of doorways and the incidence of graffiti messages per street in Pompeii as an index of the level of social interaction and cross-town traffic in various parts of the city.[34] Perhaps predictably, the highest incidence of doorways and graffiti messages occurred along the major thoroughfares connecting the city gates with the urban centre and/or along streets exclusively connected to the forum. This suggests a fairly continuous flow of traffic moving through the city, probably including many visitors. It also indicates that the social, political and commercial attention of many of Pompeii's inhabitants focussed on this flow of traffic. The data suggest that, as an urban landscape, Pompeii 'worked', in the sense that it actually succeeded in guiding the majority of those passing through from the city gates directly to the centre, to the buildings and spaces constituting the social, economic, political and religious heart of the community. The recent study by Alan Kaiser of Roman urban street networks (based on a comparison of four cities: Pompeii, Ostia, Silchester and Spanish Empúries [Emporiae]) partly echoes this conclusion but takes the analysis to a new level by differentiating between streets that integrated urban space ('primary streets', fora), and those that segregated it ('secondary streets', some plazas).[35] Integrating streets and squares connected the central areas of the city and united inhabitants and visitors. They were the primary arteries of commerce, constituted the crucial venues for the display of elite social power, in the form of statues and luxurious housing and provided access to the most important civic amenities (e.g. fountains, bath houses and temples). They had the most doors opening onto them. Segregating paths, which were often short and narrow 'secondary' streets and smaller plazas, by contrast, 'kept out people who did not live or work in that area', allowing a somewhat more private neighbourhood atmosphere.[36] Kaiser notes important similarities between cities across the Roman world with regard to this particular differential use of public space.[37]

[33] Yavetz (1958); Scobie (1986) and the next section of the present chapter.
[34] Laurence (1994) 88–103.   [35] Kaiser (2011a).
[36] On neighbourhoods, in this case in Augustan Rome, see the recent work of Bert Lott (2004).
[37] Kaiser (2011a) 200–201.

Innovative approaches to urban space are currently in the forefront when it comes to revealing something of the 'lived experience' in ancient cities.[38] This involves work on the flow of traffic around cities, on nuisances obstructing this flow, on 'space syntax' (a method for calculating how integrated particular streets are within the overall urban street network), on ancient street life, on the differentiated experiences of walking around the city ('ambulatory movement') for different social groups, on the smells and sounds of civic life in relation to space ('multisensory experience of movement') and so on.[39] Crucial in all these studies is a shift in focus from particular spatial settings and monuments to analysis of movement and flow.

Urban Living Conditions

Consideration of the ancient urban experience also invites us to take a look at the darker side of life in the city. For all of their architectural splendour, both ancient and comparative evidence suggests that Greek and Roman cities may not in all respects have been particularly pleasant places to live in. The sources offer disconcerting glimpses. The author of the Aristotelian *Constitution of Athens*, discussing the duties of officials called the *astynomoi*, mentions in passing that they employed public slaves to 'remove for burial the bodies of those who die in the streets' (*Ath. Pol.* 50.2). Suetonius tells of a street dog carrying in a human hand while the emperor Vespasian was having breakfast (*Vesp.* 5.4), while one of the characters in Petronius' *Satyricon* mentions treading on refuse and corpses in the streets at night as if this were a normal occurrence (*Satyr.* 134.1). Martial describes a scene in which a beggar, dying in the street, hears dogs howling in anticipation of eating his corpse while he is trying to keep away vultures (10.5.11–12). Archaeological discoveries confirm the impression created by the written sources: at Rome in the Esquiline graveyard huge pits (*puticuli*) have been discovered, into which the human corpses were unceremoniously thrown along with animal carcasses and sewage.[40] Often bones from ancient graveyards show traces of having been gnawed by dogs or other animals,

---

[38] See Scott (2012), in this series, for an excellent overview of recent approaches to the use of space in the ancient world.

[39] See the contributions in Laurence and Newsome (2011), particularly those of Van Nes (space syntax), Betts (multisensory experience), Hartnett (nuisances), Kaiser and Poehler (traffic), Holleran (street life) and Macaulay-Lewis (walking).

[40] Hopkins (1983) 207–11.

suggesting that the bodies had been lying in the street for some time or had been poorly buried.[41] Death, it seems, was omnipresent in ancient cities.

This situation should hardly cause surprise when viewed from a comparative historical perspective. Historical demographers have long known of the high death rates in pre-modern cities. In pre-modern cities, especially larger ones, the annual number of deaths often exceeded the number of births. This has been called the urban graveyard effect. The decrease of the urban population caused by this phenomenon could be offset only by a continual influx of migrants. The urban graveyard effect resulted from the high population densities and generally extremely insanitary conditions prevailing in most pre-modern cities, which turned them into hotbeds of infectious diseases. Ancient cities were certainly very dirty and unhygienic by modern standards. Fernand Braudel's evocative description of sixteenth- and seventeenth-century Paris can easily be applied to Greek and Roman cities: 'Chamber pots . . . continued to be emptied out of windows; the streets were sewers. For a long time Parisians "relieved themselves under a row of yews" in the Tuileries; driven from there by the Swiss guards, they betook themselves to the banks of Seine, which "is equally revolting to the eye and nose"'.[42] At home, Greeks relieved themselves in chamber pots, which were emptied in the house's cesspit (*kopron*), if it had one. The contents of this, in turn, might be sold to dung collectors (*koprologoi*), who sold it to farmers as fertiliser. Given the absence of public latrines in Archaic and Classical Greek cities, people out of doors generally relieved themselves in the streets, as Aristophanes has his character Blepyrus do immediately after getting up in the morning (*Ecclesiazusae* 311–375).[43] Roman houses might have an indoor latrine, built over a cesspit, and, judging by the evidence from Pompeii, often situated in or near the kitchen. The inhabitants of *insulae*, Roman apartment blocks, did not have the luxury of indoor latrines and made do with chamber pots, the contents of which were tipped out of the window (night-time passers-by in cities were well aware of the risk, according to Juvenal). During the day, people used the public latrines available in many Roman cities. It is clear, however, from the many threats against perpetrators found in inscriptions, legal texts and wall graffiti that many people relieved themselves in public space, in the street, in tombs, in doorways and behind statues.[44] Sewers might be open but in any case often

---

[41] Scobie (1986) 418, referring to excavated cemeteries in Roman Britain.
[42] Braudel (1981) 310, cited by Scobie (1986) 417–18 as comparable with conditions in the city of Rome.
[43] Garland (2009) 133.   [44] Scobie (1986) 417.

overflowed after heavy rain or river flooding. Add to this the dung and urine from countless animals (horses, donkeys, cattle, dogs etc.), household refuse and the skins, blood and organs of slaughtered animals dumped casually in the streets by butchers, and it becomes easy to see that the ancient city represented a serious health hazard. It constituted an ideal environment for the flourishing of both pathogens and their vectors (animals transmitting the pathogen, such as the mosquito in the case of malaria).

The close physical proximity of people in the urban environment further contributed to morbidity since many infectious diseases are density-dependent, i.e. they need a certain level of population density to become endemic. Thus, the larger a city was, the more virulent its disease environment. In the imperial city of Rome, for instance, with over a million inhabitants, some diseases, such as malaria, had exceptionally high transmission rates, a situation known as hyperendemicity.[45] In large pre-modern cities, mortality, especially among infants and young children, was therefore very high (with an average expectation of life at birth in the lower twenties), resulting in a failure of the urban population to reproduce itself. To prevent urban decline, and especially to allow urban growth, exceptional rates of immigration were necessary. Willem Jongman has calculated, for instance, that under conditions of high urban excess mortality, 'to maintain the urban population of Roman Italy at late-Republican and early-Imperial levels required an annual inflow of 14,000–15,000 immigrants, corresponding to 32,000–35,000 rural births'. Two-thirds of these immigrants went to the city of Rome.[46] The upside of the situation, of course, was that in smaller cities and rural areas with lower population densities, mortality rates were lower. This difference between (metropolitan) urban and rural mortality levels is crucial to the urban graveyard model: the demographic surplus of the countryside (or in smaller cities), it is argued, compensated for the excess mortality in large cities in the form of migration from the countryside or small towns to these large cities. This surplus, if sizeable, might even allow for migration-fuelled urban growth, precisely the scenario in late-Republican Rome.

The urban graveyard model was most famously applied by E. A. Wrigley to explain the remarkable growth of London between 1650 and 1750 CE.[47] Subsequently, the theory was generalised for cities in early

[45] Scheidel (2003a) 164; see Sallares (2002) on malaria in ancient Rome and Italy.
[46] Jongman (2003) 107–8.
[47] Wrigley (1967). The intellectual roots of the model, also often termed the theory of urban natural decrease, go back much further to seventeenth- and eighteenth-century authors: see Sharlin (1978) 126–7 and Cipolla (1994) 133–5 for references.

modern Europe.[48] Applications to the ancient world, mostly to Rome and other Italian cities, have followed Wrigley's model, adopting his calculations for early modern London and adapting them to the ancient situation.[49] Criticism of Wrigley, however, appeared early on, in the form of an alternative model by Alan Sharlin in which he stressed urban fertility rather than mortality as the crucial variable.[50] Sharlin argued that urban excess mortality in early modern European cities could be explained by taking into account differences in fertility between a core population of long-time urban residents which was (just) able to reproduce itself and an immigrant population consisting mostly of young men and women who migrated to the cities to become servants, artisans and journeymen and who faced institutional barriers to marriage in the city. Thus, with rates of illegitimate fertility being low, the immigrant group hardly reproduced itself. Immigrants did, however, often die in the city, where their deaths were duly registered. The overall impression from city records would be one of significant urban excess mortality in cities with large migrant populations although that concealed underlying demographic differences between the various groups making up the urban population.

One implication of Sharlin's model is that pre-modern urban mortality levels, though higher than in the countryside, might have been less severe than proponents of the urban graveyard model tend to assume.[51] Otherwise, how could the core population of permanent urban residents have reproduced itself? Some scholars have indeed attempted to revise the negative image of ancient urban living conditions. Ray Laurence argues that the modern vision of ancient Rome as a metropolitan dystopia of overcrowding, filth and disease, such as we find in the works of Scobie and others, has more to do with Victorian outrage over urban squalor and modern ideals of urban planning than with ancient reality. These preoccupations have led modern commentators to accept the ancient literary sources for urban living conditions (e.g. Juvenal and Martial) too uncritically. In particular Laurence attacks Scobie, who 'takes a modern Western standard and compares this with Rome's pre-industrial cities ... These standards need not have occurred to the inhabitants of Rome'.[52] Yet, as

---

[48] Cipolla (1994) 133–5.   [49] Morley (1996); Jongman (2003).   [50] Sharlin (1978).

[51] Sharlin (1978) 138. Another implication is that in Sharlin's model rural-urban migration was mostly driven by 'pull factors', i.e. people went to the city to become economically better off. The urban graveyard model 'needs' many immigrants to explain urban growth, but it is less good at explaining why rural people should feel the need to migrate to the cities at all, in the absence of a grave rural subsistence crisis, if indeed cities were such filthy and deadly environments; see Tacoma (2008) 8.

[52] Laurence (1997) 12, 14.

Walter Scheidel notes, dying from pathogens does not require awareness of their existence, nor does it require knowledge of the fact that filth and overcrowding cause germs to flourish.[53]

Nonetheless, in an attempt to compare like with like, Elio Lo Cascio has argued with the aid of comparative evidence that in terms of population densities and hygienic and sanitary conditions, imperial Rome was not significantly different from other pre-industrial cities that did manage a natural (i.e. non-migration-fuelled) increase of their population. In fact, Lo Cascio argues, conditions in Rome were probably better than in most pre-modern cities, given the capital's abundant water supply through its system of aqueducts and the public grain distributions (*annona*). Following the lead of Sharlin, Lo Cascio identifies the *plebs frumentaria*, that is, those citizens benefitting from the grain dole, as Rome's core population, given that (since the emperor Augustus' reform of the *annona*) recipients had to be regularly domiciled at Rome, and argues that this group was able to reproduce itself.[54]

The two models of urban demography seem structurally opposed, with proponents of the urban graveyard theory stressing severe mortality and the inability of urban populations to reproduce themselves, while Sharlin, though not denying that urban mortality was higher than rural mortality, stresses (differential) fertility. However, the models can be combined. On the basis of data for early modern York, Chris Galley has argued that expansion or contraction of the urban economy was a crucial factor influencing the level of migration to the city and the extent to which immigrants were able to gain employment, settle down, marry and start families. Thus, when the urban economy flourished, the urban population might increase naturally because many immigrants married and reproduced, while in times of economic contraction, cities might face natural decrease.[55] Again, the important variable is fertility, not mortality. This seems an interesting line of inquiry to pursue for ancient cities.

Recently, but with different arguments, Laurens Tacoma too has argued that the models may be combined, in this case for early imperial Rome.[56] There is, he argues, no evidence for a level of fertility among the resident population of Rome high enough to compensate for the high mortality

---

[53] Scheidel (2003a) 159–60.
[54] Lo Cascio (2006). He argues (67–8) that the fact that membership of the *plebs frumentaria* was hereditary, combined with the attested use of the lot to select actual beneficiaries from among those who had inherited the potential right to the dole, presupposes a situation in which the *plebs frumentaria* was able to reproduce itself, and perhaps even increase in number.
[55] Galley (1995).   [56] Tacoma (2008).

prevailing in such an exceptionally large and densely populated pre-industrial city (which accords with the urban graveyard theory). At the same time, it is likely that among Rome's (free) immigrant population (probably mostly young men), levels of fertility were below average, i.e. lower than among the resident urban population (which accords with Sharlin's model). Fertility again is the key variable.[57]

Ongoing research into the ecology and disease environment of ancient cities has further nuanced our understanding of the Greek and Roman urban demographic experience. Strong variation across time and space is increasingly being detected. For instance, strongly density-dependent diseases, such as smallpox, measles and rubella were not endemic in Archaic and Classical Greece, simply because population densities were too low, even in the largest poleis. Similarly, well-known childhood diseases, such as diphtheria and mumps, are not attested as such in Classical Greece, again because population densities were too low for these diseases to prey endemically on small children.[58] Only with the rise of truly large cities with hundreds of thousands of inhabitants during the Hellenistic period can we expect the urban disease environment in these cities to have become more virulent, especially for infants and young children.

Mortality levels have also been shown to vary *within* cities throughout the year. In the city of Rome, for instance, mortality peaked in late summer and early autumn, indicating a seasonal pattern associated primarily with a high prevalence of malignant forms of malaria and diseases aggravated by it.[59] Local and regional differences in mortality patterns are also becoming increasingly visible, underscoring Horden and Purcell's emphasis on the micro-ecological fragmentation of the ancient Mediterranean environment.[60] In Classical Greece, there were, for instance, clear regional variations in the prevalence of certain illnesses and afflictions (e.g. the inhabitants of Boeotia suffered from tapeworms while the Athenians did not), with mountainous regions being generally healthier than low-lying areas, such as Attica.[61] For the Roman period, pronounced differences in seasonal mortality patterns between regions within Roman Egypt and between these regions and other parts of the empire (late Roman Carthage and Palestine, the city of Rome) have been found, suggesting

---

[57] See now also Hin (2013) 221–8 for a further revision of the urban graveyard model. She argues that frequent and bidirectional flows of migrants (e.g. seasonal migration between city and countryside) would have eased the spread of disease pathogens, which would have caused urban and rural disease environments to become somewhat more similar, reducing the urban/rural mortality differential.
[58] Sallares (1991) 232.   [59] Scheidel (1994), (2003a); Shaw (1996), (2006).
[60] Horden and Purcell (2000).   [61] Sallares (1991) 226–7 with references.

different disease ecologies.[62] Even within (large) cities, there might be pronounced differences in the risk of exposure to disease between various areas: at Rome, the hills were more salubrious than the low-lying regions of the city.[63] Skeletal evidence, finally, has revealed interesting differences between various ancient cemetery sites in and around Rome and in cities throughout the empire with regard to the frequency of stress markers indicative of nutritional deficiencies and exposure to disease and parasites on bone material.[64] The study of this type of evidence, which, through scientific analysis of the bone material can provide a host of information on the health and nutritional status of ancient city populations, despite many methodological problems, probably constitutes the best way forward to advance our understanding of urban demography in antiquity.

Demographic conditions in ancient cities had consequences beyond the immediate quality of life and life chances of individuals. We already saw the possible implications with regard to rural-urban migration. The growth in size and number of cities and the urban networks created within the Mediterranean region and beyond during the Hellenistic and Roman periods, together with a strong increase in the geographical mobility of people, greatly facilitated both the spread and the prevalence of infectious diseases. As Scheidel has noted for Rome, the resulting low urban life expectancies and the great fluctuation in survival chances made larger urban populations highly unstable bodies, something which surely had effects on 'family formation, social structure, political activity and the preservation of civic memory'.[65] Studies of agriculture in early modern Italy have noted 'the debilitating effect' of repeated chronic infections on farm workers in malarial regions, 'particularly at harvest time in late summer or early autumn'. In antiquity, as Robert Sallares has shown, the situation is unlikely to have been different.[66] Thus, the character of urban and regional disease ecologies appears closely linked to patterns of urbanisation, migration, civic sociopolitical dynamics and agrarian productivity, a set of correlations that strongly invites further study.

---

[62] Scheidel (2001).   [63] Scheidel (2003a) 165–6.
[64] See Gowland and Garnsey (2010); also Scheidel (2012b).
[65] Scheidel (2003) 158. See, for example, Zuiderhoek (2011) for the impact of demographic volatility among urban elites on patterns of civic munificence; Holleran and Pudsey (2011) collect various studies on the social, economic and political consequences of ancient demographic dynamics.
[66] Scheidel (2007) 36 for the quotes; Sallares (2002) 242–4.

CHAPTER 5

Politics and Political Institutions

Greek and Roman cities were political communities, which possessed the institutions required for autonomous collective decision-making. This remained a characteristic of ancient cities from one end of antiquity to the other, even if under monarchical or imperial rule the autonomy of poleis and civitates was somewhat more restricted. At the basis of ancient civic politics lay the institution of (adult male) citizenship. It was this artificial common denominator, independent of kinship, class or locale, that allowed the early poleis and the Roman civitas to overcome the rifts created by differences of wealth, power and prestige between individuals and the stubborn regionalism of local patronage networks, at least to the extent that widespread political participation and collective decision-making became possible. In both the Greek and Roman conceptions, therefore, the freedom associated with citizenship (*eleutheria/libertas*) was primarily of an active character, a freedom *to* participate, in the governing of the community, but also in civic and religious rituals (festivals, public commensality). In what follows we shall review the political systems and most important political institutions of ancient cities and some of the debates concerning them.

Politics and Political Systems

All ancient cities were organised according to the same institutional blueprint: they had one or more deliberative councils, a series of (committees of) magistrates, and one or more citizen assemblies. At a lower administrative level, citizens were generally divided up into units called *phylai* or *tribus* which carried an element of fictive kinship but often had a geographical connotation as well, and which in many poleis constituted the organisational building blocks of the higher level institutions. For instance, in Athens, the council (*boule*) contained fifty members from each *phyle*.

All these elements could, however, be internally structured and/or combined in such ways as to produce a variety of political systems. In democratic cities, such as Athens, all adult male citizens, rich or poor, had access to, and the right to speak in and make a proposal to, the public assembly (*ekklesia*), which had final say in all public decisions. In addition, each and every citizen could be selected annually to magistracies (*archai*), usually via allotment, and serve on the deliberative council (*boule*) and popular jury courts (*dikasteria* or *heliaia*). Athenian citizens received payment for serving as magistrates, councillors and jurors, and, from the 390s BCE on, for participating in the assembly, but such financial rewards, though known from other poleis as well, may not have been universal, even among democratic cities.[1]

Popular political participation, mostly via assemblies, was a general feature of Greek cities, and, in a more limited sense, of Roman ones. Classical democratic Athens did manage to realise the participatory ideal to the fullest. Yet Athenian democratic credentials have not gone unchallenged in modern scholarship. In line with a general tendency among historians and social scientists during the first half of the twentieth century to assume the existence of 'informal oligarchies' in ostensibly democratically organised institutions and states, classical scholars started to probe the Athenian political system in search of such an elite behind the scenes. According to the so-called elitist school in political theory, the main proponents of which were Gaetano Mosca, Vilfredo Pareto and Robert Michels, eventually every democratic organisation or state would evolve into an informal oligarchy as bureaucratisation occurred or wealthier, more experienced or more talented individuals managed to take control of affairs officiously, aided by the 'natural apathy' of the mass of ordinary citizens/voters.[2] Michels called this the Iron Law of Oligarchy. Parallels for this idea may be found in Max Weber's concept of an informal 'aristocracy of office' (*Honoratiorenschicht*) developing in republican political systems,[3] and in the sociologist C. Wright Mills' notion of an – economic – 'power elite' informally controlling US politics.[4] Ancient historians have looked for a locus of elite control in the Athenian *boule* or Council of 500 or in Athenian office holding, particularly the

---

[1] De Ste. Croix (1975) assembles the evidence for political pay outside Athens. See most recently Robinson (2011), esp. 227.
[2] Mosca (1980); Pareto (1963); Michels (1959).
[3] A concept adopted by Quass (1993) for an analysis of the post-Classical polis, see below.
[4] Mills (1956).

directly elected board of generals (*strategoi*), or have pointed to so-called middle-class domination of the popular assembly.[5]

Yet Athenian political practice guaranteed that the composition of both the council and the assembly was socially far too mixed and their 'membership' too ephemeral (that of the *boule* changing every year, that of the assembly more or less with every meeting) ever to constitute the basis for the formation of an enduring elite cadre. Magistrates, meanwhile, were subject to numerous checks, and the politically adventurous had to convince the assembly or popular juries of their point of view time and time again, risking banishment if they were judged too powerful or divisive (ostracism) or prosecution if their proposals were judged 'unlawful' (the *graphe paranomon*). For such reasons, during the past decades scholars, such as Moses Finley, Mogens Hansen and Josiah Ober, have argued that Athenian popular participation was a reality. The stability of the democratic regime should, according to their accounts, be explained not by the assumption of elite control behind the scenes but by socioeconomic power (empire, slavery), a uniquely subtle and effective constitutional set-up, or the continuing political and ideological negotiation between elite and *demos* in assembly and popular jury courts.[6]

Many poleis, however, had a far more oligarchic system than Athens, in which council membership and magistracies were the preserve of the wealthy, or, as was common in the early Archaic period, an aristocracy of birth. In such communities, the council was often the most important political organ, but all citizens had a say in public decision-making via the assembly (with the proviso that citizenship might be based on a property qualification). They were, in effect, 'weak oligarchies', i.e. limited by an institutionalised popular element.[7]

This type of system – with a strong oligarchic element in the form of councils and magistracies dominated by the wealthy but with a citizen-assembly as a 'democratic' or popular counterweight – was in fact typical of the Greek poleis of Hellenistic and Roman times. Alexander and his Hellenistic successor kings granted democratic constitutions loosely modelled on the Athenian system to most of the poleis they freed from Persian dominance or founded, but, as far as we know, without the financial compensation for political activities characteristic of Athens. This, and a

---

[5] De Laix (1973) on the *boule*; Pearson (1937) on the *strategoi*; Jones (1957) for 'middle class' democracy at Athens. On the presence of middling groups but the absence of a proper 'middle class' in ancient cities, see Chapter 7.

[6] Finley (1983), (1985); Ober (1989); Hansen (1991).

[7] Morris (2009) 74–75; Ostwald (2000) on *oligarchia* as a constitutional form in the Greek polis.

combination of other factors, such as the increasing dependence of cities on their wealthy citizens who might serve as ambassadors or indeed as 'friends' (*philoi*) of the king at the royal courts to secure favours for their polis, stimulated a process of 'informal oligarchisation' that produced in most cities a class of wealthy notables (Weber's *Honoratiorenschicht* again) who monopolised the councils and the more important magistracies. The Romans, when they eventually came to dominate the Greek world, gave constitutional backing to this oligarchic tendency, mostly through *leges provinciae*, laws regulating the administration of a newly established province. Under the terms of such laws, Greek city councils were often turned into mini-senates on the Roman model, with a lifelong membership of ex-magistrates, a property qualification (whether in the shape of a census requirement, or a payment upon entering office – *summa honoraria* – or both), and control through urban censors (*timetai*). The popular assemblies, however, were not abolished, and they continued to function well into the third century CE if not later.[8]

A strong focus on the Greek urban elites and their relations with kings, governors and emperors, coupled, at least until recently, with a general pessimism regarding the fate of the Hellenistic and Roman-era polis which, like the Hellenistic world more generally, was unfavourably contrasted with Classical times, has led many scholars to deny the reality of a true element of popular politics in the post-Classical Greek city. Particularly for the Roman imperial period, assemblies are often regarded as 'applause machines' that did little more than rubber-stamp decisions made by small elites of notables in the council.[9]

This view however ignores the scattered but by no means inconsequential epigraphic evidence for assembly-involvement in civic public decision-making from Hellenistic and Roman times and contrasts with the picture of contemporary civic politics sketched by participant-observers, such as Plutarch and Dio Chrysostom, who presented the assembly as a force to be reckoned with in the cities of the Roman East.[10] Oligarchic control of the council and major magistracies was certainly a reality, yet so too was the continuing political activity of the public assemblies.[11] Arguably, therefore, the most typical polis system was not the radical democracy of Athens and a number of other Classical cities

---

[8] Jones (1940); Veyne (1976); Quass (1993); Dmitriev (2005).
[9] E.g. Jones (1940) 177; Magie (1950) 640; De Ste Croix (1981) 518–37; Pleket (1998) 211; Gleason (2006) 234.
[10] Zuiderhoek (2008a) for references.
[11] Rogers (1992); Ma (2000); Zuiderhoek (2008a); Heller (2009).

but a 'republican' type of mixed constitution combining both oligarchic and 'democratic'/popular elements. This is the system that we find most often in the cities of the later Hellenistic and Roman imperial East, when there were more poleis than ever before in the history of the Greek cities.

Greeks recognised yet another political system besides democracy and oligarchy, namely monarchy. Classical Sparta had not one but two kings (*basileis*) in addition to a council (here called *gerousia*) elected from the most prominent senior citizens and including the kings among its members. Sparta also had an assembly of all adult male citizens, and magistrates (the board of five ephors, among others) who were elected annually from among the entire citizenry. Hence to ancient commentators Sparta seemed the perfect constitutional mix of monarchy (dyarchy, strictly speaking, for there were two kings), oligarchy (council) and democracy (ephors, assembly).[12] Yet Sparta as a whole was also in some sense oligarchic, for its citizenship was reserved for a select group of male warriors who met a property qualification that allowed them to contribute their share to the common messes in which they were normally required to dine every night. They called themselves the *homoioi*, or peers, and effectively constituted the elite of the Spartan polis, which also contained numerous families of free non-citizen *perioikoi* ('dwellers-around') as well as a large population of slave-like helots, who worked the estates of the *homoioi*.

It has often been thought that the Spartan kings were some sort of archaic left-over from a supposed Dark Age Greek kingship (in Greek myth, cities are often ruled by kings), yet Dark Age communities were probably governed by small elites of *basileis* with one *primus inter pares* chief assisted by a warriors'/citizens' assembly, rather than by proper monarchs (see Chapter 2). Anyhow, the Spartan kings were not sovereign, and their chief duties were military and religious, though they sat on the council. They could be tried and banned if necessary and had to respect the authority of the ephors.[13]

Even though kingship was not a common form of city-government in Greco-Roman antiquity, one city certainly had powerful kings in its early history, and that was Rome, even though here too the kings were, typically, assisted by a council (the early Senate, whatever its precise

[12] On the Spartan 'constitution', see Andrewes (1966), who stresses the role of the assembly; De Ste. Croix (1972), esp. 124–51; Thommen (1996).
[13] Cartledge (2001) and Millender (2009) on Spartan kingship; also briefly Mitchell (2006) 378–9.

form) and an assembly, the *comitia curiata*.[14] Rome's subsequent republican government, however, conformed to the general Greco-Roman civic-political blueprint of council (Senate), magistracies (open only to elite citizens) and assembly, though Republican Rome, uniquely, had several of the latter.[15] Oligarchic republican systems of a similar kind also existed in other cities of Latium, and in the urban communities of other Italic peoples, such as the Oscans and Umbrians.[16] The Etruscan cities, on the other hand, seem to have been oligarchic monarchies for the most part during the sixth and fifth centuries BCE, organised socially according to a gentilicial clan system but with a hierarchy of magistracies below the kings.[17] The cities of Latium Vetus, of which Rome was one, seem to have developed republican constitutions during the sixth and fifth centuries BCE. At Rome, Etruscan influence may have been stronger though, since it originally had kings, which the Latin cities never had, and a hierarchy of collegiate magistracies instead of a single collegiate one, as seems to have been the norm in the Latin cities.

When the Romans expanded their power, first in Latium and Etruria, then in the rest of Italy, they used the republican political model of the original Latin cities of Latium Vetus (an annual board or boards of magistrates elected from among elite candidates by a popular assembly of citizens, supported by a council or senate composed of former office holders) to reorganise or found cities that could guard their newly acquired territory. The same political model they would also later use for cities founded or reorganised in their western provinces.[18]

The model could, however, be translated into various legal-administrative formats. Thus an incorporated city could become a *municipium*, an autonomous, self-governing community of Roman citizens. Before the Social War (91–87 BCE), these citizens either received full Roman citizenship, including the right to vote in the assemblies at Rome (*suffragium*), or, more often, citizenship without political rights (*sine suffragio*) which meant that they were included in the Roman census and served in the Roman army but could not vote in Rome. But the Romans also founded urban communities called *coloniae*. These came in two varieties. 'Latin colonies', whose inhabitants had 'Latin citizenship', a sort of intermediate stage between the status of foreigner

---

[14] Cornell (1995) 114–50, 248. C. Smith (2011) on the complexities of the evidence for Roman kingship.
[15] Lintott (1999) for an overview of Roman Republican institutions. [16] Cornell (1995) 230–2.
[17] D'Agostino (1990); Cornell (1995) 230-2. [18] Cornell (2000).

(*peregrinus*) and full Roman citizen, and 'Roman colonies' whose inhabitants had full Roman citizenship.[19]

Colonies of both varieties as well as *municipia* could eventually be found in Rome's western provinces, yet initially many provincial cities had the status of *civitas peregrina* ('community of foreigners'). This was the formal legal status of most Greek poleis in the eastern provinces, and wherever the Romans organised existing non-urbanised tribal societies into civic communities, they gave them this status. In the West, civitates often had a political structure roughly resembling the republican model (i.e. with a council and magistrates), although local offices and institutions might persist. While in the East, if Roman emperors founded a new civitas, they generally made it a polis, though there were also colonies in the eastern provinces.[20] Under the empire, an existing civitas might be upgraded to a *municipium*, but then usually one with Latin rights, where only the chief magistrates and their families acquired full Roman citizenship, or later, after a reform implemented by Hadrian, the entire city council. One of the highest honours a provincial city could receive was, finally, to be made a Roman colony, with full Roman citizenship for all of its inhabitants.[21]

There is an intense and ongoing debate over whether the Roman republican political system can be thought of as (partly) democratic. In antiquity it was regarded, like Sparta, as a prime example of a mixed constitution (Polybius 6.11–18), part monarchy (the consuls with their *imperium*), part oligarchy (the Senate, plus the fact that Rome's magistrates were not responsible to the people), part democracy (the electoral and legislative assemblies). Among modern historians, however, Republican Rome has long been viewed as deeply oligarchic, run by an elite of powerful senatorial families (the *nobiles*) who controlled the political system (including elections and voting in the assemblies) through their extensive patronage networks.[22]

The problem with this argument has always been that it reduces the entire constitutional structure of the Republic to a mere façade and that it takes all ideological substance out of its politics, concentrating purely on shifting alliances. Besides, there is precious little evidence for the complete dominance of Roman politics by patronage.[23] In recent times, some scholars, Fergus Millar most prominently among them, have therefore

[19] Cornell (1995) 301–4, 348–52; Lomas (1996) 31–9.
[20] Jones (1940) 51–84; Mitchell (1993) 1:80–99; Levick (1967) on colonies.
[21] Edmondson (2006) 256–60 for references.   [22] Gelzer (1969); Münzer (1920); Gruen (1974).
[23] Brunt (1971), (1988); Finley (1983); Garnsey (2010) 40–4 for some nuance.

returned to the ancient (Polybian) vision of Republican politics, with a strong focus on its democratic element, the assemblies, particularly the *comitia tributa*, through which in the late Republic virtually all legislation was passed.[24] It has also been pointed out that Roman election campaigns were 'real', in the sense that outcomes were not fixed beforehand, and elite candidates really had to win the hearts and minds of the Roman *populus*.[25] The 'democratic model' of Republican politics thus taking shape has been criticised on the grounds that, by the late Republic, the Roman territorial state had simply grown too big, and the number of Roman citizens too large, for it to function as a proper direct democracy, and that the majority of people were uninterested in politics because issues relevant to their socioeconomic situation rarely cropped up.[26] Yet if we simply look at the *city* of Rome in the late Republic, there is something to be said for the argument that ordinary citizens often played an influential part in policy making via the *comitia tributa* (reinforced by the fact that many citizens belonging to rural tribes had migrated to Rome since the mid-second century BCE) as well as in elections. As for the argument about voter disinterest, its is both anachronistic (transposing modern western concerns about supposed voter apathy to the ancient world) and one-sided in its reliance on the unproven assumption that 'political engagement is necessarily based solely on material interest' and is belied anyhow by the mass participation evident in those ancient cities with institutional structures that, more so than Rome, explicitly encouraged the primacy of popular politics (i.e. the democratic poleis).[27]

Roman cities in Italy and the western provinces retained their electoral systems (with magistrates being elected annually by the *populus*) for many centuries. Though we have evidence suggesting actual campaigns, particularly in the form of the electoral graffiti preserved at Pompeii, scholarly opinion is divided on the role played by elite machinations, co-optation and bribery.[28] As with the city of Rome itself, however, it would go too far to think of these communities as static and stifling oligarchies. For one thing, it seems obvious that the very existence of an electoral system implies that ordinary citizens had some kind of say in deciding who should take up office, even if, as some scholars think, elites exercised a tight

---

[24] Millar (1998).
[25] Yakobson (1999). It should be noted, though, that the *populus* did not *vote* democratically in its assemblies, i.e. according to the 'one man, one vote-principle' that prevailed in Greek popular assemblies. Rather, Roman citizens voted in groups, see below.
[26] Mouritsen (2001); for a survey of the debate, see Hölkeskamp (2010) .
[27] Mackay (2002) 400 for the quote.   [28] Mouritsen (1988) on Pompeian politics.

control over the number and identity of the candidates.[29] Moreover, the prevailing demographic regime of high and unpredictable mortality affecting the masses as well as the (political) elite meant there would have been considerable room for upward social mobility. The middling groups in urban society (primarily the higher echelons of the urban professional classes of traders and manufacturers) often appear to have provided the personnel, causing a partial social renewal of the political elite every generation or so (see Chapter 7).

One crucial aspect of ancient civic politics should finally be stressed, and that is the very public, open and direct character of political activity in ancient cities. Politics was, most of the time, essentially an open air, outdoor activity, involving large numbers of people gathering in a relatively confined yet highly symbolically charged urban landscape of squares, theatres, council houses, all in close physical proximity to one another (see also Chapter 4).[30] Assemblies of thousands of citizens met in the agora or forum, in theatres, or in other especially assigned places (e.g. the hillside of the Pnyx in Athens) to be addressed by (elite) speakers, vote on proposals and/or elect magistrates; large crowds would gather to participate, either as jurymen or onlookers, in court cases, often conducted in or near the agora or forum, and taking place in the open air or in publicly accessible buildings. Town councils, numbering in the hundreds, would meet in council houses, but again within close range of the *demos* or *populus*. Roman senators, debating a controversial issue, would have been keenly (and uncomfortably) aware of the shouts of the crowds in the forum outside while the citizens of Greek poleis might follow discussions in the council by standing in the galleries by the doorway of the council house (*bouleuterion*).[31]

Several observations follow. One is that ancient civic politics entailed frequent, close-range contact between sociopolitical elites and ordinary citizens, physical contact even, as elite candidates for magistracies came round to shake the hands of plebeian voters, or when wealthy citizens sat or stood amidst ordinary shopkeepers, craftsmen or farmers in the assembly. Another related observation is that Greco-Roman civic politics was not for the faint-hearted. It often took real courage, especially given the absence of anything resembling an organised police force in most cities, for a magistrate or politician to take the stage and address a crowd of thousands of angry or frightened people, particularly during periods of war or crisis, or put to the vote a deeply controversial proposal. The assembly,

---

[29] Franklin (1980); Jongman (1991), but see Mouritsen (1990).
[30] A point particularly stressed by Millar (1998) for Republican Rome.   [31] Mitchell (1993) I: 203–4.

Cicero wrote (*Amic.* 26/97), resembled a *scaena*, a theatre stage, but the blood, when it did flow, was real.

The Main Political Institutions: City Councils, Popular Assemblies and Magistrates

City Councils

In civic decrees from the ancient world, councils are generally mentioned first: 'The *boule* (council) and *demos* (assembly) have decided . . . ', '*Senatus populusque romanus* . . . ' Clearly, in the Greco-Roman conception of civic government, councils played a central role. In the *Athenian Constitution* (*Athenaion Politeia*), a description of the Athenian political system written most likely by a pupil of Aristotle in the late fourth century BCE, much attention is paid to the council, the numerous magistracies and the law courts while the assembly is taken more or less for granted. When Kleisthenes around 508/507 BCE introduced democratic reforms at Athens, his reorganisation of the Athenian citizen body focussed first and foremost on the creation of a new council. It is also the Senate which plays a central role in the pages of Livy describing the turbulent history of the Roman Republic (though we should note that the Senate's actual political role was very different from that of Kleisthenes' *Boule* of 500, see below).

All this does not necessarily imply that ancient cities were inherently oligarchic, even though many were. What it does imply, however, is that it was often the particular composition, structure and functioning of the council within a city's political system that determined whether it tended towards oligarchy or democracy. Small councils were oligarchic, according to Aristotle (*Pol.* 1299b.34), while large ones were democratic. The Council of 500 at Athens consisted of a wide cross section of the citizenry, selected by lot, and changing annually. In more oligarchic cities, membership of the council would often be for life and be subject to some kind of property qualification (as was the case, for instance, in both Greek and Roman cities under the empire) and hence consist of the more affluent citizens, while magistrates, though elected by the people, tended to be wealthy men too. According to Aristotle again, in democratic cities, the assembly should be powerful and not the magistrates (*Pol.* 1317b.28–30). Hence the focus of the fourth-century *Athenaion Politeia* on council and magistrates. It was the way these were organised in Classical Athens, with, crucially, payment for council membership, office-holding and jury service, so that the poor could fully participate, that made the city a radical democracy.

In most Greek cities, the council fulfilled the function of *probouleusis* (lit. 'prior consideration'), that is, it prepared meetings of the popular assembly by determining which business was to be brought before it, and, often if not always, by formulating proposals (*probouleumata*) for deciding on the matters concerned. In democratic cities, such as Athens, the assembly might accept, amend or reject a *probouleuma*. Moreover, any citizen had the right to address the assembly and propose an alternative. In more oligarchic poleis, proposing motions might be the sole prerogative of the council and/or magistrates, and debate in the assembly is likely to have been restricted or absent.[32]

In Roman cities, the councils functioned somewhat differently. The Senate of Republican Rome advised the magistrates (consuls, praetors) who proposed laws for ratification to the public assemblies. Its counsels, the *senatusconsulta*, were not legally binding but were usually followed. In Italian or provincial cities with a Roman-style constitution (*coloniae*, *municipia*), however, it was mostly the councils and magistrates who made political decisions while the role of the assemblies was restricted to the election of magistrates.[33] The membership of Roman city councils (including the Senate at Rome) consisted of ex-magistrates, current magistrates and those directly admitted via *adlectio*. Subject to a property qualification, they served as councillors/senators for life. They thus stand in sharp contrast to the democratic Greek city councils where membership changed on a regular basis, though, as was noted above, councils of Greek cities that became part of Roman provinces were often reformed along Roman lines.

In addition to their probouleutic councils, many Greek poleis also had a council of elders (*gerousia*). Sometimes, the *gerousia* effectively played the role of a probouleutic council, as at Sparta. At Athens, the council of elders was called Areopagus, after the rocky hill where it met, and was composed of former archons (Athens's chief executive and judicial magistrates). It had great influence in Archaic times, until 462 BCE, when a constitutional reform robbed it of most of its powers. It became more important again later in Athenian history, particularly in Roman times. Councils of elders are fairly widely attested in other poleis as well, particularly during the Hellenistic and Roman periods, although their actual function is not always clear.[34]

---

[32] Ehrenberg (1969) 59–65; Mitchell (2006) 373–4. Even in Athens, however, actual debate in the assembly, in the sense of a group discussion among the citizens present, may have been comparatively rare, see Cammack (2012).
[33] Lintott (1993) 147.   [34] Mitchell (2006) 374 for references; Jones (1940) 225–6.

Popular Assemblies

Most ancient cities from early Archaic times until well into the third century CE or later had public assemblies of citizens, in some form or another, even those cities that were oligarchies. As Aristotle wrote, the operational difference between oligarchy and democracy was that in a democracy, the assembly was sovereign (*Pol.* 1298a.3–35).[35] At Athens, all male citizens of c. 20 years or older could attend, debate, propose motions to and vote in the assembly (*ekklesia*), but in some cities, attendance was restricted to a specific group of citizens. Intriguingly, this could be the case in democratic as well as in oligarchic cities. Thus, at democratic Argos, there was a property qualification for assembly 'membership', whereas in Sparta, the property qualification was for citizenship, but all citizens could attend and vote in the assembly.[36]

Voting in Athens was by show of hands (*Ath. Pol.* 44.3; 61.1); in Sparta it was by acclamation. According to Aristotle (*Pol.* 1272a.4–12), there were no debates in the Spartan assembly. The assembly simply voted on issues put to it by the council (*gerousia*) via *probouleusis*. Yet other sources, chiefly Thucydides, appear to present a different picture, and scholars are divided on the issue.[37] If Aristotle is right, Sparta was in this respect probably not typical of Greek poleis generally, not even of the oligarchic ones. In the Hellenistic and Roman imperial poleis, portrayed as strongly oligarchic by many historians, debates did take place, as is clear from the writings of authors such as Plutarch and Dio Chrysostom, even if it was mostly the wealthy who were doing the talking.[38]

The Romans, uniquely, voted by group instead of individually in their assemblies (*comitia*). Under the Republic, the *comitia centuriata*, which voted per *centuria*, and was therefore deeply oligarchic, since the higher census classes controlled the majority of *centuriae*, elected the chief magistrates (censors, consuls, praetors), while most legislation was passed via the *comitia tributa*, which voted per *tribus* or geographical district, i.e. a fairly random selection of citizens, and was therefore arguably somewhat less dominated by the elite.[39] There was no debate; citizens simply voted for or

---

[35] Yet the *class* difference between these two types of constitutions was that oligarchy was the rule of the (few) rich over the (many) poor and democracy the rule of the (many) poor over the (few) rich: see *Pol.* 1279b; De Ste. Croix (1981) 71–6.

[36] Mitchell (2006) 371; Tomlinson (1972) 193 on Argos.

[37] Andrewes (1966) for references to the Spartans debating in their assembly; Mitchell (2006) 372–3 summarises modern opinion.

[38] Zuiderhoek (2008a) for references.

[39] Taylor (1966); North (2006) 260–3 provides a useful schematic overview of the Republican assemblies and their workings.

against a proposal presented by the magistrates or for or against a candidate for office. Often assemblies were preceded by a *contio*, a more informal public meeting in which the issues involved were presented in speeches by magistrates; even here, however, there was little room for popular discussion.[40] It might be argued though that with the group voting system, the locus of debate and consensus-seeking was simply transferred from *comitia*-in-session to *centuria* or *tribus* beforehand since within the voting group consensus, or at least a majority, first had to be found to decide on the group's vote.[41] The assemblies in the city of Rome lost their political role during the early Principate. In Roman cities in Italy and the provinces, however, citizen assemblies (*populi*), voting in groups called *curiae* (or *vici*, at Pompeii) for the election of magistrates, remained part of the political system.

Magistrates

The rules and regulations concerning magistrates take up quite a lot of space in many ancient laws and constitutions. The earliest Greek law that we have, from the polis of Dreros on Crete and dating to 650–600 BCE, is solely concerned with precluding anyone from holding the office of *kosmos* (chief magistrate) for successive terms – ten years should pass between one term as *kosmos* and a subsequent one – and with outlining the penalties for those who disregarded this rule.[42] A similar concern with officials' precise responsibilities and the limits thereof can be found in other Archaic Greek laws, as well as in later ones.[43] The Aristotelian *Athenaion Politeia*, as noted above, devotes a great deal of space to the numerous officials of fourth-century BCE democratic Athens, the way they were elected (mostly by lot, sometimes directly) and their various duties. Extant Roman municipal charters, such as those from Málaga and Irni in Spain and Tarentum in Italy, also have a fair bit to say on the election and duties of the municipal magistrates.[44]

One reason for such emphasis on magisterial responsibility and its limits was the Greek propensity to classify laws and procedures according to the

---

[40] Morstein-Marx (2004).

[41] Note that during elections in the *comitia centuriata*, one *centuria*, the so-called *centuria praerogativa*, which was selected by lot from the first property class, voted before the other *centuriae*. Its result, which was announced immediately, may well have swayed the other *centuriae* in the same direction.

[42] Meiggs/Lewis no. 2 = Fornara no. 11.

[43] Osborne (1997) 79 lists and discusses a range of examples.

[44] Spitzl (1984); Gonzales and Crawford (1986); Lomas (1996) 203–5, no. 323.

magistrate responsible, rather than according to a typology of regulations and offences, a pattern that we can also recognise in the Roman municipal charters.[45] Another, arguably more important reason, however, was that Greek poleis and Roman civitates were citizen-communities organised on the principle of the collective political participation of all adult male citizens. Consequently, a strong need was felt precisely to circumscribe and also to limit (in time, in content and in terms of personal accumulation) the level of executive power with which an individual citizen could be entrusted. This was most obviously the case in democratic cities – the Athenian preference for selecting most officials by lot (apart from generals [*strategoi*] and treasurers [*tamiai*], who were elected) – was surely in part motivated by the fact that it prevented magistracies from falling too often into the hands of wealthy and influential citizens who would find it easier than a poorer man to abuse (and get away with abusing) the authority with which they were entrusted. In oligarchic communities, where offices were generally the prerogative of the wealthy, limits to power and a system of rotation primarily functioned (and were surely designed) to prevent destructive internecine conflicts among the elite.

These were some of the reasons behind the two most distinctive characteristics of Greek and Roman civic magistracies: they were collegial and annual. Barring a few exceptions, magistrates operated in pairs or in committees. Thus the famed Roman *imperium*, or supreme power to command of magistrates, was generally shared among those magistrates endowed with it: each year, these were the two consuls and the two (later four, and, still later, eight) praetors.[46]

Partly due to this principle of collegiality, ancient cities, especially Greek ones, often had great numbers of officials, well over one thousand in the case of Classical Athens if we include the councillors (who at Athens were selected annually by lot).[47] For Greek cities generally from the Archaic period until well into the later Roman Empire, the sources refer to an astonishingly large number of magistracies, many of them probably quite similar in terms of their duties but often going by different titles in different cities.[48] There was less variety in Roman cities. Unlike the

---

[45] Osborne (1997) 79.
[46] Other magistrates with *imperium* were the dictator – nominated by the consuls at the request of the Senate, who had power superior to all offices but was only appointed in emergencies and for just six months – his aide the 'Master of the Horse' (*magister equitum*) and, within the boundaries of their provinces and also for a fixed period of time, promagistrates (i.e. propraetors and proconsuls).
[47] Hansen (1991) 230.
[48] Ehrenberg (1969) 65–71; Mitchell (2006) 375–8; on post-Classical poleis, see Jones (1940) parts III and IV; Dmitriev (2005).

Greeks, the Romans were more systematic, organising their magistracies according to a strict sequence of increasing seniority, the famous *cursus honorum*. Also, the administrative structure of Roman civitates, *coloniae* and *municipia* was originally modelled on that of the civitates of Latium Vetus (see above), which led to a greater degree of uniformity (despite some differences between the various legal categories of city).[49] Still in Republican Rome the number of holders of some magistracies increased considerably over time, largely due to the demands of empire; there were, for instance, eight praetors by the time of Sulla instead of the original two, and forty quaestors by the time of Julius Caesar.[50]

Despite such overall variety, we can generally group magistracies in Greek and Roman cities according to several broad categories. First, there are the chief political, judicial and/or military officials (e.g. archons and *strategoi* at Athens, ephors and nauarchs at Sparta, consuls and praetors at Rome and *duoviri* and *quattuorviri* in Roman colonies and *municipia*). Regarding chief magistrates, there was an important difference between Greek poleis and the city of Rome. The notion of *imperium* was alien to Greek governmental practice. Greek magistrates were essentially servants of the people (*demos*), whereas, if we accept Theodor Mommsen's influential theory, the chief magistrates at Rome had inherited their *imperium* from the old Roman kings, who, of course, stood *above* the people (*populus*).[51]

Next, we can generally distinguish a category of officials concerned with various civic services and infrastructure, such as *agoranomoi* (market supervisors), *sitonai*, *sitophylakes* (overseers of the grain supply), gymnasiarchs (directors of gymnasia/bath houses), *epimeletai* (building overseers), *agonothetai* (festival directors), *aediles* (overseers of markets, roads, drains, public buildings, festivals and games) and a category of financial/secretarial officials of all kinds (e.g. quaestors, *tamiai* and *grammateis*). We might add a further category of officials responsible for public order (e.g. eirenarchs in Greek cities and in western Roman towns the *aediles*).

Naturally there are many attested offices that do not fit this broad categorisation. For instance, the tribunes of the *plebs* and the censors at Rome, councillors and jurors in Greek cities (if counted as magistrates), and the many prefectures of the imperial city of Rome, to name but a few.

---

[49] Mouritsen (1988) on Pompeii; Lomas (1996) 195–214 and Lassère (2007) 339–87 present and discuss evidence for civic elections, magistracies and municipal careers.
[50] Lintott (1999) 94–146; North (2006) 263–6.
[51] North (2006) 263; Mommsen (1887–1888) 1.27–75.

But as a summary, the overview just presented is fairly indicative of the kinds of public tasks that needed to be performed in ancient cities.

Magisterial overzealousness was sometimes mocked, as when Apuleius, in his comical novel *The Golden Ass*, has an aedile destroy the fish a customer has just bought from a market stall because the price charged was too high (*Metam.* 1.24–5). Corruption was the opposite charge: in his *Satyricon*, Petronius has one of the characters accuse *aediles* of colluding with the city bakers and wealthy grain hoarders to keep bread prices high (*Sat.* 44).

In general, however, commitment seems to have been high. For what was often only modest remuneration, great numbers of ordinary Athenian citizens devoted years of their life to the numerous magistracies of the democratic polis. Countless inscriptions from the post-Classical Greek poleis and Roman Italian and western provincial cities list the many magistracies held by scores of prominent citizens, without pay and often at considerable private expense. Of course, status and prestige were to be gained, and there were perhaps other emoluments as well, yet we should realise that without the concerted effort of many generations of such individuals ancient cities could not have functioned. It is after all surely significant that precisely when, for various reasons, such civic commitment started to flag from the late second and early third centuries CE onwards, that the Roman Empire for the first time began to get into serious trouble.[52]

---

[52] See Chapter 10. Of course, flagging commitment of the *decuriones* was by no means the only factor responsible for the troubles of the third century CE, but it was certainly an integral component.

CHAPTER 6

Civic Ritual and Civic Identity

At some point between 2 BCE and 2 CE, the citizens of Kyme in Asia Minor decided to honour their prominent fellow-citizen Kleanax, who had been holding the office of *prytanis* for the last year. As the inscription recording the honorific decree of the council and people states, they did so because:

> [N]ow as *prytanis* [Kleanax] has performed at New Year's Day the sacrifices for the gods in the ancestral manner and has treated everyone in the polis to sweet wine and has put on expensive stage shows and has made the vows for prosperity and the sacrifices in the ancestral manner and has for several days entertained in the town hall (*prytaneion*) many citizens and (resident) Romans; he has also performed the sacrifices for the dead on the accustomed day in the ancestral manner and distributed the remains of the sacrifice and a milk-and-flour porridge to all in the city, free men and slaves. At the Festival of the Lark he himself, being the first to do so, by proclamation invited to breakfast in the town hall the citizens, the Romans, the (non-citizen) residents (*paroikoi*) and the (non-resident) foreigners (*xenoi*) and performed the throwing out (into the crowd) of presents in the same way as earlier *prytaneis* had done. He organised the Procession of the Laurel[1] and gave breakfast to the priests, the victors in the sacred games, the city magistrates and many of the citizens. He also, at the festival for the emperor organised by the province of Asia, just as he had promised, provided sacrifices and festive banquets.[2]

Yet the benefactions of Kleanax to his city went further than this. At an earlier stage in his career, as priest of Dionysus, he had treated the inhabitants of the city to many a banquet and invested much of his own wealth in the adornment and elaboration of the cult festivities for the god. At his daughter's wedding, he had put on yet another lavish public banquet.

Kleanax, of course, is a typical example of the grand public benefactor, a stock figure of civic life during the later Hellenistic and Roman imperial

---

[1] A cult ritual for Apollo.   [2] Merkelbach (1983). Schmitt Pantel (1992) 255–60 for discussion.

periods, the 'honour-loving' rich citizen (*philotimos*) who uses his (or, less often, her) wealth for the benefit of the community and gains fame and prestige in return.[3] Such people often used their money to pay for a certain category of events, events that cities also often organised themselves with public funds and which were typical of the public life of Greek and Roman cities from their earliest beginnings until (very) late antiquity. We find such events here as well in the inscription erected in honour of Kleanax. They are what Pauline Schmitt Pantel, in her work on public banquets in the Greek poleis, has called 'collective practices' (*pratiques collectives*): public, festive events involving the entire civic community or large parts of it, such as religious festivals, games, cult rituals, processions, public feasts, distributions and so on.[4]

Typical of such collective activities is that they effortlessly blend together elements belonging to what a modern western observer would regard as separate social spheres: the political, the religious, the cultural (in the sense of entertainment and sociability), the social and economic. Kleanax at Kyme was engaged in the organisation of religious rituals (public sacrifices, processions) whilst holding an important political office, yet at the same time these events, at all stages, involved entertainment and sociability among participants in the form of public distributions (of sweet wine, porridge, sacrificial meat and 'presents'), games and shows, and, especially, public banquets, which on several occasions were organised in one of the city's most important political buildings, i.e. the town hall (*prytaneion*). Among those invited were Kleanax's fellow-citizens, some of whom were singled out according to function, status or merit, and thus clearly distinguished from ordinary citizens: priests, victors in the sacred games and magistrates (observe again the mixture of religion, politics and 'play' or entertainment). Notable, however, is the presence, among those invited to the banquets, of groups that did not belong to the citizenry of Kyme, but were nonetheless inhabitants of the city: resident Roman citizens, slaves and other unspecified fellow-residents (*paroikoi*). Even those visiting the city, 'foreigners' (*xenoi*), were occasionally involved. As we shall see in Chapter 7 as well, even though in terms of politics and political institutions, the ancient city can be defined as a community of citizens, since the adult male citizens were the only inhabitants with full

[3] On Greco-Roman civic munificence (euergetism), see Veyne (1976); Zuiderhoek (2009a).
[4] Schmitt Pantel (1990), (1992). Note also Iddeng (2012) 19: a Greco-Roman festival 'was a public, inclusive event – inclusive at least for the community; indeed, it was a visible manifestation of, for, or within a community, which was often made up of the inhabitants of a polis/*civitas*'.

political rights (only citizens could legislate, vote, judge and hold office), in other contexts, the city might well be perceived as a much broader community, involving, in addition to the citizens, a whole variety of non-citizen and semi-citizen groups: women, children, freedmen, resident foreigners and slaves.

Particularly in the context of religious ritual, a crucial ingredient of most of the events that fall under the heading of 'collective practices' in the ancient city, the civic community could be defined very broadly. In Classical Athens, for instance, *metoikoi*, that is, resident foreigners, male and female, routinely participated in important religious festivals alongside Athenian citizens, most famously in the grand procession during the Panathenaea, the annual festival for the goddess Athena, but also in other rituals, and the same happened in other poleis as well.[5] Theatres and amphitheatres in Roman cities often had specially assigned areas for lower status and non-citizen groups (women, freedmen, non-citizen residents or *incolae* and even slaves), thus allowing them to share the experience of watching the games, shows and spectacles taking place there with the full citizens.[6] Of course, the fact that collective events or the settings in which they took place were often so structured that it was clearly possible to distinguish the non- or semi-citizens groups from the citizens proper (and that our sources do the same) might well signify hierarchy or segregation as much as it signals inclusiveness, a point to which I shall return below.

In the remainder of this chapter, we shall observe civic culture and identity through the lens of collective practices/collective events. Naturally, one might study Greco-Roman civic culture from a variety of perspectives. The reason I opt for the perspective of collective practices is that it offers a way to study civic culture at the level of the community, which is the appropriate level of analysis in a book focussed on the ancient city as a historical entity. In addition, collective practices or events were a remark-ably prominent feature of pre-modern civic life, in Classical Antiquity, but also in other historical periods and regions. We might note, for instance, the vibrant civic ceremonial life in early modern Italian cities, which has long been an important field of study among historians of that period.[7]

Most pre-modern cities were probably too large to be able to rely entirely on continuous face-to-face interaction between all community members to ensure social cohesion, as was possible in a village. Yet at the same time, pre-modern cities were small enough, even the very large

[5] Maurizio (1998); Blok (2007); Wijma (2014).
[6] Kolendo (1981); Moore (1994); Van Nijf (1997) 212–15.   [7] Trexler (1980); Muir (1981).

ones among them, such as imperial Rome, not to have to rely *entirely* on symbolic communication via monuments or images or the dissemination of the written word to maintain cohesion and a sense of belonging, in the way a territorial state often has to.[8] Most territorial states, due to their size, can only be 'imagined communities'.[9] Instead, pre-modern cities developed a form of collective identity management at a level somewhere in between these two extremes (the face-to-face society of the village and the imagined community of the territorial state), that is, mass collective events, involving a sufficiently large number of community members so that those present at the activity or event could be thought to 'represent' the entire urban community. Thus, for example, the mass of spectators, gathered in the theatre, amphitheatre or circus for the games, the Roman collective event *par excellence*, could be thought to represent the urban *plebs* of Rome in its entirety. They behaved accordingly, by publicly expressing pleasure or displeasure with the acts and decisions of the reigning emperor, who was generally present too, and their utterances were also interpreted as such by the emperors, i.e. as if they represented the feelings of the entire city.[10] The continuous mass gatherings for games and spectacles in the imperial city of Rome were, in terms of sheer scale, the most impressive example of civic collective events in the ancient world. Yet why, exactly, were collective practices such a prominent element in ancient civic culture? And if they stimulated cohesion, how precisely and to what end(s)? We shall now examine civic collective practices and events from various different but sometimes overlapping perspectives, partly suggested by research from the past few decades, in an attempt to answer these questions.

Memory and Identity

Collective practices played a crucial role in the cultivation of civic memory. Keeping alive the community's history through civic ritual, moreover, contributed in important ways to establishing and maintaining a sense of collective identity. In the agora of Cyrene in Libya, for instance, stood the tomb monument of the city's founder, Battus, a citizen of Thera, who, according to tradition, had led a group of colonists to found a polis in

---

[8] Of course, monuments and public buildings were essential to a city's communal identity as well (see Chapter 4). Yet it was precisely the constant involvement of public architecture and monuments in civic collective practices which ensured that the urban landscape became loaded with meaning, see below.

[9] Anderson (2006). [10] See Hopkins (1983) 14–20 on gladiatorial shows as 'political theatre'.

Libya on the advice of the Delphic oracle in late seventh century BCE (Hdt. 4.150, 155–157).[11] The citizens of Cyrene worshipped Battus as a *heros*, that is, a deceased individual (real or legendary) to whom demigodlike powers were ascribed, and who merited cult.

Hero-cults were widespread in the Archaic and Classical Greek word, and they had several distinctive features. Among them was that, in contrast to the cults of actual divinities (say, the Olympic gods), the hero-cults often contained elements of death rituals that were also carried out for ordinary deceased individuals. Like the ordinary dead, heroes were thought to be present in their graves and were thus ritually offered food and drink (though, due to their semi-divine aspect, they also received actual sacrifices, often resembling those of the cthonic or 'earth gods' such as Hades or Persephone). Another related feature was that the cults of heroes generally focussed on their (real or supposed) tomb monuments. That is, hero-worship was mostly firmly anchored to a specific locality, a family, a group, but most often a city. In other words, a hero-cult functioned, in Walter Burkert's formulation, as 'a centre of local group identity'.[12] Thus the collective practice of hero-worship of Battus, Eireann Marshall has argued, 'united Cyrenaeans just as the commemoration of a deceased relative united ordinary Cyrenaean families'.[13] Since Battus was Cyrene's founder, moreover, the cult provided Cyrenaeans united in worship with a direct symbolic link to their city's glorious origins, and thus functioned as a potent nexus of civic identity and social memory. Given that heroes were as a rule thought to have played some exemplary role in their cities' past, real or imagined, as founders, (legendary) rulers or heroic warriors, the Cyrenaean situation was by no means unique, and civic hero-cult thus constitutes an excellent example of the ways in which collective practices (in this case, public cult rituals) might play an important role in fostering both collective identity and social memory in ancient cities.

Roman imperial Ephesus provides us with a similar example of strong links between elements of the civic landscape, memory, identity and collective practices, albeit that the latter in this case took the shape of a festival procession. In accordance with the terms of a foundation endowed in 104 CE by one of Ephesus's prominent citizens, C. Vibius Salutaris, about every two weeks a procession carrying type statues of members of the imperial family, personifications of Roman and Ephesian political and social institutions (e.g. the Senate, Roman people, city council, *gerousia*,

---

[11] See Scott (2012) 14–44 for a detailed spatial analysis of the Cyrenaean agora.
[12] Burkert (1985) 206.   [13] Marshall (2000) 13.

city tribes and *ephebeia*), important figures from the city's historical and mythological past (e.g. Augustus, Lysimachos and Androklos) and the city's patron-goddess Artemis wound its way through the civic landscape. The procession, according to the analysis of Guy Rogers, followed a route which, in its various stages, exemplified 'the successive foundation legends of Ephesos, walked in reverse chronological order'. Starting at the great temple of Artemis, in the story of whose birth at the grove of Ortygia the Ephesians found their ultimate civic identity, the procession made its way through the city walls that had been built by the Hellenistic dynast Lysimachos (who in the early third century BCE had moved Ephesus to a new location), and into the upper city, which 'had essentially been refounded since the reign of emperor Augustus', so thoroughly had it been filled with Roman temples and monuments. Thus the procession, by entering this part of the city first, emphasised the 'new' Roman element in the civic identity of the old Greek polis while also harking back to its Hellenistic relocation or 'second foundation'. Moving along through the city and passing a wide array of buildings and monuments linked to Ephesus's past and present, the procession eventually passed out of the city again through the Koressian gate, recalling the region of Koressos, where, according to legend, Androklos, an Athenian prince, had founded the original city of Ephesus. From there, the procession moved back to the temple of Artemis, thus coming full circle, both physically and historically.[14] The regularly recurring ritual of this procession, just one example, from one single city, of countless similar festivals and processions throughout the Greco-Roman world, would have allowed Ephesians ample opportunity to internalise the messages concerning their present and past which it evoked. The ritual underwrote and reinforced their civic identity, their sense of belonging and their cohesion as a civic community.

Cohesion and Sense of Unity

If collective practices served, among other things, to reinforce civic social memory and collective identity, and if these in turn contributed to the cohesion of the civic community, then it could be argued that collective practices were highly functional in a sociopolitical sense. Because if Greek and Roman cities were indeed politically decentralised communities – that is, communities lacking a permanent institutionalised centre of power (a professional government and bureaucracy) both separated from the rest

---

[14] Rogers (1991) 80–126 for a detailed analysis.

of society and responsible for holding the community together administratively as well as symbolically – then collective practices might have had an important sociopolitical part to play.[15] For, as Moshe Berent notes with regard to the polis, decentralised political communities, lacking a proper state government, are prone to disintegration unless held together by other forces that integrate their members into the community and provide cohesion and a sense of unity. One such force, identified by Berent, was warfare: the incessant war-making among Archaic and Classical Greek poleis, involving the majority of the full (i.e. adult male) citizens of the polis community, strongly contributed to the sense of cohesion among the citizens.[16]

Collective practices, it could be argued, might be another such force. Civic festivals, feasts, games and public cult rituals all had the effect of emphasising the unity and collectivity of the citizenry. Indeed, the reach of collective events often went beyond the citizens proper, involving women, children, freedmen, slaves and resident foreigners as well, as we saw above, symbolically integrating these groups into the civic community via festive participation. It should be noted in this context that historians have often analysed Greek and Roman religion in similar terms, that is, as a public set of rituals and practices involving the entire civic community (or at least significant sections of it), and thereby symbolising its essential unity.[17] Particularly the repetitive character of many collective practices and events, such as cult rituals and periodic festivals, may have been essential to their role as stimuli of integration; given the absence of a permanent, institutionalised political centre, integrating forces in decentralised political communities need to be continuously 'switched on', which, as Berent argues, explains why war, given that it had the effect of integrating political communities, was the normal state of affairs in Classical Greece, and peace the exception.

If collective practices and events indeed fulfilled a similar integrating role (and if one accepts the theory of the ancient city as a decentralised political community, which is controversial – see Chapter 9), we have here at least a partial explanation for the sheer intensity of festive culture in Greek and Roman cities. In fact, the integrating function of collective practices and events might have increased in importance over time. As scholars have noted, starting from an already very rich festive life in Classical times, the number of attested civic festivals and games seems to

---

[15] See e.g. Berent (2000a). For further references and discussion see Chapter 9.   [16] Berent (2000a).
[17] Thus the concept of 'polis religion' coined by Sourvinou-Inwood (1992); but see Kindt (2012), esp. 16–35 for a critical reappraisal.

increase exponentially in the Greek poleis of the Hellenistic and Roman imperial periods.[18] Could it be that this trend was related to the fact that warfare increasingly became the prerogative of kings, Roman generals and, later, emperors with their standing armies, and that consequently polis citizens had fewer and fewer chances to reinforce group cohesion on the battlefield? The great increase in civic munificence (*euergetism*), which began in the later Hellenistic period and continued under the empire, might at least partly be accounted for in similar terms.[19] It was a mechanism through which many new festivals and games were created, and which, moreover, produced its own collective practices, i.e. the public rituals of praise during which benefactors were honoured by the community.

As noted above, our analysis of the sociopolitical functions of civic collective practices might well be extended in comparative terms. We could conceive of collective practices as a form of cohesion-building typical for pre-modern cities, which analytically could be placed between the face-to-face interaction of villages, on the one hand, and the 'imagined community' symbolism of territorial states, on the other. However, the *intense proliferation* of such collective practices and events in Greek and Roman cities can arguably in part be explained by the political decentralisation typical of the ancient city.

'Naturalising' Civic Social Hierarchy

If collective practices could serve to emphasise civic unity, they could also be instrumental in reinforcing civic social hierarchy and stratification. Greek religious public banquets during the Classical period, it has been argued, served to underline the political equality (*isonomia*) of their citizen-participants, symbolised by the equal portions of meat of the sacrificial animal distributed among them and the *koinonia* ('togetherness') of the citizen-community, expressed through their public commensality.[20] Roman public commensality, by contrast, is thought to have expressed primarily the social hierarchy among participants. During sacrificial banquets (*epulae*), portions were distributed according to social rank, with the highest-status individuals or groups taking their portions first (and receiving the largest portions and finest quality meat), then those ranking immediately below them and so on.[21] Non-religious public meals (*cenae*) operated on the same principle, as did private dinner parties (*convivia*).

---

[18] E.g. Chaniotis (1995) 148–9; Mitchell (1990).   [19] Zuiderhoek (2009a).
[20] Schmitt Pantel (1992).   [21] Scheid (1985); Van Nijf (1997) 152–6.

Suetonius, for instance, compliments the emperor Augustus on the close attention the latter paid to the status of guests at his banquets (*Aug.* 74).[22]

A closely related type of civic collective practice, public distributions of food or money, functioned in a similar manner in Roman cities. Great care was taken to distinguish the various status groups within the civic community, and those occupying a higher place in the social hierarchy received larger or better quality handouts. Thus, at Ferentinum in Italy, a wealthy citizen named Aulus Quinctilius Priscus probably during the reign of Trajan provided funds for an annual distribution, on his birthday, of pastry snacks, honeyed wine and money among the city's inhabitants. City councillors (*decuriones*) and their sons, that is, the city's political elite, received ten sesterces each as well as honeyed wine and pastry (*mulsum et crustulum*); *seviri augustales*, who were mostly wealthy freedmen, received eight sesterces each plus wine and pastry, while ordinary citizens (*municipes*), non-citizen residents (*incolae*) and married women received just pastry and wine. In addition, nuts were to be scattered among the young boys of the *plebs*, who also received a drink of wine (*CIL* 10.5853 = *ILS* 6271). Evidence from other Italian cities under the empire confirms that cash handouts followed a similar hierarchical pattern everywhere, with *decuriones* consistently receiving most, followed by *augustales* and then the ordinary citizens/plebeians. Subgroups among the *plebs*, such as the members of professional associations (*collegia*), might be singled out and receive (slightly) more per person than ordinary citizens or *incolae*.[23]

It has been observed that, during the course of the Hellenistic and Roman imperial periods, public banquets and distributions in Greek cities also increasingly came to emphasise the internally stratified nature of the civic community. Over time, the focus shifted from emphasising political equality among citizens (*isonomia*) to representing the social hierarchy.[24] Note, for instance, how clearly the *prytanis* Kleanax distinguished between the various status groups at Kyme (citizens, non-citizens, foreigners, freedmen and slaves) in the organisation of his public meals. At Ephesus, Vibius Salutaris in addition to funding a procession also set up an elaborate scheme of lotteries and distributions along distinctly hierarchical lines, distinguishing a great number of civic subgroups.[25] While in its later phase, this development was no doubt partly inspired by the Roman example, it has also been related to the growing oligarchisation of Greek civic society

---

[22] Mrozek (1992); Donahue (2004).
[23] Duncan-Jones (1982) 141–3; Mrozek (1987); Van Nijf (1997) 152–5.
[24] Schmitt Pantel (1992) 253–420; Van Nijf (1997) 156–60.   [25] Rogers (1991) 39–72.

during the preceding Hellenistic era, and to the increasing prominence of wealthy citizens as public benefactors, who paid for many of the banquets and distributions in question. As such, the shift in distributional and banqueting practices represents a change in 'the collective self-image of the Greek polis during the late Hellenistic and Roman periods'.[26] There is something to be said for this argument, given that under the empire, the civic elite of councillors and their families in the poleis does start to assume the characteristics of an *ordo decurionum* on the Roman model, which arguably triggered a further development towards hierarchisation among the citizen body.[27] Another telling sign is that in the Greek East during the imperial period, theatres, the venues *par excellence* for civic collective practices, increasingly came to adopt the Roman custom of emphasising the civic social hierarchy through the seating arrangement by reserving blocks of seats for specific status groups.[28]

On the other hand, hierarchical distinctions among the citizen body had by no means been absent during the Classical period – one need think only of the Solonian property classes in democratic Athens – although these seem to have lost much of their political relevance during the later fifth and fourth centuries BCE. Moreover, as mentioned earlier, religious festivals in the Classical Greek poleis were often characterised by the participation of a variety of status groups, citizens as well as non-citizens. In processions, the various groups might be clearly marked out, as they would be during festivals and distributions in the post-Classical poleis. Interestingly, scholars of Classical Greek religion have mostly interpreted such wide cultic participation as a sign of the inclusiveness of civic ritual, and here, I think, lies the key to the interpretation of socially stratified collective practices in the post-Classical poleis as well.[29]

Like the Classical poleis, Hellenistic and Roman-period Greek cities remained first and foremost citizen-communities, and taking part in civic collective practices, such as a festive distribution, served to emphasise one's belonging to the civic community.[30] This impression is confirmed by the main thrust of civic euergetism during the imperial period: local benefactors overwhelmingly focussed their munificence on their fellow-citizens.[31]

---

[26] Van Nijf (1997) 157.
[27] Van Nijf (1997) *passim* refers to this process as 'ordo-making'; Zuiderhoek (2008a) 425–9.
[28] Small (1987); Van Nijf (1997) 209–40.
[29] Parker (1996) 91; Maurizio (1998); Wijma (2010) 42 analyses cultic participation of non-citizens (*metoikoi*) in terms of 'a sliding scale of membership [of the polis community]'.
[30] See e.g. Dio Chrys., *Or.* 7.49 with Jones (1978) 60; Van Nijf (1997) 156.
[31] Veyne (1976); Zuiderhoek (2009a).

Thus, while the differentiation of status groups during processions, theatrical shows, public meals and festive handouts certainly served to mark civic hierarchy, the collective rituals of which such events were part functioned at the same time as celebrations of the civic community as a whole. Collective practices in Roman cities similarly focussed on both status differentiation *and* community spirit. For instance, whilst at Roman sacrificial banquets there certainly was differentiation between status groups, as stated above, the feasts might also be highly inclusive, involving the entire *plebs* of a city.[32]

Legitimation of Power

If social hierarchies could be confirmed and 'naturalised' during and by means of civic collective practices, the implication of course is that the power held by those at the top of the civic hierarchy was thereby legitimated. In Greco-Roman culture, such power, and its legitimation, had to be earned. Greek and Roman citizens generally awarded political position, social status and prestige to those among their fellow-citizens who (or whose families) had proved themselves particularly valuable to the community in some way, e.g. in terms of political leadership, military success, athletic prowess or public generosity.[33] Collective practices in the form of public rituals of honour were instrumental to the awarding and legitimation of status, power and prestige in Greek and Roman cities – we might think of the triumph awarded to successful Roman generals, the festive entrance into their native cities of athletic victors in one of the crown games (Olympic, Pythian, Nemean or Isthmian) or the mass acclamation of the generous civic bene- factor in the theatre, which could go on for hours.[34]

Aristotle noted a clear connection in the Greek cities of his day between political office holding, public gifts – particularly contributions to festivals and public buildings – and the awarding of public honours, especially in oligarchic poleis (*Pol.* 1321a; *Rhet.* 1.5.9). Even in Athens, however, that most democratic of Classical poleis, high social prestige could be gained and maintained through the performance of liturgies (which often involved [co-]funding and [co-]organising some public event, e.g. a theatre show or a public banquet), especially when one performed liturgies more often, or contributed more per liturgy, than was legally required.

---

[32] Mrozek (1987) 41–2; Van Nijf (1997) 154–5.   [33] See e.g. Adkins (1972) 60–1.
[34] Beard (2007) on the triumph; Slater (2013) on athletic victors' return; Zuiderhoek (2009a) 113–53 on euergetism, rituals of honour and legitimation.

Nonetheless democratic Athens long remained averse to rewarding its generous citizens with explicit public honours.[35] Post-Classical Greek poleis and Roman cities were less scrupulous when it came to honouring the generously wealthy among their citizens, most of whom were also holders of important civic magistracies. Time and again in our sources we see the nexus of office holding, contributions to civic collective events (e.g. festivals, distributions and banquets) and public rituals of honour, whether unequivocally expressed in large honorific inscriptions, or analysed with some misgivings in the writings and speeches of Cicero, Plutarch and Dio Chrysostom.[36]

Greco-Roman civic collective events were particularly suited to what political scientists would refer to as the expression of consent to existing power structures by free subordinates – an essential element of the process of the legitimation of power.[37] Thus a grateful citizenry would honour publicly a civic benefactor, who often was also an important office holder, thereby expressing consent to this individual's social and political power by actually increasing it. Or, more formally, the people would (re-)elect to a magistracy a politician who had proved his worth by benefitting the community, politically, militarily or materially (think e.g. of Roman Republican electoral gift-giving). At their most poignant, civic collective events displayed a seamless interweaving of power, legitimation, expression of civic identity and glorification of civic memory, as happened, for instance, in the case of the munificence of Vibius Salutaris at Roman Ephesus, thus presenting a vibrant tableau of the city's past, its present, and, in the ambitions and strivings of its political elite, its possible future.

---

[35] Wilson (2000); Deene (2013) 99–157 for a thorough analysis of the 'honours system' in Classical Athens.

[36] Zuiderhoek (2007).

[37] This is based on the model of political legitimation developed by Beetham (1991); see Zuiderhoek (2009a).

CHAPTER 7

Urban Society: Stratification and Mobility

In Western thought, the urban social milieu is commonly conceived as open, dynamic, ever-changing and prone to innovation. *Stadtluft macht frei* ('city air makes one free'), as the medieval proverb goes, stressing the escape from the bonds of agrarian feudalism that urban living afforded. This idea of city life is embedded deeply in Western European social science and historiography, from Max Weber through Henri Pirenne to Fernand Braudel, who stressed the electrifying transformative effects of cities on their inhabitants and the hinterlands surrounding them.[1] It is still a leading trend in studies of European urbanisation to this day. Thus, in a recent survey of European cities and towns between 400 and 2000 CE, we read that '[t]his book will contend that from the high Middle Ages cities have been an essential driving force in European transformation', and stress is placed on cities as 'crucibles for new ideas' in all spheres of life, on their 'creative milieu' and the 'relative openness of the [urban] social order'.[2]

Historians of medieval and early modern Europe have often linked the development of the supposedly unique open and dynamic European urban milieu directly to the rise and increasing social and political dominance of a new social group within the cities: the urban middle class or bourgeoisie, whose wealth derived from manufacture, trade and commerce rather than agriculture, and whose value system differed radically from that of the landed gentry. 'The cities', Carlo M. Cipolla wrote in his classic synthesis on the economic history of pre-industrial Europe between 1000 and 1700 CE, 'became the seats and centers of the power of the triumphant bourgeoisie ... [T]he political and social triumph of the urban middle class, and its peculiar set of values, had revolutionary consequences ... With the appearance of the medieval city, a new Europe was born. Every

---

[1] Weber (1958); Pirenne (1939); Braudel (1981) 479. Note also the classic formulation of Postan (1975) 239: '[medieval European cities] were non-feudal islands in the feudal seas'.
[2] Clark (2009) 13.

sector of social and economic life was transformed. Sets of values, personal circumstances and relations, types of administration, education, production and exchange, all underwent drastic transformation'. This transformation, he argues, 'paved the way for the Industrial Revolution'.[3]

Here we have, of course, the familiar story of European urban exceptionalism that we already encountered in Chapter 1. In that chapter we also saw that the urban exceptionalism-thesis is no longer an uncontested explanation for the rise of capitalism and industrialisation in Europe. For our purposes in the present chapter, however, what is relevant about the traditional grand narrative of European urbanism is that it locates the origins of Europe's exceptional development precisely in the *social structure* of its cities, even more precisely, in the specific value system of the social group that dominated these cities, the middle class or bourgeoisie. If the key to the supposed socially transformative powers of cities was to be located in their social structure, in what sense then did the social structures of cities in other societies differ from the European model? Or were they rather similar? Did, for instance, Greek and Roman cities also harbour a middle class, a bourgeoisie? Some ancient historians have thought so.

Most famously perhaps, Michael Rostovtzeff in his classic studies of Hellenistic and Roman social and economic history has argued that the Hellenistic world and the early Roman Empire owed their prosperity to the efforts of a 'city bourgeoisie', which was actually an analytically inappropriate conflation of urban professionals, such as traders, shopowning manufacturers and money lenders, on the one hand, and the landowning urban elites, on the other.[4] Others have sought their middle class elsewhere: the Roman equestrian order has long been a favourite candidate, particularly because of the involvement of a minority of equestrians, as *publicani*, in provincial tax-farming and money-lending during the Late Republic.[5] However, the *equites* were a strictly juridically determined group, an *ordo*, not a loosely defined social class, and nearly all of them were large landowners. As a subset of the Roman imperial elite, there was nothing 'middle' or 'bourgeois' about them. Most recently, Emanuel Mayer has argued for the existence of a proper middle class in Roman imperial cities, a group which, he claims, exhibited most of the features of later European middle classes (e.g. a strong work ethic, commercial pride

[3] Cipolla (1994) 120–2.
[4] Rostovtzeff (1941), (1957); see Reinhold ([1946] 2002) for a penetrating analysis and critique of Rostovtzeff's historical conceptualisation.
[5] E.g. Hill (1952). Note in particular the trenchant criticism of Finley (1999) 49–50.

and attachment to the nuclear family) and had a distinct, non-elite cultural identity which they expressed in the art which decorated their houses and funerary monuments. Mayer's analysis falters, however, at the same point as Rostovtzeff's in that his 'middle class' is an artificial conflation of separate social strata. At first, Mayer focusses on the urban non-elite commercial and professional groups, while in his analysis of supposedly middle class housing and artworks he appears to include the urban elites in the definition as well.[6]

In truth, there was no bourgeoisie in ancient cities, in the common early modern European sense of a politically prominent city-based class of well-to-do people, fairly uniform in terms of their cultural outlook and education, whose wealth derived from commerce, finance, industry or civil service. The wealthy and politically prominent groups in ancient cities, we already saw, were landowners, agrarian rentiers mostly, not businessmen. This is not to say, however, that there was no social stratification in ancient cities beyond the crude division between the landowning elite and 'the rest', just that this stratification was of a different character, with different social and political ramifications, than that found in later European cities.

As ancient historians have long recognised, both the elite and the non-elite populations in ancient cities were highly differentiated internally. In recent decades, scholarly attention has particularly focussed on the internal stratification of the non-elite urban population. So-called middling groups, located socially and economically between the poorest and the wealthiest strata of urban society, have attracted much attention. These groups encompassed a broad range, from the not-so-very-poor to the quite well-to-do at an almost subelite level, and consisted of individuals belonging to a range of different status groups, including freeborn and freed, citizens and non-citizens. They might be farmers, manufacturers, traders, retailers or service providers of some kind. Although they were not middle class in the sense defined above, recognition of their presence and role in urban life is vital to our understanding of the functioning of ancient urban society.

During the past half century, it has also become increasingly clear that Greek and Roman cities were characterised by a significant degree of social mobility. Urban social groups were not static entities: individuals and

---

[6] Mayer (2012). For criticism, see Mouritsen (2012), (2015); Flohr (2013b); Wallace-Hadrill (2013). It should be pointed out, however, that Mayer is certainly right to emphasise the importance of 'middling groups' in Roman urban society. Yet these groups should definitely *not* be confused with a 'middle class' or bourgeoisie.

families might indeed be confronted with the opportunity, or might face the risk, of moving upwards or downwards through the social hierarchy. Recognition of the causes and implications of such mobility has considerably advanced our understanding of the dynamics of social and political life in ancient cities. In this chapter, I shall discuss some of the research on stratification and social mobility in Greek and Roman cities, with a particular emphasis on recent work concerning the identification and role of middling groups. Again, as in other chapters, my aim is to outline what might be thought of as typical features of the ancient city and to provide some insight into what I consider important developments in the study of ancient urban society.

State and Society

Yet can we actually isolate 'society' in the ancient city? It may seem like a strange question, but one which has figured especially in debates on the Greek polis. The polis, it is often argued, represented a fusion of state and society, that is, the polis was, in essence, the community of citizens and their *oikoi* (households). Thus, in any analysis of the polis, the social sphere cannot effectively be separated from the political sphere.[7] Whether this viewpoint implies that 'the polis ... *controlled* the behaviour of its citizens in every department of life: religion, family, upbringing, education, housing, production and trade', as Hansen, who criticises the fusion of state and society-thesis, would have it, remains to be seen. Thus formulated, Hansen argues, it fits Classical Sparta but not Athens, nor, presumably, other (democratic) poleis, where citizens distinguished between a public and private sphere and where there were few regulations concerning – and the assembly only rarely discussed – matters such as upbringing, education, agriculture, crafts, trade and the like.[8]

To my mind, however, the theory of the inseparability of social spheres in the ancient city is indicative of something more profound than a supposed totalitarian control by 'the polis' over all social life. It has much more to do with the fact that for the members of the citizen community, their political status as citizens had profound repercussions for their activities in other social spheres. For instance, it afforded them economic, social and legal privileges (e.g. the right to own land, exemption from direct taxes, protection from certain judicial procedures and punishments, rights of appeal and so forth) and assigned them certain roles in the

---

[7] E.g. Finley (1963) 49–50; Ostwald (1986) xix.   [8] Hansen (2006) 122–4, quote from 122.

religious sphere, while politics itself was pervaded with religious rituals and civic festive life (games, plays) had a decidedly political dimension. In addition, if, as some scholars maintain, poleis were not states but stateless societies lacking professional politicians and administrators, which were governed by the community of adult male citizens through mass councils and assemblies, it makes more sense to argue that *society* (or at least the citizen-element of it) controlled the polis and its politics, rather than the other way around.[9]

There is, however, another, and for our purposes in this chapter, more useful way to view ancient urban society. For, in the same way that we can equate an ancient city in its *political* aspect with the citizen community, and in its *material* aspect with a specific urban landscape, so we can equate the city as a *society* with the totality of its inhabitants (citizens and everyone else), their internal stratification and ways of life. As a society, a Greek or Roman city was far more than the sum of its citizens, even if they constituted an integral part of the entire, complex whole.

Stratification and Mobility

A Greek or Roman city would of course be home to its citizens and their wives and children but would also contain sometimes very large groups of non-citizens and their families, ranging from strangers temporarily present to legally registered resident aliens (*metoikoi, incolae*) to dependent native populations (in cities planted in newly conquered territories), serf-like groups (e.g. in Sparta and the poleis on Crete) and of course slaves. There would also be freed slaves (*exeleutheroi/apeleutheroi, liberti*), who in Roman cities gained a qualified form of citizenship (they were barred from holding political office), but in Greek poleis acquired the status of resident foreigners (*metoikoi*). In addition, we might find a variety of other categories (e.g. bastards or disenfranchised citizens).[10]

There was a lot of diversity *within* these various groups as well, some of it institutionalised. At Athens, for instance, the citizen population had been officially divided into four property classes since the reforms of the early sixth-century BCE lawgiver Solon. At Rome, a reform ascribed to King Servius Tullius, but perhaps of later date and certainly elaborated further during the Republic, similarly divided the Roman citizen body into a property-based hierarchy (see below). These divisions owed their

[9] See Chapter 9 for discussion and references.
[10] See e.g. Cohen (2000) 70–2 and Kamen (2013) 62–78 on such groups in Classical Athens.

institutional formality to the fact that (at least for a time) they served clear political and military needs. However, much of the socioeconomic or status differentiation within the main sociolegal groups that made up ancient urban society – citizens, resident foreigners, freedmen and slaves – was of a more informal kind, if no less significant.

In an attempt to come to grips with the complexities of status differentiation in Greco-Roman society, Moses Finley developed the notion of a 'spectrum of statuses', with the chattel slave at one end and the full (adult male) citizen at the other, 'and with a considerable number of shades of dependence in between'.[11] Though the model has been criticised, it actually provides us with an excellent analytical tool for understanding the gradations of status (defined as a combination of an individual's social standing and legal rights) particularly among the non-citizen population in ancient cities.[12] It allows us, in Finley's words, 'to locate the slave with a *peculium* in relationship both to the slave-farmhand and to the free independent craftsman and shopkeeper'.[13] Thus a nuanced picture can be constructed of status differentiation in Greco-Roman society.

Stratification and Mobility in the Classical Polis

It was precisely the application of Finley's spectrum model that has recently allowed Deborah Kamen to produce a fine-grained analysis of status gradations in Classical Athens, incorporating a great deal of earlier research.[14] Focussing on the rights and privileges of individuals in various spheres (e.g. claims to property, control of their own or others' labour, corporal inviolability, freedom of movement, judicial privileges and liabilities, possibility of political, religious or military participation, and opportunities for social mobility), Kamen is able to delineate the many, sometimes subtle distinctions that existed between a wide variety of status groups in Athens. These groups include chattel slaves (e.g. those performing manual labour in the fields or the mines) and what she calls 'privileged chattel slaves', i.e. slaves who worked and/or lived separate from their master, often in artisanal, commercial or service positions, and were able to keep some of their earnings, or public slaves, who were owned by the polis. She similarly

---

[11] Finley (1981b) 98; see also Finley (1981c) 147–8, (1999) 67–8.
[12] See Kamen (2013) 3. Criticism: see e.g. de Ste Croix (1981) 92–3, who prefers a class-based analysis; Garlan (1988) 85–118; Hedrick (1994) 307; for a defence of the model, see Kamen (2013) 4–7.
[13] Finley (1999) 68. [14] Kamen (2013).

distinguishes between conditionally freed slaves, who by law still owed some services to their former master, unconditionally freed slaves, who became a category of *metoikoi*, 'true' (i.e. freeborn) *metoikoi*, privileged *metoikoi* (for instance, those who had been granted the right to own land in the polis, normally a privilege of full adult male citizens), bastards, disenfranchised citizens, naturalised citizens and, finally, full citizens (female and male). Some of the non-full citizen categories Kamen discusses have already received a great deal of attention from scholars, for instance slaves, (privileged) *metoikoi* and naturalised citizens, while others have been studied less often.[15] Athenian civic ideology may be partly to blame here, Kamen suggests, since it dominates much of our literary evidence and relentlessly foregrounds the tripartite division citizens-*metoikoi*-slaves so as to underline the centrality of the citizen community.[16]

Scholars studying the Classical Greek economy in particular have long recognised the economic importance of slaves and, particularly, *metoikoi* (including freedmen), since these were the groups that carried out most of the manufacture, commerce and financial activities in the polis. The separation between citizens and non-citizens in this respect was by no means absolute, however, since citizens were involved in these economic activities as well, either directly, by carrying them out for themselves, or through co-operation with non-citizens. Some non-citizens became particularly wealthy. The extreme example is the non-Greek Pasion, once a slave of the Athenian bankers Antisthenes and Archestratos, who, after having been freed by his owners, took over the bank, became extraordinarily wealthy and eventually even gained Athenian citizenship (in return for generous benefactions to the Athenian people).[17]

Such wealthy non-citizens, who freely interacted with the Athenian citizen-elite, have often been regarded as exceptions by scholars.[18] In recent decades, however, Greek historians have increasingly focussed on the evidence for all kinds of interaction between citizens and non-citizens in Athenian life, in terms of residence, use of public spaces (agora, gymnasia), participation in religious ritual and, particularly, economic

---

[15] For slaves, see e.g. Garlan (1988); on *metoikoi* Whitehead (1977) is the classic study; on naturalisation at Athens, see M. J. Osborne (1981–1983).

[16] Kamen (2013) 5, 109–15.

[17] See Davies (1971) 428–9; Trevett (1992). Other wealthy non-citizens, particularly *metoikoi*, are known as well, such as Cephalus, in whose house Plato situated the dialogue of the *Republic*, and his sons Polemarchus and Lysias, the famour orator. See also Cohen (2000).

[18] E.g. Whitehead (1977) 120, 150; also Raaflaub (1983) 532; Todd (1993) 173. Yet see Austin and Vidal-Naquet (1977) 103–6 for a notable exception to the traditional view ('The legal categories do not correspond to social classes').

cooperation.[19] Edward Cohen has gone furthest in this respect, arguing that in their financial operations and transactions (which are the focus of his research) Athenian bankers and wealthy citizens frequently disregarded the status system and worked closely with *metoikoi*, women and slaves. Particularly the latter could acquire wealth and influence through banking, something which leads Cohen to a strong conclusion: '[t]he appearance of banking *oikoi* [households] of slave origin signalled the rise of a new "mixed" Athenian establishment, which was infusing the traditional Athenian upper classes with wealthy resident foreigners, former slaves, naturalised citizens'.[20] Cohen's claim of the rise of a new mixed social class of well-to-do citizen and non-citizen entrepreneurs was in fact foreshadowed in the work of Victor Ehrenberg, who, based on an analysis of Athenian Old Comedy, argued for a fusion of citizens and *metoikoi* into (as Whitehead writes) 'a middle-class *bourgeoisie*'.[21]

Several objections, however, can be made against Cohen's (and Ehrenberg's) arguments. First, critics have pointed out that there is in fact little direct, concrete evidence for the wholesale emergence of a mixed citizen/non-citizen economic establishment along the lines suggested by Cohen.[22] Second, and more important, while among both *metoikoi* and citizens we can find groups of middling wealth (for 'middling citizens', see below), and while there certainly was some economic cooperation between citizens and non-citizens at Athens, it simply makes no analytical sense to regard these groups as constituting part of a unified social class, a middle class, for the same reasons that invalidate Rostovtzeff's and Mayer's attempts to identify a Roman bourgeosie. The individuals concerned were members of different sociolegal categories (citizens, *metoikoi*, freedmen, slaves) with different political, juridical and economic rights and privileges, and they did not have the uniform economic underpinning of the later European bourgeoisie (for instance, many middling citizens probably derived the bulk of their income from agriculture).

[19] See e.g. Whitehead (1986) 82–5 on the presence of *metoikoi* in almost every Athenian deme (neighbourhood-district); Millett (1998) on interaction between citizens and non-citizens in the Athenian agora; Vlassopoulos (2007b) on the blurring of identities between citizens, *metoikoi*, women and slaves in what he calls 'free spaces', e.g. the agora, the workplace, the tavern, the house and the trireme; on blurred identities at Athens, see also Cohen (2000). See Wijma (2014) on the participation of *metoikoi* in Athenian polis religion. On economic cooperation note e.g. Cohen (1992); Deene (2014).
[20] Cohen (1992) 87–8.
[21] Ehrenberg (1962) 113–64, esp. 152–4, 161–2; Whitehead (1977) 120–1 for a sharp retort.
[22] E.g. Morris (1994) 354–5.

The Athenians were actually well aware of the socioeconomic differentiation within the various categories of non-citizens in their polis.[23] However, when it comes to the citizens proper, many of the texts at our disposal often appear to distinguish only between the *plousioi*, that is, the rich, and the *penetes*, the less wealthy or labouring men.[24] Yet these terms were flexible and could mean very different things in different (rhetorical) contexts. J. K. Davies has argued convincingly that the wealthiest Athenians were those able to pay for the substantial public contributions called liturgies, and that this required a minimum fortune of at least three to four talents (18,000–24,000 drachmas). During the fourth century BCE, this 'liturgy-class' consisted of some 300–400 individuals.[25] Davies has also argued that a fortune of about one talent (6,000 drachmas) placed one in the leisure class, a group which may have comprised some 1,200–2,000 citizens.[26] Our sources almost always equate the *plousioi* with those belonging to the liturgical class.[27] Consequently, nearly every citizen who was not a *plousios* could be considered a *penes*, even if he owned a fortune of, say, two talents.[28] The *penetes*, then, were a highly differentiated category, consisting of many gradations of wealth, from fairly well-to-do individuals to subsistence farmers or day labourers and anything in between.[29]

In fact contemporaries were clearly conscious of the existence of a middling category between rich and poor citizens. Aristotle states that in all poleis, the citizenry are divided into three parts, the rich, the poor and the middling sort (*hoi mesoi*), and that those poleis are most stable in which the middling citizens are numerous (*Pol.* 1295b–1296a). Solon's system of property classes at Athens, which clearly included a group of middling citizens, the *zeugitai* (to be distinguished from the wealth-elite, the *pentakosiomedimnoi* and *hippeis*, on the one hand, and ordinary citizens or *thetes* on the other), has already been referred to (Plut., *Solon* 18.1–2), and we can

---

[23] Note for example the grumblings of the Old Oligarch (an anonymous fifth-century BCE pamphleteer) about rich slaves and *metoikoi* at Athens, and on the impossibility of distinguishing ordinary citizens from slaves or *metoikoi* on the city's streets, [Xenophon], *Ath. Pol.* 1.10–12.

[24] Ober (1989) 194–6. Note, however, that down at the bottom end of the socioeconomic scale, some of our sources again distinguish between the *penes* and the *ptochos*, the beggar who has no means of living (e.g. Aristophanes, *Plut.* 537–554).

[25] Davies (1971) xx–xxx, (1981) 9–37.

[26] Davies (1981) 6–14, 28–35, esp. 28–9 and 34–5; Ober (1989) 128n58.   [27] Davies (1981) 10–11.

[28] Ober (1989) 195. Alternatively, however, our sources sometimes simply identify the *plousioi* with the leisure class while the *penetes* were those who had to work for a living. According to this definition, our owner of two talents would of course be a *plousios*.

[29] In the context of a court speech even rich litigants who obviously belonged to the liturgical class could portray themselves as *penetes*, arguing that they were less wealthy than their equally liturgical oponents, whom they would then describe as *plousioi*, see Ober (1989) 196.

also point to the plan of the oligarchic conspirators at Athens in 411 BCE to limit political rights to a group of 5,000 property-owning citizens (Thuc. 8.65.3; *Ath. Pol.* 29.5).[30] For fourth-century BCE Athens, modern scholars have assumed a 'middling' stratum of about 7,000–9,000 citizens who possessed property to the value of 2,000 drachmas or more (out of a total citizen population of about 20,000–30,000) and hence were of hoplite status.[31] Recently, Josiah Ober has posited a middling group at Athens amounting to some 40–60 per cent of a total Athenian population of just under 250,000 persons during the later fourth century BCE. Ober's 'middling group' covers a fairly broad socioeconomic spectrum and consists of individuals with an income in a range of 2.4 to 10 times minimum subsistence (which he puts at 100 drachmas per year). It includes mostly citizens (men, women and children) but also some *metoikoi* (men, women and children) and slaves.[32] Ober cautiously suggests that for the fourth-century BCE Greek world as a whole (thus factoring in many poleis that were much smaller and less prosperous than Athens), we should perhaps assume a middling stratum of approximately 20 per cent of the total population.[33]

This is of course a speculative reconstruction which should certainly not be taken as fact, yet it does give us a sense of orders of magnitude. It then becomes interesting to explore the economic and sociopolitical implications of the assumption that Classical Athens and other poleis were home to a fairly sizeable group of individuals of middling wealth. Do our findings from Greek economic and sociopolitical history provide a context in which such an assumption would make sense?

We can start with the economic side of the question. Revisionist accounts of Classical Greek agriculture that have been developed since the 1970s suggest that ordinary farmers could achieve greater levels of productivity than was formerly envisaged by intensively working concentrated sections of land (rather than scattered small plots), by pasturing animals on their land during fallow periods (the dung would restore nutrient levels in the ground) or through reducing fallow periods by using various kinds of manure.[34]

---

[30] On the *zeugitai*, 'a broad class of middling peasants' (277), see most recently Valdés Guía and Gallego (2010) who have summarised a great deal of earlier debate.
[31] On the size of the hoplite stratum and the value of their property in fourth-century Athens, see e.g. Jones (1957) 8–9, 81, 142, n. 50; Strauss (1986) 43, 78–80; Ober (1989) 129.
[32] Ober (2010), who bases his analysis on data for Athenian wage levels and conventional population estimates for citizens, slaves and *metoikoi*.
[33] Ober (2010) 265–6.
[34] See e.g. Jameson (1977–1978); Halstead (1987); Garnsey (1988) 93–106; Hodkinson (1988), (1992); Gallant (1991); Hanson (1995) 41–89; Morris (1994) 363–6, (2006) 41 for references to the archaeological survey data supporting what he calls the 'New Model' of Classical agriculture.

Population pressure most likely constituted the impetus for this development towards a more intensive agricultural regime, which began in the sixth century BCE, but it is certainly possible that productivity gains outpaced population growth, thus creating the surplus necessary to support an above-subsistence stratum of some magnitude. Recently, Ian Morris has tried to sketch just such a scenario of economic growth for Archaic and Classical Greece. Based on various archaeological indices, such as changes over time in the median size of ordinary houses and improvements in building standards, Morris argues for an average annual improvement of *per capita* living standards between 800 and 300 BCE of somewhere between 0.07 and 0.14 per cent. Overall *per capita* consumption may have shown a 50–95 per cent increase during this 500-year period.[35] Though modest by industrial standards, this growth-scenario looks fairly impressive when compared to the 0.2 *per annum* increase in living standards in early modern Holland, arguably the highest-performing pre-modern economy on record, during the period 1580–1820.[36] It would clearly leave room for the development of sizeable middling groups in Classical Greek poleis.

Much is uncertain about Morris's growth-scenario, based as it is on inferences from archaeological data that are often hard to interpret, yet the estimates he presents seem broadly to be within the range of what one might expect from a complex pre-modern economy. Yet if we want to make a plausible case for the existence of sizeable middling groups in Classical Greek poleis, we need not just look at growth, but also and primarily at the distribution of wealth. As usual our information is best for Athens, and, as the above-mentioned guesstimates concerning the internal differentiation of the citizen community already suggest, there we do not find a particularly strong concentration of wealth at the top. Studies of landownership in Attica conclude that about 7.5–9 per cent of citizens possessed approximately 30–35 per cent of all land, while 20 per cent of citizens owned little land or no land at all. This means that 70–75 per cent of the citizens owned 60–65 per cent of all land, which, in comparative historical terms, suggests a strikingly equal distribution of wealth.[37] Analysis of house sizes based on data from across the Archaic and Classical Greek world tentatively confirms the Athenian picture. Median house size during the Classical period outstrips that of nineteenth-century England or the United States in the twentieth century. House sizes also tend to cluster

---

[35] Morris (2004) 726. See also Von Reden (2007) 399–402; Ober (2010) 249–53, (2015).
[36] Morris (2004) 726.
[37] Foxhall (1992), (2002); Osborne (1992); Morris (1998b) 235–6; Ober (2010) 258–9.

tightly around the median, suggesting, again in comparative historical terms, a fairly equitable distribution of wealth and the presence of sizeable middling groups.[38]

Some scholars have argued for a strong correlation between the development of the new intensive agricultural regime in the Greek world from the Archaic period onwards and the rise of the polis. Taking his cue from Aristotle's idealisation of 'farmer-democracy' in the *Politics* (1291b–1292b, 1295b, 1318b), Victor Davis Hanson, for instance, has argued that the agricultural innovations of the Archaic age led to the development of a broad stratum of sedentary, middling farmers, a group who would eventually come to constitute the social backbone of polis democracy.[39] Others have stressed a more general link between the development of the idea of – and the institutions and practices associated with – adult male citizen political egalitarianism and economic growth during the Archaic and Classical periods, even though there is still much debate about the precise causal relationships.[40]

What seems clear, however, is that over the centuries from the early Archaic period onwards, the socioideological climate in the poleis became increasingly favourable to the middling citizen. This has been argued most forcefully by Ian Morris, who has pointed to the development of a 'middling ideology' in the Greek polis from the sixth century BCE onwards, but with roots dating back to at least the eighth century BCE.[41] Its origins lay in long-standing conflicts between sections of the elites in the developing poleis, which were expressed ideologically in Archaic poetry.

According to Morris, in this literature we see an 'elitist' ideology associated with aristocratic inter-community guest friendships, the culture of the symposium (aristocratic drinking party) and eastern cultural influence coming into conflict with a 'middling' ideology, adopted by other sections of the elite (aristocrats as well as non-aristocratic *nouveaux riches*), in which the polis and its citizen community were viewed as the primary sources of power and authority. The social ideal type of the middling ideology was the *metrios*, the 'middling man', a self-sufficient farmer owning his own land, neither too obviously rich or poor (thus avoiding extremes), a member of the hoplite phalanx, a head of household, 'married with children, pious, responsible and self-controlled'.[42] It was an image

---

[38] Morris (2004) 721–2; Kron (2014) 128–9, 131–3.   [39] Hanson (1995).
[40] E.g. Morris (1994) 365, (2004) 722; Ober (2010) 270–5.
[41] Morris (1996), (2000). See also Kurke (1992); Hanson (1996); Ober (2000).
[42] Morris (2000) 116.

that could be adopted as a form of self-representation by the large land-owner, if he displayed his wealth sparingly and used part of it for the benefit of the civic community, as well as by the small citizen-farmer.[43] It well fitted the political egalitarianism of the Greek polis, either in its weak oligarchic form (with an elite council but a citizens' assembly) as well as in its more radical democratic variety. Indeed, Morris argues that the mid-dling ideology was a necessary condition for the development of democracy in Greek poleis.[44]

On the whole, then, research in Greek economic and sociopolitical history suggests that in economic, political and ideological terms the Archaic and Classical Greek polis was an environment highly conducive to the rise of a broad segment of middling citizens (and non-citizens), and that such middling groups played an important part in the development of polis society. Yet such social differentiation, stimulated by both economic developments and political and ideological changes, suggests a certain level of social dynamism: individuals and families should to some extent have been able to traverse the social hierarchy, either within the span of a personal lifetime or over the generations. Here we turn to this chapter's second theme, social mobility. How socially mobile were the inhabitants of Greek poleis?

As the preceding paragraphs will already have made clear, it was cer-tainly possible for Classical Greeks, whether citizens or non-citizens, to accumulate wealth over the course of their own lifetimes or in a generation or two, and hence to advance themselves and/or their families economic-ally. For Athens, J. K. Davies has shown that from the later fifth century BCE onwards, sources of wealth beyond agriculture *sensu stricto* were increasingly being exploited by Athenian citizens (e.g. employing slaves in workshops and the silver mines, renting out real estate, money-lending etc.), and that this diversification of sources of wealth went hand in hand with the appearance of many *nouveaux riches* in the propertied class and on the Athenian political scene, whose income partly derived from these non-traditional sources.[45]

What Davies demonstrates with equal clarity, however, is the fragility of wealth. In his survey of Athenian propertied families for the period

---

[43] Ober (1989) 220–1, 226–33.

[44] Morris (1996). Of course this does not imply that other ideologies ceased to exist in the poleis during the Classical period, nor that all poleis became democracies (many did not). Even in that most democratic of poleis, Athens, we find a vibrant elite counterculture of anti-democratic thought, see Ober (2001).

[45] Davies (1981) 38–72.

600–300 BCE, he could identify only one family that managed to remain part of the Athenian wealth-elite, the so-called liturgical class, for five generations. Five families were part of the liturgical class for four generations, 16 for three generations, 44 for two generations, and 357 for just one generation.[46] No doubt the fragmentary nature of our sources has its part to play here, yet the pattern revealed by Davies is certainly plausible and can be confirmed from the study of other pre-modern elites, particularly those in Roman cities.

Davies suggests various explanations for the observed lack of intergenerational stability of the Athenian elite, some of them economic and political (the cost of liturgies; the irregular incidence of special taxation, e.g. the *eisphora*, an extraordinary property tax paid by wealthy Athenians, both citizens and non-citizens; the effects of attacks by political opponents etc.), others demographic and legal. High mortality among infants and young children meant that patrilineal extinction was a relatively frequent occurrence. Alternatively, the absence of any principle of primogeniture meant that a family with a number of surviving heirs might face a fragmentation of its patrimony, causing the individual heirs to 'drop out' of the wealth-elite.[47] Studies of such demographically-induced social mobility, and particularly of strategies developed to prevent mortality's adverse effects (adoption, marriage within the patrilinear or matrilinear kingroups or joint ownership by heirs to counter the fragmentation of estates), have revealed much about the pressures governing the behaviour of Athenian households.[48] Needless to say, the downward mobility or extinction of some families created opportunities for newcomers either to occupy high status positions that had become available or even to acquire significant new wealth.[49]

We have already discussed the possibilities for various categories of non-citizens (slaves, *metoikoi*) to acquire wealth in Athenian society, but social mobility entails more than just an increase in (or decrease of) individual economic prosperity. Social privileges, status and prestige also come into play, as commodities that could be gained or lost while people traversed

---

[46] Davies (1981) 85–7.   [47] Davies (1981) 73–87; Deene (2013) 30–52.
[48] E.g. Cox (1998). See Hodkinson (2000) on the fragmentation of holdings and familial strategies to prevent its adverse effects among the citizen-elite in Classical Sparta.
[49] For example, Athenian citizens with ties to more than one household might experience an instantaneous increase in prosperity when one of these households faced patrilineal extinction. Thucydides (2.53.1) relates how, during the epidemic that struck Athens in 430 BCE, many people suddenly became rich through inheriting the property of wealthy relatives who fell victim to the disease. The plague, however, merely accelerated processes that were already at work. See Deene (2013) 49–52.

the social hierarchy. Just like citizens, *metoikoi* might win prestige and privileges through benefitting the polis, by, for instance, paying for liturgies.[50] In return for such contributions, *metoikoi* could receive privileges such as *enktesis*, the right to own real property (a house and/or agricultural land) at Athens, or *isoteleia*, the right of 'equal taxation', which in practice primarily meant exemption from the *metoikion*, the special poll tax *metoikoi* had to pay. A privilege far more rarely bestowed upon *metoikoi* was the grant of citizenship, or naturalisation.[51] Acquiring citizenship might be thought of as the crowning achievement of the socially ambitious *metoikos*, but, even though we are aware of some well-documented cases, citizenship was not awarded to *metoikoi* very often.[52]

Edward Cohen has tried to circumvent this issue by arguing that *astos*, the word commonly used for citizen and regarded as an equivalent of *polites*, did in fact mean 'free local person/resident of Attica', thus subsuming citizens (*politai*), *metoikoi* and several other groups under one heading.[53] Philologically, however, this is unsound: there are hardly any passages in the sources that support such a reading. Moreover, this view of *astoi* would make nonsense of Pericles' famous citizenship law of 451/0 BCE.[54]

An alternative approach would be to let go of the notion that citizenship and naturalisation were necessarily overarching concerns of all socially ambitious *metoikoi*. As recent research has shown, Athenian social life in fact offered multiple avenues for participation, integration and acquiring status and prestige. Thus Kostas Vlassopoulos has pointed to the continuous interaction between (adult male) citizens, women, *metoikoi* and slaves in what he calls 'free spaces' (i.e. the agora, the workshop, the tavern etc.), which led, in effect, to a 'blurring of identities' between the various categories of Athenian inhabitants and created room for profitable cooperation.[55]

Other scholars, in search of a more inclusive model of Athenian society that goes beyond the strict adult male citizen/non-adult male citizen divide, have defined the concept of 'polis membership', based on the notion of 'sharing in the polis' (*metechein tes poleos*) as mentioned in the

---

[50] Whitehead (1977) esp. 6–26, 80–2; Kamen (2013) 55–61 for an overview of debates on 'privileged metics'.

[51] M. J. Osborne (1981–1983); Deene (2011) on naturalisation and social mobility; Kamen (2013) 79–86 with many references.

[52] M. J. Osborne (1981–1983) 4: 207: 'naturalization (honorific or otherwise) was never very common in Athens prior to the second century [BCE]'.

[53] Cohen (2000).

[54] See the long and subtle review of Cohen (2000) by Robin Osborne (2002) for substantial criticism of Cohen's argument.

[55] Vlassopoulos (2007b).

sources. This was a form of 'sharing' that might *inter alia* be expressed through differentiated participation by the various groups of polis inhabitants in religious rituals (the *hiera* and *hosia* of the polis, see e.g. Dem. 23.65). Thus *metoikoi* could become integrated into, and acquire status within, the Athenian community through actively sharing in and contributing to the religious life of the polis along with the full citizens (e.g. in sacrifices, festivals, feasts). According to this analysis, participation in polis religion was a crucial marker of 'community membership' and of much broader significance than adult-male-citizen-only political participation.[56]

Scholars have also pointed to the role of associations as constituting both a forum for expressing econonomic differentiation among citizens *and* a vehicle for interaction between (wealthy) citizens and non-citizens. At Athens, public associative institutions that were connected to the political and administrative functioning of the polis, such as the demes and *phylai*, generally reflected the political egalitarianism of the democracy and could therefore not give institutional expression to socioeconomic differentiation among the (non-elite) citizenry. Other associations less tied to public administration *could* do so, however, and scholars have pointed to the phratries and their subdivisions in groups of citizens of different levels of wealth and status as one example.[57] In such subgroups of the phratries, based on kin, cult, economic activity or otherwise, Athenians could fraternise with fellow-citizens of similar wealth and status, escaping for a while the relentless political equalising of the democratic polis. Nicholas F. Jones has argued that even women and non-citizens could become members of such associations (*thiasoi*) that were only loosely connected to the phratry itself (which, officially, was strictly male-citizens-only).[58] If true – and the hypothetical nature of the argument should be stressed – this suggests that (occasionally?) similarities of wealth and social position could override political and status barriers, which leaves us with the interesting conclusion that *thiasoi*-type associations served the double function of, on the one hand, underlining socioeconomic differentiation among the (non-elite) citizenry and, on the other, integrating into the polis community 'qualifying' individuals who belonged to otherwise socially and politically marginal groups.

---

[56] Blok (2005), (2014); Wijma (2014) on *metoikoi* acquiring 'polis membership' through participation in Athenian religious rituals.

[57] Lambert (1993) 59–141; Jones (1999) 214–20, referring to *gennetai* (clans, that is, the traditional aristocracy), *orgeones* (cultic groups), *oikoi*, a variety of *thiasoi* (associations) and other less well-defined groups of *phrateres*.

[58] Jones (1999) 218–20.

Interaction-focussed and inclusive, participation-based analyses of Athenian society like the ones just presented are very promising, even if they need to be refined through further research. Arguably, they can more easily accommodate the evidence for economic and social differentiation both within and across the main legal status categories and the dynamics of social mobility than the standard tripartite 'citizens-*metoikoi*-slaves' model. In any case these approaches are to be preferred to anachronistic attempts to construct a bourgeoisie out of the socially and politically highly diverse middling strata of Athenian society.

The presence of middling groups was not restricted to the poleis of the (later) Archaic and Classical periods of Greek history. We should point, for instance, to the large number of mainly epigraphical attestations of private associations in the poleis of the Hellenistic period. Such clubs (*thiasoi, eranistai, koina* etc.) often provided a haven for citizens and non-citizens of the 'middling sort', craftsmen, traders, soldiers, sailors, artists and so forth.[59] Indeed, private associations, whether primarily religious, occupational or convivial in nature, or, as was often the case, consisting of a mix of such elements, continued to prosper later on, in the cities of the Roman imperial period, to which we shall now turn. For this period in particular, the flourishing of associations in the cities has often been associated strongly with the presence and increasing social visibility of urban middling groups.

Stratification and Mobility in Roman Cities under the Empire

Anyone wishing to study stratification and mobility in Roman cities is faced with something of a paradox. On the one hand, literary and legal sources produced by and for the elite tend to present a dichotomous picture of Roman society as consisting of a tiny elite of senators, knights (*equites*) and municipal city councillors (*decuriones*) – the three *ordines* – set over and against a vast mass of poor plebeians, free non-citizens and slaves. From the later second century CE onwards, Roman penal law increasingly came to reflect this dichotomy, as *honestiores* (senators, knights, decurions and army veterans) were distinguished from *humiliores* (the rest, i.e. poor citizens, free non-citizens and slaves), for whom the harsher punishments were reserved.[60] This top-down binary ordering has found its way into

---

[59] See e.g. Gabrielsen (2001), (2009); Arnaoutoglou (2011); Trümper (2011). For Roman associations (*collegia*) and their relation to middling groups, see below.

[60] Garnsey (1970).

most modern accounts of Roman social structure, and even though scholars generally insist that the legal categories do not adequately reflect actual social and economic divisions, one suspects that Walter Scheidel is right when he states that 'no matter how often the formal ordering of imperial society into a tiny elite and a vast humble mass is explained as a purely legal construct, it nevertheless continues to seep into our evaluations of lived realities'.[61]

On the other hand, Roman historians have always been aware of the presence of a particular category of people in Roman urban society (in Italy above all, but also in many provincial cities) who have often been regarded as 'middling', namely freed slaves (*liberti*).[62] The Romans freed many of their slaves, particularly those they employed in an urban context, and, once formally manumitted, *liberti* became Roman citizens, yet their citizenship came with some qualifications. Freedmen were barred from public office, some priesthoods and legionary service. How to fit freedmen into the binary status scheme outlined above? For the Roman elite, the answer to that question was in principle straightforward: since freedmen could not become senators, knights, decurions or legionary veterans (due to being barred from office-holding and legionary service), they belonged to the *humiliores*.

Yet freedmen were hardly a homogenous group. Freedmen belonging to the imperial household or large senatorial *familiae* could become very rich and influential due to their closeness to the sources of wealth and power.[63] At the local urban level too, we find many well-to-do freedmen. This was due to the fact that many urban freedmen had been employed by their former masters (or had even worked alongside them) in administrative, commercial or manufacturing jobs, in which they had picked up skills and expertise that could be put to good use once they were manumitted. Many continued in the same professions, as artisans, traders and service providers, generally earning above-subsistence incomes, as numerous epigraphic monuments testify. Those who were most successful might achieve a level of wealth on a par with members of the civic elite. Such

---

[61] Scheidel (2006) 44. For analyses of Roman society in dichotomous terms (few rich vs. many poor), see e.g. Brunt (1987) 383 (excepting rich freedmen); Kloft (1992) 203; Jongman (2000b) 271 (but note that Jongman [2007a] offers a considerably more nuanced picture); Toner (2002) 50–1.

[62] Duff (1958); Treggiari (1969); Garnsey (1998c); Mouritsen (2011) 207 and *passim* on scholars' mistaken identification of freedmen with a 'middle class' or 'bourgeoisie', with many references to earlier literature. See De Ligt and Garnsey (2012) on the particularly high numbers of freedmen in central Italian cities during the early empire (their case study is Herculaneum).

[63] Weaver (1972) on imperial slaves and freedmen.

freedmen, barred as they were from civic office-holding, often became members of the *augustales*, civic associations which may have been linked to the imperial cult and membership of which consisted mostly, but not exclusively, of wealthy *liberti*.[64] According to some scholars, the *augustales* increasingly acquired the trappings of a proper *ordo*. Located between the civic elite of city councillors (*ordo decurionum*) and the *plebs*, the *augustales* have sometimes been thought to constitute some kind of formally instituted municipal middle class, a second order.[65] As Henrik Mouritsen has shown, however, the degree of local variation between cities and regions with regard to the associations of *augustales*, their structure, functions and the social profile of their membership, is so great as to defy any attempt to present them as a clearly delineated class or order in civic society.[66]

The contrast between the actual levels of wealth and power some freedmen achieved and their low servile descent might well have caused occasional resentment among the senatorial and equestrian elites, yet there is little indication that freedmen were systematically looked down upon among the broader (urban) freeborn population. Urban freedmen generally seem to have blended easily into the professional trading, manufacturing and service-providing sections of the urban population, while for wealthy freedmen the possibility to become *augustalis* offered the ultimate means of integration into civic society: through euergetism. Like members of the freeborn civic elite, *augustales* were frequent benefactors of their cities.[67]

All in all, then, freedmen *per se* were too diverse a category to be termed a middling group, though, given the administrative, commercial or manufacturing skills urban freedmen had often acquired as slaves, and the continued support of their patrons which many among them enjoyed after manumission, many *individual liberti* would stand a good chance of becoming part of such a middling stratum. Yet we have to cast our net wider. In a recent exercise in controlled parametric conjecture, Walter Scheidel and Steven J. Friesen have estimated that 'middling groups' (not all of them urban, of course) possibly made up roughly one-tenth of the empire's population, but may well have accounted for about one-fifth of total (i.e. aggregate gross) income, which in terms of overall economic significance put them on a par with the elite (senators, equestrians, *decuriones*), who also accounted for about a fifth of gross income but of

---

[64] Duthoy (1978); Mouritsen (2011). On the internal structure of the associations, see most recently Vandevoorde (2013).
[65] See chiefly Abramenko (1993).   [66] Mouritsen (2011) 248–61.   [67] Mouritsen (2011) 258.

course made up only a tiny fraction of the total population.[68] If this reconstruction approximates reality, the empire's middling groups were of considerable socioeconomic significance. Yet can we locate them, sociologically, in Roman cities?

Paul Veyne, Andrew Wallace-Hadrill and others have pointed to a distinction drawn by Pliny the Elder (*NH* 26.3) between the so-called middling plebeians (*plebs media*) and the lowly plebs, the truly poor (*plebs humilis*).[69] Adopting the Plinian usage, Veyne proceeds to flesh out the social profile of the *plebs media*. He identifies these individuals as freeborn, mostly moderately well-to-do citizens: shopkeepers, traders, professionals and owners of medium-sized estates. In short, according to Veyne, the *plebs media* included all of those freeborn citizens located, in social and economic terms, below the equestrian order in the city of Rome or below the elite of town-councillors (*ordo decurionum*) in other Italian and provincial cities but above the truly poor citizens, who owned no form of property and lived from hand to mouth, day to day (the *plebs humilis* or *plebs sordida*).[70] Wallace-Hadrill, in an attempt to locate the social group that might have owned or inhabited 'the enormous number of houses of middling size and middling rank' that can be found at Pompeii and Herculaneum, likewise adopts Pliny's terminology and suggests that they were the *plebs media*, 'a large and disparate group between elite and poor ... [t]o judge by the nomenclature of almost all the documentary evidence we have from the Campanian towns, a high proportion of them are likely to have been of servile origin. To judge by the archaeological evidence, they were extensively involved in the trade, craft and commerce of the city'.[71]

Following Wallace-Hadrill's observations, it seems indeed realistic to envisage the middling plebs as consisting of both freedmen and freeborn, and not solely of freeborn, as Veyne would have it. This is also the perspective of historians working on Roman professional associations

---

[68] Scheidel and Friesen (2009).
[69] Wallace-Hadrill (1990) 146–7, 191; (1994) 143–4, 168–71; Veyne (2000) 1170; see also Pleket (1998) 208. In the passage in question, Pliny talks about a contagious skin disease that broke out in Rome under the emperor Tiberius. As Pliny notes, it affected the upper orders (*proceres*), who kissed upon greeting each other, but did not spread among women, slaves or the poor and middling plebeians (*plebes humilis aut media*). Note also e.g. Tacitus, *Hist.* 1.4, where the historian contrasts the *pars populi integra*, the 'respectable part of the people', with the *plebs sordida et circo ac theatris sueta*, 'the squalid populace accustomed to circus and theatre', and the epitaph of the commedian Ti. Claudius Tiberinus: *Roma mihi patria est, media de plebe parentes*, 'Rome is my fatherland, and my parents derive from the middling plebs', *CIL* 6.10097 = 33960. For further source references, see Veyne (2000) 1170–4.
[70] Veyne (2000).   [71] Wallace-Hadrill (1990) 190–1, (1994) 173.

(*collegia*), who have plausibly argued that the *plebs media* was the social stratum from which the *collegia* derived the bulk of their membership, which included many freedmen.[72] *Collegia*, from this view, were crucial to the integration of the *plebs media* into civic society. The associations (which we find in many cities of the empire, both East and West) had a formal structure, with by-laws, membership requirements, magistrates and often a common treasury. They arguably served to further their members' economic and business interests, to engage them in common worship and to provide a focus for sociability. Through participation of their members in civic rituals, festivals and processions, *collegia* functioned as a vehicle for the incorporation of the *plebs media* (including freedmen) into the civic social hierarchy.[73] In addition, *collegia* probably provided a social and political platform for their members, allowing them to negotiate and establish enduring contacts with powerful individuals within the civic elite, who frequently acted as patrons and benefactors of associations. *Collegia* could perhaps operate as pressure groups serving the interests of the *plebs media*, and yet might also on occasion have assumed a mediating role between the elite and the rest of the urban population.[74]

The link between urban professional associations and the *plebs media* lends further support to the notion of the latter's extensive involvement 'in the trade, craft and commerce of the city'. [75] Yet as Veyne had already argued, the economic basis of the middling plebs is unlikely to have been restricted to trade and manufacture. Substantial numbers among them may have owned some land, either deriving their income solely from this, or combining agriculture with manufacture or retail.[76] Starting from the property thresholds of the Roman Republican census classes, Scheidel conservatively estimates that there may have been some 225,000 citizen-households in late Republican Italy (out of a total of 1.15 million house-holds with 4 million citizens) belonging to the third and fourth census classes, i.e. those owning landed property to the value of at least 50,000 sesterces (HS) or HS 20,000, a middling group when compared to the HS 100,000 required for the first class, and the HS 375 required for the fifth.[77]

---

[72] On *collegia*, see Royden (1988); Van Nijf (1997); Tran (2006); Verboven (2007), (2009), (2011); Liu (2009); Broekaert (2011); on the *plebs media* as the stratum from which most *collegiati* derived, see in particular Van Nijf (1997) 18–28; Patterson (2006) 261; Verboven (2007), (2009); Liu (2009) 162–3; on freedmen as *collegiati*, see Mouritsen (2011) 129, 207, 249, 294–5 with references; Royden (1988) 228–34 on freedmen as *collegia* magistrates.

[73] Van Nijf (1997); Harland (2003).   [74] Patterson (2006) 258–60; Zuiderhoek (2008a) 437–45.

[75] Wallace-Hadrill (1990) 190–1, (1994) 173.   [76] Veyne (2000) 1174–5.

[77] Scheidel (2006) 48–50, based on the analysis of census rankings by Rathbone (1993).

Estates in the HS 25,000 to HS 100,000 range predominate in the surviving land register from the town of Ligures Baebiani in imperial southern Italy (early second century CE), while in the contemporary land register from Veleia in northern Italy (from which estates below HS 50,000 were excluded) most estates fall in the HS 50,000 to HS 75,000 range.[78] By way of comparison, in the imperial period the minimum property requirement for a city councillor (*decurion*), that is, a member of the civic elite, was HS 100,000. The registers are of course isolated pieces of data, yet they do at least tentatively suggest the presence of a fairly broad range of middling land owners in Roman imperial Italy (thus offering some support for Scheidel's late Republican reconstruction). A similar property-owning stratum has been identified in Roman Egypt.[79] Such owners of medium-sized estates were not all urban residents (certainly not in Egypt), but a substantial number of them probably were.

Veyne, Wallace-Hadrill and historians working on *collegia* emphasise that the *plebs media* by no means constituted a commercial bourgeoisie along later European lines.[80] Like their Greek counterparts, the Roman urban middling strata were internally diverse, and they lacked a clear social profile. They may also have been fairly transient in terms of their membership, with individuals frequently rising socially or sinking depending on economic and demographic contingencies and the extent of patronal support from the elite.[81] Nonetheless the middling groups were a vital component of Roman urban society, in that they provided many essential tasks and services, populated the numerous workshops (*tabernae*) and modest yet comfortable houses (alongside the elite's grand residences) that were characteristic of Roman cities, erected the majority of still-extant funerary monuments (where we can read their names in the inscriptions and see them depicted in reliefs, with the tools of their trade or proudly toga-clad with their wives and children) and, through their *collegia*, put an indelible stamp on urban social, political and cultural life.

---

[78] Ligures Baebiani: *CIL* 9.1455, Duncan-Jones (1990) 131, Scheidel (2006) 51; Veleia: *CIL* 11.1147, Duncan-Jones (1990) 132, Scheidel (2006) 51; also Garnsey and Saller (2014) 95–7.

[79] Bagnall (1992) esp. 142, with Scheidel (2006) 52–4.

[80] Veyne (2000) 1174; Wallace-Hadrill (1990) 191, (2013); Van Nijf (1997) 22.

[81] Mouritsen (2015) 17–18. Mouritsen argues on the basis of a brief analysis of housing patterns (18–20) that the Pompeian middling groups were already in decline during the first century CE. If true, this would make the city rather unrepresentative of Roman cities in many parts of the empire, where, for instance, the remarkable flourishing of professional *collegia* during the second and early third centuries CE attests to the increasing prominence of urban middling strata. Of course, Vesuvius has made it impossible for us to know how Pompeii would have developed beyond the later first century. On the potential social mobility of middling individuals, see below.

The urban middling groups were of crucial significance to Roman civic society in yet another sense, however, and this brings us to the final topic to be considered in this chapter, social mobility in Roman cities. Roman urban elites were basically elites of office-holders (magistrates and city councillors) and were in principle open to newcomers (*novi homines*) who were sufficiently wealthy, popular and socially adept. Two factors in particular could lead over time to a depletion of the ranks of city-councillors (who generally numbered about a hundred in the West and two hundred in the East, though totals varied). The first, as in the Greek cities, was high and unpredictable mortality, particularly among infants and young children. The twin effects of the mortality regime, i.e. patrilin-eal extinction of elite families and fragmentation of estates,[82] have been much studied, both for the senatorial elite at Rome and for the urban elites in Italian and provincial cities.[83] Strategies were of course available to mitigate mortality's worst effects, in the form of adoption or marriage alliances, yet on the whole the mortality regime appears to have comprom-ised elite social and genetic continuity to a significant extent. A second, lesser force of depletion of local city councils was the integration of cities into the larger social and administrative system of the empire. Increasingly, the wealthiest and most able members of local urban elites were co-opted into the imperial elite of knights and senators.[84]

To fill in the gaps in the *ordo* created by these two processes, cities often had to fall back on recruiting new members from wealthy but socially less elevated groups, particularly when the customary annual supply of new members entering the *ordo* as ex-magistrates did not suffice to fill all the vacancies and suitable recruits from established families were lacking. The higher echelons of the *plebs media*, i.e. rich traders and manufacturers, wealthy shop owners, owners of medium-sized estates and veterans, espe-cially retired centurions, then provided the most obvious candidates.[85] As the Roman jurist Callistratus grudgingly admits, cities should not deny council membership to 'those who are engaged in the trading and selling of foodstuffs' (*eos qui utensilia negotiantur et vendunt*) when confronted with a

---

[82] As in the Greek case, if families tried to avoid extinction by having a large number of children, and, fortuitously, many survived, the absence of primogeniture and the partible inheritance system could result in a situation where the individual heirs were no longer sufficiently wealthy to remain part of the elite, which in Roman cities meant being able to meet the census criterion for *ordo* membership.

[83] Brunt (1982); Hopkins (1983); Jongman (1991) 311–29; Saller (1994); Mouritsen (1997); Scheidel (1999); Tacoma (2006); Zuiderhoek (2011).

[84] For the effects of this process on the cities of Roman Italy, see Patterson (2006).

[85] See Zuiderhoek (2011) 190–1 for evidence and discussion.

needful shortage of 'honourable men' (*honesti viri*) (*Dig.* 50.2.12). Some of those recruited were (freeborn) *collegiati* (generally *collegia* magistrates), suggesting that the *collegia* might occasionally have acted as a springboard for such social mobility.[86] Sons of wealthy freedmen, whose fathers might have been *augustales* and might even have been awarded the honorific *ornamenta decurionalia* (while still being barred from actual office holding and from entering the council), constituted another group of promising candidates.[87] Unlike their fathers, they were freeborn (*ingenui*).

The result of such social mobility was of course civic elites, *ordines decurionum*, that were as internally stratified and as dynamic – with newly 'arrived' families ascending the ranks, and some older ones dying out, becoming impoverished, or moving on to higher things in the imperial service – as the non-elite urban populations. This was a state of affairs not lost on the Roman authorities, who in their official communications casually distinguished between the *primores viri* or *honesti* (the 'first men' or 'the honourable') in the city councils and those councillors who were *inferiores* or *e plebe*.[88] Yet such condescension from up high probably did little to damage the self-esteem of the baker, the purple-dyer, the goldsmith, the ship owner, the merchant, the *collegium* magistrate or the ex-centurion who had achieved wealth and civic prominence, invested his profits in land, as befitted a gentleman (if he did not already own some landed property) and saw his efforts richly rewarded with council membership.[89] Who knows, his son might scale even greater heights . . .

'We should guard against the blind insistence', Ramsay MacMullen once observed in a book on Roman social relations, 'that there *must* be a middle class and that it must be sought where we are used to finding it today, in the urban commercial and industrial segments of the population'.[90] As will be evident from the above, I agree, provided that by 'middle class' is meant a bourgeoisie on the later European model (as is clearly MacMullen's intention here). I would add, however, that equally, we should not allow ourselves to be blinded by the simplistically dichotomous picture of society sometimes propagated by Greek and Roman elite

---

[86] Royden (1988) 232–3.   [87] Garnsey (1975); Mouritsen (2011) 261–3.

[88] For *primores viri* vs. *inferiores* in the city councils, see *Dig.* 50.7.5.5, a letter from the emperor Hadrian to the city of Klazomenai. For *honesti* vs. those *e plebe* among the city councillors, see Pliny, *Ep.* 10.79, a letter he wrote as governor of the province Bithynia-Pontus to the emperor Trajan. See Mouritsen (2015) on the internal stratification of the Pompeian curial class.

[89] Zuiderhoek (2011) 190–1. See Petronius, *Sat.* 76 and Cicero, *Off.* 1.151 for references to merchants investing in landed property to achieve civic prominence and respectability.

[90] MacMullen (1974) 89.

commentators, who might write and speak as if their world consisted only of rich and poor, *plousioi* and *penetes*, *honestiores* and *humiliores*. Greek and Roman cities were complex and stratified societies, with a range of middling groups located between the elite and the truly poor. These groups did constitute a crucial component of ancient civic life: Greco-Roman cities would have looked and functioned decidedly different without them. Yet, as I have tried to show in this chapter, they were no bourgeoisie. To paraphrase another observation of MacMullen, social and political terminology appropriate to our world often simply does not fit the ancient.[91]

However, it is precisely this difference from the later European model that matters in comparative historical terms. That the medieval/early modern European city came to be seen as *the* city is an accidental by-product of the fact that industrialisation and modernisation happened to take place in Europe first, and that influential European historians and social scientists thought the European city pivotal to these processes. Yet the European city represents just one model of urban social development. The ancient Greco-Roman city represents another (equally workable given the purposes it served): a dynamic urban community, headed by a land-owning social and political elite but otherwise diversified into a range of socioeconomic strata active in a wide variety of occupations, and ranging from very poor to moderately wealthy. A community, moreover, in which social mobility was not only possible but necessary, to replenish elites but also the groups below them, whose energies and resources were needed to keep going a complex urban economy catering for the city's many needs. It is to this topic that we shall turn in the next chapter.

---

[91] MacMullen (1974) 92. This does of course not preclude the conscious and controlled use of modern social-scientific techniques, models and concepts in research on antiquity; rather, it is the casual employment of modern-day terminology in historical description, without due attention to possible anachronistic connotations, that has the greatest potential to mislead. Note e.g. Wallace-Hadrill's (2013) 606 comment on Mayer's (2012) use of the term 'middle classes': '[a]t stake, then, is not merely what word we use, but how much of the baggage associated with it we are prepared to smuggle in' (in this case, an anachronistic association with capitalism and the Industrial Revolution).

CHAPTER 8

The Urban Economy

The occupations and trades in the city, if all are considered, are many
and of all kinds, and some of them are very profitable . . . But it is not
easy to name them all separately on account of their multitude, and
equally because that would be out of place here.

(Dio Chrysostom, *Or.* 7.109–10).[1]

Cities are places of craft and commerce. That was as true of the cities of the
pre-Columbian New World, such as the sprawling metropolis of Teotihuacan (which flourished in the highland Basin of Mexico during the first
millennium CE) where patient excavation and surface survey have revealed
many traces of workshops and of obsidian, stone, ceramic and textile
industries, as of pre-modern Islamic cities, with their souks and bazaars,
of the cities of medieval and early modern Europe, and indeed, of ancient
Greek and Roman cities.[2]

Noting this strong association in urban cultures the world over,
V. Gordon Childe famously included the presence of 'full-time specialist
craftsmen, transport workers, merchants, officials and priests' among his
ten criteria for distinguishing pre-modern cities from villages.[3] Also, it was
precisely the highly commercial character of many western European
medieval and early modern cities which, according to Adam Smith, Karl
Marx, Werner Sombart and Max Weber, provided the most important
reason why capitalism and the Industrial Revolution arose in Europe first.

Even though, as we saw in Chapter 1, this latter idea has now been
disputed for some time, it was adhered to by Moses Finley, who pointed to
what he perceived as a stark contrast between the later European cities and
their dynamic commercial relationship with the countryside, exchanging
manufactured products for agricultural produce and raw materials, and

[1] Tr. J. W. Cohoon, Loeb Classical Library, slightly altered.
[2] Cowgill (2003b) 38–41 on Teotihuacan.
[3] In his classic paper on 'The Urban Revolution', see Childe (1950) 11.

Greek and Roman cities which basically laid claim to and consumed the agrarian surplus from their territories on the basis of extra-economic (legal, social, political) entitlements (mostly rents and taxes).

As we saw in Chapter 3, however, while many Greek and Roman cities could indeed be described as consumer cities, this does not in the least imply that their manufacturing or commercial sectors were necessarily small-scale or unproductive. As spin-offs of the citizen-elites' agrarian rent income expended in the town, they catered for what especially in larger cities (say, with 10,000 inhabitants or more) was a considerable and diversified urban demand for manufactured goods and services, including 'foreign' demand from other towns, as not every product could be produced as easily in every city. Indeed, if the comparatively high rates of urbanisation in the Mediterranean region during Classical, Hellenistic and Roman times are anything to go by (particularly in areas such as Greece, Italy and western Asia Minor), as well as the presence of a fair number of what were, by pre-modern standards, true metropoleis especially during the latter two periods, we should certainly be wary of underestimating the productive potential of the non-agrarian sectors (see Chapter 3).

Recently, moreover, scholars have begun to argue in favour of comparatively high standards of living among broad swathes of the population during the central periods of antiquity, in particular Classical Greece and the Roman world during the Late Republic and early Empire.[4] As these claims rest for the most part on difficult-to-interpret archaeological data sets, debate is ongoing. Yet even if only half true, such claims are highly relevant for our present purpose, given that within the discipline of economics, growth and rising living standards are commonly associated not just with an increase of agrarian productivity, but particularly with development and innovation in the typically urban-based commercial and manufacturing sectors.

All this prompts two important questions with regard to the internal economy of Greek and Roman cities. First, how were manufacture, service provision and trade in ancient cities structured and organised, and second, were they structured and organised in such a way as to make them comparatively efficient given the specific constraints imposed on them and the context in which they had to function. In what follows, we shall focus on some typical characteristics of ancient urban economic activity. As in the other chapters of this volume, I cannot provide an exhaustive

---

[4] E.g. Morris (2004); Ober (2010) on Greece (see Chapter 7). For Rome, see Jongman (2007a); Kron (2012) and Scheidel (2012b) for diverging views and many references to other contributions.

survey of the topic but hope to address some essential issues and perhaps provide some pointers for further research.

(Sub)urban Agriculture

First, a caveat. Just as some economic activities that we associate with the city also took place in non-urban settings (i.e. manufacturing on estates or in army camps, commerce on rural fairs, see Chapter 3), so some agricultural activity did also take place in and closely around cities.[5] Since in pre-modern economies transport, especially over land, was slow and expensive, it made sense to produce the most perishable agricultural products in close vicinity to the city. Thus we commonly find a zone of intensive dairy farming and horticulture in the suburban areas and immediate hinterland of (larger) pre-modern cities. Classical Athens and the imperial city of Rome provide good examples of this, but similar zones will have existed in and around other cities.[6]

Animals we tend to associate with farm life were also omnipresent in ancient cities (as they were in pre-modern cities generally). Although raised outside the city, on rural or suburban farms, particularly food animals might be present in large numbers. In and around the imperial city of Rome, for which we have relatively good archaeological data, there were present at any one time a great many pigs, sheep, goats, cattle as well as many work animals (horses, donkeys, mules and oxen) and domestic fowl (chickens, ducks and geese).[7] Early imperial Rome, with its one million inhabitants, was of course an exceptionally large city, but these types of animals were abundantly present in smaller cities as well.

Within cities, people kept kitchen gardens, either for home consumption or for selling the produce to supplement their income. At Pompeii many gardens reveal traces of having been planted with a variety of crops, including fruit, nut and olive trees as well as cabbages, onions and herbs. The urban landscape even included some commercial vineyards and orchards.[8] Although in most cities, except perhaps the smallest agro-towns, manufacture, trade and services would have been dominant forms of economic activity, agriculture did in fact penetrate into the very heart of the Greco-Roman city.

---

[5] Clark (2009) 44–5. [6] See Chapter 3 for references. [7] MacKinnon (2013) 121–3.
[8] Jashemski (2007).

Specialisation

In cities, specialised craft production can take place because the concentration of population ensures a large and stable demand. In a small village, a shoemaker might not find enough customers for his products to earn a living, forcing him to engage in other forms of productive activity (agriculture, other trades) as well. But in the city, he would have been able to focus on his craft. People who perform the same task over and over, day in, day out, generally tend to become very skilled at what they do. Thus, specialisation, or division of labour, leads to higher quality and increased output per unit of time. Adam Smith's parable of the pin factory in his *Wealth of Nations* is of course the modern *locus classicus* for this view, but the point was in fact not lost on the ancients. According to Xenophon, 'the other crafts too are in detailed fashion pursued in the great cities' (*Cyr.* 8.2.5). He writes:

> It is impossible for a man engaged in many arts to pursue them all well. In the great cities by reason of the fact that many people have need of individual items, each craft suffices for the livelihood of one individual. And often not even an entire craft. For one man makes men's shoes, and another women's. And in some cases in shoemaking one craftsman makes a living sewing, another cutting, and another trimming the uppers, and yet another doing no more than assembling the pieces. Therefore, the craftsman who exercises his function in the most restricted sphere must of necessity do it best.[9]

In this famous passage, Xenophon mentions two types of specialisation, which in modern parlance are known as horizontal and vertical specialisation. Horizontal specialisation implies that people specialise in the production or provision of a specific good or service. The greater the diversity of goods and services, the greater the need is for specialists to produce these different goods and services, hence the greater the level of horizontal specialisation. Vertical specialisation concerns the number of different specialist skills involved in the production of a single good or service, as in Xenophon's example of a shoemaking workshop where one craftsman specialises in sewing, another in cutting, another in trimming, and so on. This latter type of specialisation, in which each worker becomes a highly skilled expert in just one tiny aspect of the productive process, has the potential to increase radically both the quality and quantity of the good

---

[9] Tr. Hopper (1979) 104; see also Plato, *Rep.* 2.369a–371e.

produced.[10] It promises increasing returns to scale, given that it makes good economic sense to integrate ever more aspects of the productive process within one single enterprise, and it thus constitutes the basis of the modern industrial factory system.[11]

As the passage from Xenophon already suggests, we find both types of specialisation in ancient cities. Yet we do not find them in equal measure. Research has demonstrated that ancient urban economies were primarily characterised by a great deal of horizontal specialisation. For Athens, scholars have identified over 170 different occupations in sources dating to the period 500–250 BCE. As Edward Harris notes, the 'vast majority of [these] occupations . . . are named for the item they produce', suggesting horizontal specialisation, and not for 'a part of a complex product (e.g. boiler-maker in ship-building) or one role among several steps of production', which would suggest vertical specialisation.[12] Thus what we primarily find are terms such as *artopoios* ('bread-maker'), *anthrakeus* ('charcoal-maker'), *aspidopegos* ('shield-maker'), *daktuliopoios* ('ring-maker'), *hupodematopoios* ('sandal-maker'), *luchnopoios* ('lamp-maker'), *sakchuphantes* ('sack-maker' or 'sail-maker'), *thorakopoios* ('maker of breastplates') and so on.[13] The same is true for the late Republican and imperial city of Rome, where among the 170–200 or so different occupations attested in inscriptions and literary and legal sources, we find many titles such as *annularius* ('ring-maker'), *caligarius* ('boot-maker'), *candelabrarius* ('candle-maker'), *crepidarius* ('maker of slippers'), *scutarius* ('shield-maker'), *tesselarius* ('dice-maker'), *unguentarius* ('perfumer') etc.[14]

Now Athens and Rome were of course exceptionally large and populous cities for their time, with correspondingly large internal markets, where one would expect such a proliferation of specialised occupations. However, a similarly differentiated occupational structure has been found in much smaller cities. Thus, in late antique Korykos (a small city in Asia Minor) some 110 different occupations have been identified on funerary inscriptions, among them numerous craftsmen specialising in single finished

---

[10] As was understood in antiquity, see Plato, *Rep.* 370c: 'It follows from this that more of each thing is produced, and better and more easily, when one man performs one task according to his nature, at the right moment, and at leisure from other work'. Tr. P. Shorey, Loeb Classical Library, slightly adapted.
[11] And, by implication, of the modern oligopolistic or monopolistic multinational corporation, as those firms that most successfully (i.e. most cost-effectively) manage this process of integration inevitably win out over competitors and tend eventually to become very large indeed.
[12] Harris (2002) 71.   [13] Harris (2002) 88–99.
[14] Treggiari (1980) 56–7 and the list of occupations at 61–4; Joshel (1992); Holleran (2012), esp. 26–30; Broekaert and Zuiderhoek (2013).

products.[15] The same pattern has been detected at Pompeii, with 85 different occupations.[16] Finally, in his recent extensive survey of occupational specialisation in the eastern Roman provinces (Egypt included), Kai Ruffing also came to the conclusion that the dominant form of specialisation was horizontal, not just in manufacture, but also in trade (even if there are indeed also indications of vertical specialisation in the ancient urban economies – see below).[17]

How to explain this emphasis on horizontal specialisation? One answer is perhaps that the dominant organisational form of ancient urban production was the workshop (*ergasterion, officina, taberna*), generally combining both production and sale, and employing, as the Attic vase paintings and the reliefs on Roman funerary monuments show, only a small number of people, often a mix of free men, freedmen and slaves. Some rich people owned larger workshops, such as the knife-making and couch-making workshops owned by the father of Demosthenes, which employed 32 or 33 and 20 slaves respectively (Dem. 27.9), but these were the exception rather than the rule. Workshops might be located in or around public places such as the agora or forum, or in porticos along important thoroughfares, where space could be rented from the city or from private individuals. Just as often, however, workshops seem to have been part of larger residential structures, in which lived either the master craftsman's family, or the larger household to which he and his family belonged or with which they were connected, as slaves, freedmen or clients.[18]

This suggests that in such instances the household (*oikos, familia*) provided the social and organisational framework within which manufacture and commerce took place in ancient cities. In Classical Athens, and presumably in other Greek cities, people did not distinguish clearly between the activities of the *oikos* and the workshop, and the *ergasterion* was not recognised as an independent legal entity.[19] For instance, as Edward Cohen has noted, when speaking about banks Athenians did not differentiate between the individual banker and his bank; both were part of the same *oikos*.[20] In Roman cities, workshops might be part of elite

[15] See *MAMA* III nos. 200–788, with the useful index of 'Berufe' (Occupations) on pp. 234–5. Patlagean (1977) 156–70 for discussion, with a tabulated overview on 159–63. Also Hopkins (1978) 71–2; Jongman (1991) 185–6.
[16] Hopkins (1978) 72.   [17] Ruffing (2008) esp. 108–9.
[18] Migeotte (2009) 95–7; Wallace-Hadrill (1994).
[19] Harris (2002) 81–3: when, for instance, Demosthenes lists his father's assets in court, he does not distinguish the knife-making and bed-making workshops from the other possessions of the *oikos* (27.9–11).
[20] Cohen (1992) 64, also referred to by Harris (2002) 83.

residences, or of *insulae*, that is, clusters of shops, flats and houses that were rented out by wealthy citizens.[21] Wealthy Romans might supplement their agrarian incomes with income from urban property and urban manufacture and commerce. They might just rent out the workshop they owned, but frequently such workshops were run by slaves or freedmen of the owner, that is, people with whom he had direct social ties, who were part of his *familia*.[22]

Such elite involvement in manufacture and commerce never became total. We do not find merchant elites in antiquity, and those traders and manufacturers wealthy enough to enter the elite almost always invested in land before they did so. The fact that only a comparatively small part of ancient elite wealth was invested in non-agrarian economic activity might explain the relative absence of truly large-scale privately-owned factories in antiquity, given that most craftsmen and shopowners would have lacked the resources necessary to set up such enterprises themselves. The incentive was missing (let alone the very concept of a factory), in the case of elites because they already had income from other sources, but also, for both elites *and* craftsmen and shopowners, because the specialised workshop system was actually quite efficient and indeed profitable, given ancient market conditions.

The strong horizontal specialisation in ancient urban production was possible only because of the presence of substantial and well-functioning urban markets. Ancient rates of urbanisation were comparatively high: in the Classical period at least up to 10 per cent of cities had 10,000 inhabitants or more, a percentage that would only increase in later centuries.[23] Even in smaller towns, however, market conditions would have been comparatively healthy, because ancient cities in fact created many of the conditions necessary for urban markets to function well.[24]

Citizens of Greek and Roman cities were generally not burdened by extra-economic, 'feudal' demands of powerful local lords – the abolition of debt-bondage during the early phases of Greek and Roman history had seen to that – so they could compete on relatively equal terms.[25] Their citizen-status guaranteed them the protection of the law in case of disputes (special legal provisions were also made for resident aliens and foreigners, in the form of specialised courts and regulations, for example). Most cities developed (or took over from a founder city/ruling power) a sophisticated

[21] Wallace-Hadrill (1991), (1994) 133–4.   [22] Wallace-Hadrill (1991); Garnsey (1998b).
[23] Hansen (2006) 75–6; Scheidel (2007) 74–80.   [24] Harris (2002) 71–7; Bresson (2008).
[25] Of course, taxes had to be paid to the central government during Hellenistic and Roman times.

body of regulations ensuring the proper working of the city market, and instituted specialised magistrates (e.g. *agoranomoi, aediles*) to enforce these regulations.[26] Many cities, moreover, struck coins (or took over the coinage of the ruling power), thus facilitating monetary exchange, clearly defined weights and measures, and had a physical infrastructure of paved roads, squares and market facilities that was a notch above that of many European medieval towns.

All this meant that transaction costs within Greek and Roman cities were *comparatively* low (which does not mean that they were absent, see below). Combined with a relatively high aggregate urban demand, this created a situation in which a system of production and exchange based on numerous small specialised workshops could easily flourish. Given the strong seasonality of demand in ancient cities, moreover (with the spending power of urban consumers being greatest just after the harvest, when food prices were low – except in a bad year – and more restricted later on), and the particularised consumption patterns of the elite, who did not want mass-produced goods, small units of production, connected with one another through flexible cooperative networks (such as *collegia*), made perfect economic sense.[27] The low level of mechanisation in many crafts further militated against the rise of factories. There were no economies of scale to be had from concentrating production into larger units.[28]

The arguments just sketched are reinforced when we take a look at those situations in which vertical specialisation did indeed take place. The most obvious example is construction. Building was enormously expensive, and financing, planning, organising and executing entire building projects was generally beyond the means and capabilities of even the largest private workshops in the ancient world. Construction required the financial and organisational backing of wealthy elites and governments. These then brought together numerous small specialised groups of workmen on a single project, with each group (or several groups together) focussing on one aspect or element of the construction process.[29] The same applied to ship-building, which was also an undertaking obviously too large and costly to be handled by an individual workshop. Another case is

---

[26] Bresson (2008) on Greek cities.   [27] Hawkins (2012).

[28] Though note Flohr (2013a) 74–95 on several large fullers' workshops at Rome and Ostia. These, however, were a response to the extraordinary economic conditions created by the presence of the imperial metropolis: due to 'the enormous aggregate demand within a relatively small region', some *fullonicae* in and around Rome 'reached a scale that, probably, was almost completely unparalleled elsewhere' (94).

[29] E.g. Plut., *Per.* 12.6–7; Burford (1969); DeLaine (1997), (2000); Anderson (1997).

interregional trade. Merchants exporting grain, wine, oil or other food-stuffs from the provinces to Italy and Rome often aimed to gain control over various processes associated with their trade, such as production (grain lands, vineyards, olive plantations), ship-building, amphora production, processing (milling, baking) and so forth. Interregional markets in the ancient world were often thin and fragmented due to the slowness of communication and transport, the dangers and high costs of travel, asymmetries of information and trust and so forth. Thus it made eminent sense to integrate the various specialist activities within a single enterprise, in practice often the *familia* or extended household of the merchant.[30]

In each of the specific cases mentioned here, vertical specialisation and integration took place because the costs of investment, organisation and transaction were such that the market was not the most efficient means of bringing the various specialists together. Instead, elites, governments and wealthy merchant families intervened to draw specialist activities and groups together within a single project or enterprise. For most other forms of production and exchange, however, the internal urban market with its numerous small workshops functioned efficiently enough.

A consequence of the emphasis on horizontal specialisation and the resulting strong diversification of occupations in the urban economy was that there were very few 'specialist' cities in antiquity, comparable to, for example, the textile-producing cities of medieval and early modern North-Western Europe, in which a substantial part of urban manufacturing was concentrated in one large sector producing for distant markets. To be sure, certain cities were widely known for specific products and some of these towns may well have functioned more or less like producer cities, but such cities were the exception rather than the rule. In the case of textile manufacture, the argument has, for instance, been made for a number of cities in the Roman East, including Tarsus, the twin cities Laodicea and Hierapolis, Miletus and others.[31] Yet in Roman Italy, it was wool rather than textiles that was produced on a large scale in specialist sheep farming regions, with the organisation of urban textile manufacture following the workshop model, that is, numerous small production units catering for local urban demand. Again, there was nothing inherently 'primitive' about this organisation of production. Rather, it has been interpreted as a function of the high degree of urbanisation in the imperial heartland and the consequent high level of urban demand.[32]

---

[30] Broekaert (2012), responding to Silver (2009). [31] Pleket (1984), (1990).
[32] Jongman (2000a).

Urban craftsmen and traders especially during the Hellenistic and Roman periods were often, as we saw, members of professional associations (*collegia*) that provided them with a network for sociability, represented them *vis-à-vis* the city authorities, and arguably looked after their economic interests.[33] Workshops, stalls and booths of craftsmen active in the same trade often clustered in certain neighbourhoods (giving rise to neighbourhood-based craft associations), streets or parts of the market place. Thus the Athenian agora district included a fish market, as well as other specialised market-sections: people would go to 'the wine', or 'the olive oil', 'the vegetables', 'the garlic and the onions' and so on. In Rome we find, for instance, the *vicus materiarius* (neighbourhood of the carpenters), the *vicus lorarius* (harness-makers), the *vicus ... ionum ferrariarum* (iron workers), the *vicus turarius* (perfumers), the *scalae anulariae* (stairs of the ring-makers) and so on.[34] Such clustering, typical of many pre-modern cities, reflects the fact that, even in relatively efficient pre-industrial markets, reliable information on product quality, price levels, actual production costs and so on was still often scarce, asymmetrically distributed and generally hard to come by. Consequently, buyers often engaged in longer-term trust-based exchange relationships with particular sellers of certain goods, rather than browse the entire market anew every time they wanted to make a purchase. Since every seller thus had his own 'core-group' of regular customers, there was no need to engage in all-out, intense and continuous competition with other sellers of the same good. He (or she) was therefore free to enjoy the practical advantages of proximity to colleagues: cooperation where needed and the sharing of knowledge. This does not mean that there was *no* competition between sellers (for there certainly was), nor that intense bargaining between buyers and sellers did not take place (it did). It just means that the general processes of economic production and exchange were structured in specific ways, given the constraints of the pre-industrial urban market.[35]

The Civic Authorities and the Economy

Greek and Roman civic authorities intervened in the urban economy primarily to gather public revenues and to ensure the adequate

---

[33] Verboven (2011); Hawkins (2012).
[34] Wycherley (1956); Frank (1940) 223n15; Holleran (2012) 51–7.
[35] The anthropologist Clifford Geertz (1978) describes the type of urban market sketched in this paragraph as a 'bazaar economy' in his classic paper with the same title; see Bang (2008) for an application of the bazaar economy model to Roman trade in general; Holleran (2012) 57–60 for a discussion of additional reasons for the geographical clustering of trades at Rome.

provisioning of the community with essential goods and amenities. We start with revenues. Cities drew revenues from a variety of sources. Among them were public lands, publicly owned real estate and workshops which were rented out, fees for the use of public amenities (i.e. the gymnasium or the baths), all sorts of fines, and, in the Roman period, payments for office by civic magistrates, priests and aspiring council members (the so-called *summae honorariae*). To this may be added income from natural resources in the cities' territories, the exploitation of which was often farmed out to private individuals (think of the exploitation of the Laurium silver mines in Attica), and public monopolies on certain economic activities.

Probably the most important source of revenue, however, was taxation. This is a somewhat controversial statement. Scholars have long been sceptical about the ability of ancient cities to draw in sufficient revenues via taxation. One reason for this is that Greek and Roman civic ideology basically militated against citizens paying direct personal and property taxes; these were associated with tyranny, and citizens should be free of them (e.g. Aristotle, *Pol.* 1315b; Cicero, *Off.* 2.74). Consequently it is often argued by modern scholars that direct taxation occurred only rarely in ancient cities and that cities had to make do with income from a variety of indirect taxes (tolls, dues).

In fact, direct taxation did occur more often than is generally believed, though it was indeed rarely systematic. In the city of Rome, a direct tax on citizens' property was originally instituted only during military emergencies and great wars; it was thought to have occurred for the first time during the protracted war against the powerful Etruscan city of Veii (Livy 4.59.11–60.8). The continued warfare of the following centuries caused direct taxes (*tributum*) to occur ever more frequently until imperialist successes made it possible to abolish them for Roman citizens in Italy in 167 BCE. In Classical Athens the *eisphora*, a direct tax on wealth for the rich, was not imposed regularly, but Athens had tax revenues from its extremely profitable harbour to draw on, as well as, during the fifth century, its empire, and its silver mines. Other resource-rich communities, such as Thasos, could also spare their citizens (Hdt. 6.46–47), but in other Greek poleis citizens might have taxes directly imposed on their assets or products.[36] During the Roman imperial period, Nemausus (Nîmes), Rhodes and Celaenae-Apamea are known to have taxed directly inhabitants of dependent villages and cities in their territories.[37] And, as is of course well known, at least in Athens, but presumably in many other cities

---

[36] Migeotte (2009) 49–50, (2014).   [37] Schwarz (2001) 363–9.

as well, resident foreigners (*metoikoi*) paid a special direct tax, the *metoikion*, one drachma a month for men, half a drachma for women.

Not only was there more direct taxation in ancient cities than is often acknowledged, but cities could also draw on a wealth of indirect taxes. The most important among these were customs dues and market dues. In Greek cities the *pentekoste*, a 2 per cent (one fiftieth) *ad valorem* tax on all goods imported and exported, was the most important customs due. Collection was generally farmed out to private individuals, at Athens in 399 BCE for 36 talents, or well over 200,000 drachmas (Andocides, *On the Mysteries* 133–34). At Delos, the *pentekoste* in 279–8 BCE brought in 14,200 and 17,900 drachmas respectively, while before the Romans turned Delos into a free port in 166 BCE harbour taxes brought Rhodes an annual revenue of 1 million drachmas (Polybius 30.31.12).[38]

Cities during the Roman imperial period did levy their own import and export taxes, in addition to the *portoria* or customs dues collected by the Roman government from traders crossing a provincial tax border. Thus the city of Palmyra, according to a tax law from 137 CE, levied taxes on the import and export of anything from slaves to olive oil, dried food, purple fleeces, unguents, animal fat and salted fish.[39] At the cities of Kaunos and Myra, a 5 per cent and 2.5 per cent *ad valorem* tax respectively were placed on goods imported and exported.[40]

More important still to a city's budget, however, were market dues and other taxes on internal economic activity. In Greek cities, local retailers (*kapeloi*) paid sales taxes when buying goods from wholesale traders (*emporoi*) which they would then sell on the city market.[41] Foreigners (*xenoi*) trading in the Athenian agora had to pay a special tax (Dem. 57.34). There were taxes on all kinds of transactions, e.g. sales, renting, farming out, as well as taxes on the buying and selling of specific products, such as the dues on the buying of horses and slaves in sixth-century BCE Kyzikos (*Syll.* [3] 4B) and on the sale of wood in late Classical Teos (*SEG* 2.579). We also know of taxes on the use of public weighing equipment, on the use of market stalls, on work animals (donkeys) and so on.[42] The tax law from Roman Palmyra also lists numerous taxes on the

---

[38] Migeotte (2009) 51. To give an impression of the size of these sums: a typical daily wage for a skilled labourer in Classical Athens amounted to 1 drachma a day at the end of the fifth century BCE and two and a half drachmas during the fourth.

[39] Matthews (1984).

[40] Schwarz (2001) 385–401, though it has been argued that the Myra tax may have been a Roman *portorium* instead of a civic tax, see Marek (2006).

[41] Migeotte (2009) 51   [42] Schwarz (2001) 350; Migeotte (2009) 49–54.

production and sale of a whole range of goods and services, including clothing, skins, leather, prostitution etc. From Pompeii, we have the remains of an archive of wooden writing tablets containing the receipts of one L. Caecilius Iucundus, auctioneer and tax collector. One tablet records that for the first year of a four-year tax farming contract, Iucundus paid over HS 1,652 to the city's public slave for the fullers' tax (*CIL* IV 3340.141), not a tiny sum, and from just one tax alone.

That all such taxes put together might ordinarily provide cities with a handsome stream of revenues can also be concluded from the fact that they were often temporarily remitted during civic festivals in order to lure traders, craftsmen and service providers from other cities to the town or cater to the festival crowds. Such temporary festive exemptions are frequently attested, from which we might conclude that the strategy was a success.[43] This suggests that indirect taxes were generally high enough for their temporary removal to generate the required local trading booms.

Besides taxation, civic authorities also intervened in economic life to provide their communities with necessary goods and amenities. I shall focus briefly on two areas where this happened: public building and the food supply.

Responsibility for supervising the condition of public buildings was in many Greek cities among the duties of the *astynomoi* ('city-controllers') and in Roman cities among those of the urban censors (*censores* at Rome, *duoviri/quattuorviri quinquennales* in *coloniae* and *municipia*). City authorities also took most of the responsibility for the supply of new public buildings, increasingly assisted, from the later Hellenistic period onwards, by private benefactors, and of course by the occasional contributions of kings, and later, emperors. Expenditure might be considerable, but varied greatly from city to city, period to period. The small city of Epidaurus during most of the fourth and early third centuries BCE was engaged in building a sanctuary for the healer-god Asclepius. Its total cost, over a period of about 100 years, may have come to 290 talents. Since Asclepius and his sanctuary had a pan-Hellenic appeal, there were probably many contributions from other poleis.[44] Still, this was an expensive undertaking for a small polis.

At Athens, the Parthenon may have cost about 500 talents to construct, and the Propylaea 200.[45] Fifth-century Athenian investment in public building was remarkable: in one generation (that of Pericles, 480–450 BCE), the Athenians built about three times as much as the Corinthians

---

[43] De Ligt (1993) 229–34.   [44] Burford (1969) 81–5.   [45] Stanier (1953).

in the three centuries from 700 to 400 BCE, and Corinth was one of the most actively building poleis of the Archaic and Classical Greek world.[46] Yet Athenian expenditure on building was buttressed by the revenues from its empire. In that sense, Athens was exceptional. However, even in smaller, less powerful cities expenditure on public buildings could reach extraordinary levels. The city of Nicaea in Asia Minor during the early second century CE spent more than ten million sesterces (that is, more than ten times the legal property requirement of a Roman senator) on building a theatre, and even then, it was still unfinished, as an astonished Roman governor reported to the emperor Trajan (Pliny, *Ep.* 10.39). It has been estimated, on the basis of attested ancient building costs, that equipping an ordinary Roman city, such as Pompeii, with its entire set of public buildings might take about 9 million sesterces. This suggests that Pliny was probably correct in his assumption that the Nicaeans had a rather cavalier approach to public spending.[47]

Such figures pale, naturally, when compared with imperial expenditure on buildings in the city of Rome. The imperial capital was engaged in a constant process of rebuilding and restructuring as emperor after emperor tried to leave his mark, no expenses spared. To mention only one famous example, the Baths of Caracalla, completed in 217 CE, may have cost the equivalent of 120,000–140,000 tonnes of wheat, sufficient for feeding over 500,000 people (i.e. half the city's population) for a year![48] Yet Rome as the capital of a world empire was of course in a category all of its own. Most 'normal' cities might be able to do without any serious rebuilding for several generations once the required set of public buildings were in place, barring of course necessary repairs, renovations and extensions (an area in which, during the Hellenistic and Roman periods, private benefactors were very active).

Another area in which civic authorities regularly intervened was that of the provision of commodities necessary for the community's survival, that is, the supply of foodstuffs. Grain, antiquity's staple food, naturally received the most attention. Large cities generally had to import grain because their hinterlands did not produce enough to feed all urban inhabitants. This category of course included urban giants such as Rome, Antioch, Alexandria and Carthage, but also cities such as imperial Ephesus

---

[46] Estimated as worked surface area *per annum*: Salmon (1999) 149–50, (2001).
[47] MacMullen (1974) 142–5; Pliny, *Ep.* 10.39.6.
[48] DeLaine (1997) 219; Jongman, *Neue Pauly*, s.v. 'Roma: II. Bevölkerung und Wirtschaft der Stadt Rom, B. Wirtschaft', 1079–81.

and, during the Classical period, Athens, Corinth, Megara, Aegina and Samos.[49] Even in smaller cities that could in principle be fed from their own hinterlands, however, measures often needed to be taken to protect the population from shortages since the high inter-annual variability in the amount of rainfall typical of the Mediterranean climate meant that bad harvests occurred frequently but in a highly unpredictable manner.[50]

Civic authorities adopted a variety of tactics. Some instituted direct, regular distributions of grain to their citizens, but such schemes were rare, presumably because they were very expensive. The *annona* at Rome, monthly distributions of grain to Roman citizens living in the capital, are the most famous example, but we have attestations for some other cities as well.[51] More common were legislation and measures to forbid exports and encourage imports of grain or other foodstuffs. For example, in early sixth-century BCE Athens, the lawgiver Solon outlawed all exports except olive oil (Plut., *Solon* 24), while the city of Selymbria during the fourth century BCE explicitly outlawed the export of grain ([Arist.] *Oec.* 1348b.33–34). Athenian residents were legally forbidden to ship grain to any other harbour than Piraeus and to extend maritime loans to merchants unwilling to bring back a cargo of grain to Athens (Dem. 34.37, 35.51), while shippers importing grain into imperial Rome for the *annona* received favourable terms and special legal privileges.[52]

Cities also often regulated the price of grain or bread in the city market. This might take the form of directly imposing a maximum price but more often consisted of limiting profit margins. In Classical Athens, persuading merchants importing grain and local grain dealers (*sitopolai*) to sell at a cheap and fixed price that still included a margin of profit was the duty of the *sitophylakes* ('grain wardens').[53] During the Hellenistic and Roman imperial periods, many Greek cities had municipal grain funds, generally cash reserves managed by specially appointed magistrates (often called *sitonai*) that were used to buy grain abroad for sale at a low price or free distribution among the citizenry in times of dearth.[54]

---

[49] Garnsey (1988); Erdkamp (2005); Bissa (2009) Ch. 9.   [50] Garnsey (1988) 10.
[51] Rickman (1980); Garnsey (1988) 81–2, 265–6. Public distribution schemes are attested on Samos during the second century BCE and at Egyptian Oxyrhynchus, Hermopolis and Alexandria during the imperial period.
[52] Garnsey (1988) 232–6.
[53] Bresson (2000); see Aristotle, *Ath. Pol* 51.3–4; Lysias 22.5–8. On the food supply of Athens see also Moreno (2007); Oliver (2007).
[54] Strubbe (1987), (1989); Erdkamp (2005) 276; Zuiderhoek (2008b).

It should be noted that cities' interventions in economic life were not motivated by economic policy concerns as we would understand them. Civic authorities invested in public architecture and amenities in the first place because any city worth its salt was supposed to be equipped with a culturally/ideologically-defined standard set of splendid public structures and monuments (e.g. theatres, baths, agoras/fora, temples, gymnasia and stadia), paved roads, and, in the Roman period, aqueducts, a sewer system and so forth.[55] When civic authorities intervened in trade and the operation of markets, it was to ensure sufficient imports of goods necessary for the physical survival of their communities and to guarantee that these became available to their citizens at a reasonable price, or, as in the case of grain at imperial Rome, for free. Of course, the lack of explicit policies stimulating growth and commerce does not rule out the possibility that the functioning of ancient civic institutions had *unintended* economic effects, whether positive or negative. To this issue we shall now briefly turn.

The Political Economy of the Ancient City?

It has been suggested above that ancient civic institutions may have contributed to keeping transaction costs comparatively low within the urban economy, without, it should be stressed, this ever having been a conscious design of ancient elites or their communities. Here I want briefly to explore this idea further. Were Greek and Roman civic political institutions and their operation in fact conducive to economic development?

Insights from economic theory and comparative economic history suggest that such a hypothesis is certainly worth exploring. Economists have argued that so-called inclusive political systems, that is, polities that allow ordinary individuals real participation in the decision-making processes of the community at large, such as republics and parliamentary or direct democracies, are better at protecting individual property rights than exclusive political systems, such as absolutist monarchies or dictatorships.[56] Secure property rights, in turn, are generally viewed as a necessary condition for economic growth. The key institution here is citizenship, a characteristic feature of inclusive polities. In inclusive political communities, citizens, by means of their collective share in the process of political decision-making, by and large manage to prevent governmental elites from appropriating all or most public resources, while the shared citizenship of members of the community creates a strong moral obligation for all

[55] E.g. Pausanias 10.4.1; Dio Chrysostom, *Or.* 40.10, 47.15. [56] Acemoglu and Robinson (2012).

citizens to contribute their fair share of time, energy and resources to the functioning and welfare of the polity. Thus the institution of citizenship manages simultaneously to rein in the predatory tendencies of political elites as well as free-rider behaviour by members of the citizen community.

This ensures that citizens' property is relatively secure from government or elite predation and also that the government has sufficient resources to protect citizens and their property against threats from outside. In inclusive systems, widespread citizen-participation in politics arguably also ensures a fairly efficient use of public resources. That is, to a greater degree than in absolutist or dictatorial polities, public resources are expended on public infrastructure and amenities that increase the quality of life of citizens.[57] Furthermore, it has been argued that inclusive, democratic polities tend more than other political systems to support the growth of human capital among their citizens, either through investment in public schooling systems, or even through the very requirement of citizen-participation in the political process itself.[58]

Now, Greek and Roman cities obviously fall into the category of inclusive political systems: in most ancient cities, all or at least a clear majority of the adult male citizens participated in the decision-making process and/or the election of magistrates and councillors who represented the *demos* or *populus*. The poleis, the city of Rome and Roman *municipia*, *coloniae* and civitates all had laws and institutions that clearly defined and protected citizens' property rights. They also provided systems of weights and measures and rules to regulate the market.

Citizens in turn contributed to the well-being of their communities in various ways. As we saw, they paid many different taxes, direct ones as well as a broad range of indirect ones. They might also pool their resources by each paying a small sum to finance some amenity through a public sub-scription.[59] Wealthy citizens, moreover, were morally and, to some extent, legally obliged to contribute to public welfare through benefactions and liturgies. This is not to say that the risk of elite predation was entirely absent within the Greco-Roman civic sphere.[60] Enduring social inequalities in the poleis and the more explicit social hierarchy of Roman cities (and Roman-era Greek cities) stimulated citizens of the same profession to organise themselves in associations (*collegia*), which gave them more bargaining power in confrontations with civic elites. At the same time, the difficulties elites faced in gaining sufficient economic control over poorer but freeborn fellow-citizens encouraged them to employ members of their households,

---

[57] Van Zanden and Prak (2006).   [58] Lindert (2003); Ober (2008), (2010).   [59] Migeotte (1992).
[60] Bang (2012) on predation.

particularly slaves and freedmen, as agents in economic transactions. On the whole, however, Greco-Roman civic sociopolitical organisation seems to have provided a highly beneficial context for economic activity. Throughout most periods of antiquity, citizens also fought for their city on the battle-field, defending their communities against predation from outside.

It should be added that the participatory character of ancient cities as such may have contributed substantially to human capital formation. According to Josiah Ober, the Athenian democracy effectively functioned as a kind of collective civic learning environment: 'Athenian institutional design promoted learning – both organizational learning, so that the system as a whole became more expert, and individual learning by citizens engaged in a lifelong civic education'.[61] By 'participating in "working the machine" of democracy, the individual Athenian was both encouraged to share his own useful knowledge, and given the chance to develop and deepen various sorts of politically relevant expertise'.[62]

Levels of participation in Athens and other democratic poleis were of course exceptionally high. Yet, as we saw, most Greek and Roman cities required a level of structural involvement of their citizenry in public deliberation, elections and governance that is remarkable in comparative historical terms. In Republican Rome, Fergus Millar writes, '[t]he political life ... demanded above all the delivery of speeches, and hence the communication to the public of complex forms of information, argument, and persuasion by individual orators'.[63] This was true of virtually every Greek or Roman city throughout antiquity. Ordinary citizens were meant to understand and respond politically to such forms of information, to weigh the various arguments *pro* and *contra*, to discuss and deliberate, and it could be argued that all this had a 'schooling effect', generating a build-up of human capital that could be usefully employed in other social spheres, such as the economy.

To be sure, the all-too-brief model of the ancient urban political economy supplied in this section is strongly hypothetical still and may well turn out to be too optimistic when subjected to further research. It does, however, suggest a plausible explanatory framework for the flourishing workshop-and-specialisation-based internal economies of ancient cities that the written and archaeological records seem to reveal. This approach points the way to an interpretation of 'the ancient economy' that attributes to the cities the role of effective – if tentative and entirely unintentional – contributors to possible economic growth, and that, I think, is an intriguing suggestion.

[61] Ober (2008) 167.   [62] Ober (2008) 269, 273.   [63] Millar (1998) 223.

CHAPTER 9

City-States and Cities and States

In his comparison of the merits and achievements of the fifth-century BCE Athenian politician and general Aristides and the Roman Republican consul and censor Cato the Elder, Plutarch remarks that Cato's political abilities naturally followed from his insight into household management, since 'the city (*polis*) is but an organised sum total of households (*oikoi*)' (*Comp. Aristid. Cat.* 3.1–3). Several centuries earlier, Aristotle had already famously defined the polis as a partnership (*koinonia*) of villages, with each village in turn consisting of a *koinonia* of households (*Pol.* 1252b).

This ancient view of the city (polis/civitas) as a community of citizens and their households is an uncomfortable one for modern commentators. It does not match very well the modern connotations of common political concepts (which, ironically, in their original form were actually derived from ancient city-based political thought and practice) such as, say, politics, citizenship and republic. These are all concepts which, in modern parlance, tend to be associated with the state. Indeed, so natural is this association that many historians, political philosophers and other scholars, past and present, habitually tend to assume that the ancient city must indeed have been a state of some kind. Yet the uneasiness never quite went away, and one can find it manifested in the admission, featured in virtually every modern Greek or Roman history textbook, that the use of the term 'city-state' (*Stadtstaat, cité-état*), while handy, does not quite catch what the ancients meant when they called a community a polis or a civitas.

In this chapter, we shall consider the question whether ancient cities were indeed states of some kind, and how they related to other political entities in the ancient world, primarily kingdoms and empires, that are also often called states. Before we continue, however, we need of course some notion, or definition, of what is actually meant by the term 'state'. I shall borrow my own working definition from the *International Encyclopedia of the Social and Behavioral Sciences*, which reflects a broad consensus among legal scholars and political scientists. Thus, a state 'is constituted by a homogenous population inhabiting a contiguous territory under one single government which is characterized by complete independence from any outside authority (sovereignty) and holding the monopoly of jurisdiction and the legitimate use of violence internally'.[1]

City-States?

As we saw in Chapter 2, V. Gordon Childe in his model of the urban revolution expressly linked the rise of cities independently in various parts of the world to the rise of states, as did many of the neo-institutionalist archaeologists and anthropologists who followed in his wake.[2] For Childe, 'cities were just one component of the overall process by which complex, state-level societies came into being'.[3] The problem with this neat evolutionary model is that there are quite a number of cultures attested worldwide (e.g. in early Mesopotamia, the Indian subcontinent, West Africa and of course Archaic Greece and Italy) where cities arose and prospered for long periods in the absence of overarching state structures.[4] One way to solve this dilemma is to locate the state within the confines of the city itself, in other words, to speak of the city-state, which can then be distinguished typologically from the larger territorial state or macro-state. Several archaeologists and historians have indeed stressed that in the grand sweep of world history, states across the globe often developed into either of these two types.[5] Of course, a cluster of city-states might eventually come to form part of, or develop into, a macro-state. Macro-states in turn might fragment into a loose cluster of city-states. In other words, there is no straight evolutionary development from city-state to macro-state.

Among historians, Mogens Hansen and his colleagues from the Copenhagen Polis Centre have particularly championed this distinction. They have, however, fine-tuned it. Thus Hansen distinguishes between city-state cultures, on the one hand, which he defines as regions 'inhabited by a people who have the same language (or a common *lingua franca*), the same religion, the same culture and the same traditions, but [are] divided politically into a large number of small states, each of which consists of a city and its immediate hinterland' and macro-states or country-states, containing a large territory in which might be found numerous cities.

[1] W. Reinhard, *International Encyclopedia of the Social and Behavioral Sciences*, s.v. 'State, History of', 14972.
[2] Childe (1950); M. L. Smith (2003b) 12–16; M. E. Smith (2009) 6–8.   [3] M. E. Smith (2009) 7.
[4] See M. L. Smith (2003b) 14–15 for references to the relevant studies.
[5] E.g. Trigger (2003) 92–119 and the many contributors to Hansen (2000), (2002a).

Hansen sensibly prefers the terms 'macro-state' or 'country-state' to the more commonly used 'territorial state' as the opposite of 'city-state' since city-states, of course, also had territories, albeit smaller ones.[6] Ancient Greek and Roman cities are often considered prime examples of city-states, and Hansen considers the 'ancient Greek city-state culture' to have existed from early Archaic times until about the time of the reign of the emperor Diocletian (284–305 CE), when civic self-government became more restricted (see Chapter 10). This of course implies that Greek cities remained proper city-states when under Hellenistic monarchical and Roman imperial rule, and we might add that, if this can be said of Roman provincial cities of the polis-type, then it should in principle be possible to argue the same for cities in Italy and the western provinces. Yet was the Greek polis, or the Roman city in its various legal manifestations (civitas, *municipium, colonia*), indeed a (type of) state? For the Greek polis at least, this question has been fiercely debated.

Traditionally the question 'was the polis a state?' was hardly asked. As is suggested by the titles of two famous standard accounts of ancient Greek political institutions, Georg Busolt's *Griechische Staatskunde* and Victor Ehrenberg's *The Greek State*, the consensus among classicists and ancient historians at least for most of the nineteenth and twentieth centuries was clear: the polis was a state.[7] Yet what kind of state was it?

It was Moses Finley, writing about politics in the Archaic and Classical Greek poleis and the Roman Republic, who placed stress on one important peculiarity of the ancient city-state: neither the Greek poleis nor Republican Rome possessed a coercive apparatus to enforce political decisions. There were no police forces, and, with the partial exceptions of the Athenian navy, Sparta and some specialised forces in oligarchies and tyrannies, cities had no standing armies to maintain order and enforce the law.[8] The mercenaries increasingly employed by Greek cities from the fourth-century BCE onwards never played a role in internal civic politics. We might add that under the Hellenistic monarchies and the Roman Empire, the royal or imperial army could, of course, intervene in city politics, but this happened on surprisingly few occasions. The interventions of the Roman army, which ceased to be a citizen-militia in the late

---

[6] Hansen (2006) 9–11; 24–8.   [7] Busolt (1920–1926); Ehrenberg (1969).
[8] Finley (1983) 18–20, 24; Berent (2004) 110–11. It should also be noted that Greek magistrates often had small numbers of publicly-owned slaves at their disposal while Roman magistrates had their *apparitores* (free or slave assistants). In the case of consuls or praetors, these included the lictors. Classical Athens also employed a small contingent of Scythian archers to keep order in the public courts.

Republic, in the politics of the capital during that period were brought on by the Civil Wars that wrecked the Republic and as such constitute the exception that proves the rule. 'In general', Andrew Lintott writes, 'in Greek and Roman society a man was expected to execute through private means many acts which are now done for him by the state', including, as Moshe Berent adds, 'self-defence, bringing an adversary to justice, executing court orders and asserting other rights. Policing was by self-help and self-defence (with the help of friends, neighbours and family)'.[9]

This should give us pause since in modern definitions of the state the monopoly of legitimate violence is often considered to be a central element differentiating states from other types of political organisations (an idea which goes back to Max Weber – see also the definition quoted at the beginning of this chapter). Yet how can a monopoly of violence be maintained in the absence of an institutionalised coercive apparatus? Considerations like these have in recent times prompted several scholars to argue that in fact the polis should not be considered a state.[10] Chief among these is Berent, who argues that the Greek polis was 'what the anthropologists call a "stateless society". The latter is characterised by the absence of "government", an agency which has separated itself from the rest of social life and which monopolizes the use of violence'.[11] In a stateless society, the means of violence are distributed among (potentially) armed members of the community. In the Greek polis, every adult male citizen fought for his city when he needed to.

In addition to the absence of a 'public coercive apparatus', the polis, Berent argues, was also characterised by 'the absence of differentiation or separation of government institutions from the rest of social life', that is, from the citizen community as such, which is also typical of stateless societies.[12] Poleis had virtually no bureaucracy, i.e. no professional civil servants – not even fifth-century BCE Athens with its Mediterranean empire, the largest polis in the Classical Greek world. Polis magistrates were amateurs, ordinary citizens elected, in democratic poleis like Athens often by lot, to serve for only a short period, generally a year.

Politicians were also amateurs; that is, they were private individuals who were 'politicians' only in the sense that they devoted a lot of their time to

---

[9] Lintott (1982) 26; Berent (2004) 111; see also Hunter (1994); Nippel (1995).
[10] Osborne (1985) 7–11, (1997) 79; Cartledge (1999) 467–8, (2002b) 19, (2009) 13–14.
[11] Berent (2004) 107; see also Berent (2000a), (2006).
[12] Berent (2004) 111. Of course, this does not imply that we cannot distinguish analytically between the city as a political community (i.e. the community of adult male citizens) and the city as a society (consisting of the citizens plus all other categories of inhabitants). See Chapter 7.

politics. In Athens, where we know them best, politicians were generally wealthy, rhetorically trained and charismatic individuals (Demosthenes is a paradigmatic example), without an official constitutional position, who made or defended proposals in the assembly (and composed speeches for litigants in the popular law courts) when they wanted to. Yet they were essentially on their own, private citizens without a party machine behind them or an institutionalised coercive apparatus to back them up.[13]

The most important political institution of the polis, the assembly (*ekklesia*), was popular, not differentiated from the *demos*, the community of citizens, and the same was, with some variation, true of the council (*boule*) in most Classical and (early) Hellenistic poleis, and in Athens and other democratic poleis also of the law courts (*dikasteria*).[14] All three were essentially mass gatherings of adult male citizens, which changed in composition with every new incarnation. The polis, therefore, was a politically decentralised society. It is simply not possible to locate the state, in its modern (essentially Weberian) sense, in the Greek polis.

Berent's thesis has been vigorously contested by Hansen, who has in particular championed the notion of the polis as a city-state and a State in the strong (modern) sense of the word.[15] Hansen's arguments against Berent are for the most part empirical. Thus he questions Berent's idea that, given the absence of a coercive apparatus in the Greek polis, individuals mostly had recourse to self-help, by pointing to sources from Athens indicating that self-help (in the sense of a citizen having the right to kill an offender if the perpetrator was caught in the act) was restricted to a limited number of offences only: adultery, burglary in the home at night, treason and exiles found still in Attica. In all matters other than these four, Hansen argues 'no person was allowed to take the law into his own hands, and an offender had to be tried before a court appointed by the polis.'[16] Furthermore, even in the four cases mentioned, instead of doing the dirty work himself, a citizen could actually opt to hand over the perpetrator, once apprehended, to the magistrates and leave it to them to execute the culprit or to bring him to trial. As Berent points out, however, here Hansen confuses the rule of law with the monopoly of the legitimate use of force. Peaceful dispute resolution without resort to (private) violence, Berent argues, does not imply 'that the public has a monopoly of violence', for

[13] Berent (2004) 111; Finley (1985) 38–75; Ober (1989) 104–27; Rhodes (1995).
[14] Robinson (2011) 225–6 on popular law courts in Classical democratic poleis other than Athens.
[15] Hansen (2002b), (2006) 63–5. See also Hansen (1998), with the comments by Cartledge (1999) 467–8.
[16] Hansen (2002b) 32–3.

without a coercive apparatus, the polis 'could not have had a monopoly of violence or even come close to such monopoly'.[17] Berent also argues that Hansen operates with a rather limited concept of self-help. Apprehension and prosecution of offenders, which in Athens in most cases were performed by ordinary citizens[18], were of course also forms of self-help.[19]

Hansen's most important argument against Berent concerns the latter's characterisation of the state. By focussing on the (Weberian) notion of the monopoly of violence, Berent's definition of the state, Hansen argues, remains vague and one-sided. States are more than just their governments; they also comprise a particular population within a particular territory. One of the essential differences between states and stateless societies, Hansen argues, is that states have clearly defined territorial boundaries, whereas stateless societies (such as nomadic tribes) do not. Poleis generally had clearly defined territories, hence they were states.[20]

Berent counters this by noting that modern anthropologists recognise that stateless societies such as nomadic tribes do indeed occupy specific territories and in that sense are 'territorial units'. They are, however, not *defined* by their territories. Rather, the territory is defined through them, as the land belonging to this or that tribe. The polis as a political unit was in a very similar way not defined by its territory, as many historians have noted: it was a community of citizens that happened to live in a particular territory, and not the other way around.[21] Berent also argues, rather sophistically, that his intention, in using Weber's notion of the monopoly of violence as a key criterion, was not to define the state but rather the stateless society, to see whether the Greek polis could be described in that way. Since most modern definitions of the state incorporate a version of Weber's notion, the absence of institutions holding or aiming for the monopoly of violence in a given historical polity might well indicate that this polity was not a state.[22]

Interestingly, a number of characteristics of the stateless community as defined by Berent and applied by him to the Greek polis would also seem to fit Republican Rome, as well as Greek and Roman cities under the Hellenistic monarchies and the Roman Empire. Finley and Lintott had already noted the absence of a coercive apparatus in Republican Rome in the form of a permanent police force, and, at least until the reforms of C. Marius in 107 BCE, a standing, professional army.[23] As in the Greek

---

[17] Berent (2004) 115.   [18] Hunter (1994) 134.   [19] Berent (2004) 115.
[20] Hansen (2002b) 26–7.   [21] Berent (2004) 121–3.   [22] Berent (2004) 117.
[23] Finley (1983) 18–20, 24; Lintott (1982) 26; Nippel (1995); see Nicolet (1980) 89–109, esp. 97: 'if [Rome before Marius' reforms] were at any time at peace with all her neighbours, she might have no army in being at all'.

polis, until the late second century BCE in the Roman Republic the means of violence were distributed among the members of the political community. The Roman assemblies were popular institutions, just like the Greek *ekklesiai*. Equally, like the Greek polis, the Republic lacked a professional bureaucracy, and its magistrates and generals were amateurs as well, serving in principle for one year at a time. Thus, as in the Greek polis, governmental institutions in the Republic were not much separated or differentiated from the citizen body, and there seems not to have been a clearly definable agency monopolising the (legitimate) use of violence.

There were also differences, however. For one thing, the concept of *imperium*, the supreme power to command possessed by Rome's consuls and praetors, was wholly alien to Greek practice (see Chapter 5). The chief Roman magistrates were 'articulate law' (*lex loquens*), as Cicero wrote, 'and the law a silent magistrate' (*Leg.* 3.2), and they therefore *had* to be obeyed, whereas Greek magistrates (in democratic poleis at least) were executives of the *demos*, and under its permanent control. Also, Rome's magistrates were elected solely from among the wealthy elite, preferably from among families whose members had already held office before. Most magistrates became lifelong members of the Senate, the only permanent political body in Rome.

Thus, Republican Rome had a somewhat more clearly institutionalised political elite than the Classical Greek poleis. At the same time, however, it was the *people*, in the public assemblies, who elected the magistrates, and, despite the great respect it commanded, the Senate's actual constitutional powers were severely limited: it could not pass laws, elect magistrates or sit as a court; it could only give advice to magistrates.[24] Thus it is hard to discern anything like a state government, that is, a clear political centre, in the Roman Republic (the Senate certainly does not qualify for this role). Power was diffused throughout the community, and this makes the Republic look a lot like Berent's stateless polis.

Arguably, the same could be said of Greek poleis and Roman cities during the later Hellenistic and Roman imperial periods.[25] During these periods, of course, kings and emperors strove to monopolise the means of violence (though, especially during the Hellenistic period, 'fighting poleis' were perhaps a more common phenomenon than was long thought[26]).

[24] North (2006) 266–7.
[25] With the exception, of course, of the royal capitals and the imperial city of Rome, where the kings and the emperor naturally constituted a clear centre of power and authority.
[26] Ma (2000).

Cities had to call on their own citizens less often to defend the community, though it should be noted that, as before, the sons of citizens, armed young men (*iuvenes, epheboi*), continued to fulfil the role of temporary amateur security guards. Apart from this, civic institutions for the maintenance of order (e.g. a police force) remained absent or were developed in only a rudimentary way.[27] Authority continued to be relatively diffused throughout the community, and institutions remained little differentiated from the rest of society (i.e. the citizen body). Professional bureaucrats and administrators were still mostly lacking, and magistrates continued to be amateurs, elected for a year only. Assemblies of the people continued to meet to elect them and continued to pass decrees together with the city councils, which, like the Roman Senate, were composed of ex-magistrates but remained mass organisations of citizens, ranging in size from about a hundred to five or six hundred members (particularly in the eastern provinces). City councillors and city magistrates, in the Greek East as well as in the West, were now almost exclusively elected from among the wealthy, yet they no more constituted a clearly demarcated state government than did the senators of the Roman Republic.

As for the Republic, only during the first century BCE, with the professionalisation of the Roman legions, and the increasing prevalence of extraordinary magistracies (long-term dictatorships, endlessly renewed provincial commands, the *triumviri* and so on), did the Roman polity come to resemble a more centralised, perhaps state-like political system. But by then the Republic was dying.

The whole debate concerning the state-like or state-less character of the Greek polis (and Roman civitas) may, at first glance, seem like a rather futile exercise in historical semantics. Yet, though appearances would suggest otherwise, there is rather a lot at stake here. For instance, Berent has used his vision of the polis as a stateless, politically decentralised society to provide explanations for the frequency of war-making among poleis during the Archaic and Classical periods, the Greeks' abhorrence of *stasis* (violent internal conflict), the development of democracy and 'politics as a rational and critical discipline' in the polis and the specific nature of Greek law.[28] Hansen, in turn, has developed his notion of the 'Greek city-state culture' to enable wide-ranging comparative studies between the Greek and other historical 'city-state cultures' throughout the world.[29] In an

---

[27] See Nippel (1995), especially chapter 4; Brélaz (2005) on cities in Roman Asia Minor. See also Fuhrmann (2012).
[28] See, in this order, Berent (2000a), (1998), (2000b), (2004) 120–1.   [29] Hansen (2000), (2002a).

earlier round of the debate, Finley, though he refused in the end to let go of the term state, deployed his model of Classical Athens and, to a lesser extent, Republican Rome as true participatory political systems, in which the citizens effectively ruled themselves, to challenge the influential ideas of the Italian elitist school in political theory.[30] These are all matters of serious historical, even trans-historical, importance. So, where do we go from here?

My own view is essentially pragmatic. Is it analytically useful to call Greek poleis and Roman civitates 'states'? Does doing so, in other words, actually deepen our understanding of Greek and Roman politics, society and history? My answer, as will have been guessed from the foregoing, is no. To insist on calling ancient cities 'states', even if one resorts to the label of 'city-state' or 'citizen-state'[31], is to stretch the elements making up the common modern definition of the state to such an extent that they lose most of their meaning. Any attempt to clearly locate a government separated from the citizen body, with its associated institutionalised administrative and coercive apparatuses, in ancient cities requires a great deal of analytical and definitional acrobatics, while contributing little to our actual understanding of political processes within ancient cities.[32] It is equally unhelpful to start from very loose definitions of the state in the first place, such as the one developed by the sociologist Charles Tilly ('coercion-wielding organizations that are distinct from households and kinship groups and exercise clear priority in some respects over all other organisations within substantial territories'[33]). Again we end up with the state as a sort of broad catch-all term with little explanatory power. Finally, to come up with endless differentiations of (early) state-types ('bureaucratic states', 'military-communal slave-owning states', 'sacral states', 'imperial non-bureaucratic states' and so on) in the hope of inventing one that fits the polis or civitas, as some scholars do, serves only to increase complexity without deepening our understanding.[34]

---

[30] Finley (1983), (1985). See Chapter 5 for discussion of the views of the elitist school in relation to ancient politics.
[31] A solution proposed by Runciman (1990).
[32] See, for example, the various arguments deployed by scholars who (unlike Hansen) admit to the absence of coercive institutions and/or the absence of a clear differentiation of government institutions from the citizen community in the Greek polis/Classical Athens, yet have still tried to maintain that the polis/Athens was somehow a state: Ehrenberg (1969) 88; Finley (1983) 8–9; Morris (1991) 84; Hunter (1994) 186–8; Berent (2004) 125–31 for discussion. Note also Anderson (2009), who argues that Athens was a state because the Athenians could conceive of an abstract unified Demos as 'a discursive construct, a fictitious corporate persona', a 'fictive self . . . that was said to rule Athens' (11–12).
[33] Tilly (1990) 1.   [34] E.g. Grinin (2004).

Abandoning the term 'state' when describing ancient cities also solves the dilemma of how to label cities that became part of larger hegemonial, royal or imperial power structures (the Persian Empire, the Athenian Empire, the Sparta-led Peloponnesian League, Macedon under Philip II and Alexander, the Hellenistic kingdoms, the later, imperial Roman Republic and the Roman Empire). The traditional argument that the polis proper in fact ceased to exist after the Battle of Chaeronea in 338 BCE because Greek cities then lost their autonomy to the kingdom of Macedon (and never regained it under its Hellenistic successor kingdoms and the Roman Empire) has been convincingly refuted by Hansen and his colleagues at the Polis Centre.[35] Even in the Archaic and Classical periods, many poleis had been subject to larger powers, whether the Persian King, some hegemonic polis (fifth-century BCE Athens, Classical Sparta in the Peloponnese) or a colonial mother city. Others in turn were members of federations of poleis (*koina*).[36] Hence, autonomy in the modern sense, political independence from other powers and the freedom to conduct one's own foreign policy, had never been a typical characteristic of poleis. The incorporation of poleis into the Hellenistic kingdoms and the Roman *imperium* did not therefore create such a radical deviation from the previous situation as has often been thought. It should be noted, though, that *autonomos* in ancient Greek means 'living under one's own laws', and this poleis had for the most part always done and in fact continued to do as internally self-governing communities of citizens in the Hellenistic and Roman periods. The same can be said *mutatis mutandis* of Roman cities (civitates, *coloniae, municipia*) under the Republic and empire: they too were self-governing communities of citizens electing their own magistrates and determining their own internal affairs. Only from the reforms of the emperor Diocletian onwards, as Hansen argues, did the internal self-government of cities in the empire become significantly constrained (see further Chapter 10).[37]

Yet, by at the same time insisting that the polis was also, and in the post-Classical era continued to be, a state, Hansen wants to have it both ways, and that creates a problem. For his proposition that the polis was a state leaves us with the odd prospect, as we saw earlier, of envisaging Hellenistic kingdoms and a Roman Empire filled with mini-states. Hansen can resolve this difficulty only by radically watering down his definition of the state,

---

[35] See Hansen (2003) 269–70 and (2006) 48–50, 130–1 with many references to earlier research conducted by the Copenhage Polis Centre.
[36] Mackil (2013).   [37] Hansen (2006) 50.

scrapping autonomy in the sense of independence from any outside authority as an important feature. However, autonomy in the sense of independence from any outside authority is a crucial element in modern notions of the state as is indicated by the definition quoted at the beginning of this chapter. If Hansen is right that autonomy in the sense of independence from outside authority was never a common feature of the polis (or, for that matter, of the Roman city), as he surely is, then it makes no analytical sense to call the polis (or the Roman civitas) a state. In particular, it makes no sense for Hansen, who has always been keen to stress supposed commonalities between ancient Greek and modern politics and polities, and has always maintained that the Greek polis was a State in the strong sense of the word.[38] The pragmatic solution, surely, is to consider poleis and civitates simply to be self-governing communities of citizens that could be either independent or part of some larger political structure.

One implication of the argument just sketched is that we should probably cease to describe Greek and Roman cities as 'city-states', since they cannot be considered 'states' in any modern sense of the word. This of course in turn implies that we cannot describe Greek or Roman cities as ever having been part of a 'city-state culture'. There may well have been polities and regions in other periods of history or in other parts of the world to which these labels might be usefully applied, but my suggestion is that we have little to gain by applying them to Greek and Roman cities.[39] Here, I suggest that the comparative approach serves to highlight an essential difference between the Greco-Roman experience and the situation prevailing in (various) other societies.

Cities, Kingdoms and Empires

How did ancient cities relate to other, larger political structures that we find in the ancient world, primarily kingdoms and empires? The political history of the Archaic and Classical Greek poleis was decisively shaped by their (violent) confrontations with large territorial states, the Lydian kingdom to begin with, but in particular the mighty Achaemenid Persian Empire, and from the later fourth century BCE onwards, the kingdom of Macedon. Indeed the old poleis in Ionia (western Asia Minor) found

---

[38] See e.g. Hansen (1998), (2002b), (2003) 264–265, (2006) 106–15; Cartledge (1999) 467–8.
[39] See Hansen (2000), (2002a) for many possible examples.

themselves intermittently dominated first by the Lydian monarchy, then by the Persians and then by Alexander and his royal successors.

It was from the confrontation with Persia in particular that the Greeks drew a sort of pan-Hellenic image of themselves as a freedom-loving, independent people living in self-governing citizen-communities, an image which could be favourably contrasted with the supposed cruel, tyrannical despotism of the Persian King, whose subjects to Greek eyes were not citizens but mere slaves.[40] Yet, as was already mentioned above, in practice, in the Classical Greek world, freedom was a relative term, and it certainly did not automatically imply political autonomy. Many poleis were at one time or another members of leagues headed by a single powerful hegemonial polis, Sparta in the Peloponnese and imperial Athens in the eastern Mediterranean. Non-hegemonial leagues of cities (*koina*) also existed. Sometimes these grew out of the *ethne* or 'tribal polities' that existed in the less urbanised parts of the Greek world. The Achaean and Aetolian Leagues grew to particular political prominence during the Hellenistic period while under the Roman Empire many provincial cities belonged to a league (*koinon*) of some kind.[41]

In this section, however, I shall deal chiefly with the monarchies and the empire that came to incorporate many and later virtually all Greek and Roman cities, the Hellenistic kingdoms and the *imperium Romanum*. It is with these large-scale political entities that ancient cities had their longest-lasting relationships, and they were most determinative of the cities' fates.

Traditionally, scholars have viewed the post-Classical poleis as but pale reflections of their Classical forebears. Under the weight of the Hellenistic kingdoms, poleis lost their much-treasured political autonomy, while within the cities, popular participation on the Classical democratic model was in slow but terminal decline: behind an institutional façade of *demokratia*, wealthy elites took over.

Both developments were blamed partly on the 'weakness' of the polis-Greeks themselves, but mostly on the kings. 'The fatal weakness of the Greek city-states', W. S. Ferguson wrote, 'was their incapacity to form an all-embracing coalition'. Thus, they ended up 'completely shorn of their statehood, municipal rights and a voice in the affairs of the realm of which they formed part'.[42] As for the decline of popular participation and the rise of informal oligarchies within the poleis, A. H. M. Jones noted that '[i]n foreign politics the most important persons with whom cities had to deal

---

[40] Best exemplified in the *Histories* of Herodotus, see e.g. Cartledge (2002a).   [41] Mackil (2013).
[42] Ferguson (1928) 22, 24–5, quoted by Strootman (2011) 141.

were the kings and their ministers and later Roman magistrates. All these were much more likely to treat with respect citizens of wealth and standing . . . than plebeian demagogues'.[43]

Such views have not entirely disappeared in more recent scholarship, with the sociologist W. G. Runciman even declaring the Classical poleis 'doomed to extinction', mainly because they failed to adapt their institutions to a changed Mediterranean environment in which they now had to compete with kingdoms for scarce resources. The poleis, argues Runciman, were too democratic, even the oligarchic ones, meaning that power was shared among too many citizens, so that it never became concentrated at the top, in the hands of small ruling elites who might have caused the poleis to compete more effectively with the kingdoms.[44]

On the whole, however, the scholarly tide has turned in recent decades. We already saw that Hansen successfully argued that even during the Classical period, *autonomia* in the sense of full political independence was never an essential characteristic of the majority of poleis (barring large powerful ones like Athens or Sparta). For most poleis, therefore, the Hellenistic period implied no radical change in this respect. Moreover, in the wake of the many studies of Hellenistic polis institutions by the great French epigraphist Louis Robert, scholars have increasingly argued in favour of the continuation of popular politics in the post-Classical polis (see Chapter 5). In fact, since Alexander, after freeing the poleis of western Asia Minor from Persian domination, gave them democratic constitutions, and since this type of constitution was also the one used in most city-foundations by the kings after him, there were now in absolute terms more democratic poleis than ever before in the Greek world. Close study of institutions has revealed that offices continued to rotate annually, albeit often among wealthier citizens, and that the popular assemblies continued to exercise control over politics.[45] Yet if for most poleis a lack of autonomy was nothing new, while internal democratic self-government did not just continue but even spread more widely among poleis, how then should we conceptualise the relationship between polis and king, and what effects did the monarchies have on the poleis?

According to Rolf Strootman, the whole debate is misconceived. Historians, even those who do not support the 'Hellenistic polis-in-decline'-

[43] Jones (1940) 166.
[44] Runciman (1990); Green (1990) for an interpretation of Hellenistic history in terms of decline, *inter alia* of polis institutions and civic self-government.
[45] E.g. Gauthier (1993); Grieb (2008); Carlsson (2010); Mann and Scholz (2012).

scenario, continue to ask questions such as 'how did cities adapt to empire?' and thus remain locked in a comparative Classical vs. Hellenistic discourse with strong teleological overtones.[46] The discussion, Strootman argues, is distorted by a number of misconceptions, of which the most important are (1) that Hellenistic poleis had no independent foreign policy (not true, according to Strootman, since cities continuously had to negotiate with kings and neighbouring states and, in addition, never ceased to quarrel among themselves) and (2) that empire is bad for civic autonomy. Hellenistic kingdoms, Strootman argues, primarily the Macedonian (Argead and Antigonid) and Seleucid ones, under whose sway most poleis fell, were basically 'tribute-exacting military organisations exercising only thin administrative control, and collecting relatively little revenue, in extensive and culturally heterogeneous territories'. The kings were highly dependent on the cities because '[c]ities commanded the infrastructure and formed the loci where surpluses were collected, both of which were essential for the exercise of the empires' core business: war-making'. Using force, i.e. militarily bending cities to one's will meant besieging them, a highly costly, time-consuming and hazardous affair, so kings sought peaceful cooperation with the poleis instead.[47]

This cooperation was effected through a fine-grained network of *philoi*, or friends of the king, generally wealthy and prominent citizens of the various poleis, who might either reside at the royal court or remain in their poleis.[48] They acted as ambassadors or advocates of their cities, but also as intermediaries between king and polis, making sure that royal requests received the required political attention in the cities.[49] The shape assumed by the relationship between kings and cities, in terms of practice and discourse, was largely that of euergetism. The protection that the kings offered the cities, the grants of autonomy cities received, tax exemptions, trading privileges, donations of money or grain – all of these were construed as benefactions by the king, who could thus present himself as liberator and saviour of the cities. The poleis, in return, honoured the king by acknowledging his suzerainty, offering him divine honours, paying the tribute he required and offering military assistance when needed. This was gift-exchange, the ongoing process of giving, receiving and reciprocating.

In a fascinating study of the documents (royal letters and civic decrees) pertaining to this process of exchange between the Seleucid monarch Antiochus III and the poleis in western Asia Minor, John Ma has

---

[46] Strootman (2011).   [47] Strootman (2011) 143–5.
[48] Herman (1997); Strootman (2011) 147–50.   [49] Bringmann (1993).

demonstrated how the practices, but particularly the language of euergetism, expressed in these documents, served to lessen the (potential) violence and oppression of monarchical rule by clothing the interaction between kings and cities in a discourse that cast both parties in a favourable light, as friends who have each other's interests at heart and act out of a sense of obligation and mutual respect.[50] The seriousness with which both parties engaged in this process can be gauged from a letter by another king Antiochus (i.e. II) to the Ionian city of Erythrai, in which the king writes that the city's ambassadors presented him with a substantial gift of gold in return for a tax exemption. Neither party saw anything incongruous in this: after all, giving a gift was honourable, whereas paying taxes could be construed as a blemish on the city's autonomy.[51] Thus, although material objects and real administrative, economic and political privileges were part of the exchange between kings and cities, the true importance, for the maintenance of sociopolitical stability, lay in what these gifts signified. Together with their gifts the parties exchanged idealised images of themselves and of the other, images which both predetermined and constrained behaviour, suggesting duties and entitlements which seemed to flow naturally from the identity, status and previous actions of both city and monarch.

Broadly similar models of the relationship between cities and rulers have been developed for the Roman Empire. Like its Hellenistic predecessors, particularly the Seleucid monarchy, but on a much larger scale, the *imperium Romanum* was a far-flung territorial empire, incorporating large parts of three continents and having its own internal sea. It too focussed mainly on tax-gathering to finance its military and administrative apparatus and on keeping order. Again like most Hellenistic monarchies (with the possible exception of Ptolemaic Egypt) it had, despite its gigantic size, a remarkably small administration by comparative historical standards.[52] During the Principate, the empire was effectively 'governed without bureaucracy', which implied that many vital tasks such as the gathering of taxes and local administration and jurisdiction fell to the provincial cities and local elites.[53] Add to this the slowness of communications and the

---

[50] Ma (1999), with the review by Erskine (2001).
[51] *OGIS* 223 = Bagnall and Derow (2004) no. 22; see Strootman (2011) 145n15 for this interpretation.
[52] The contemporary Chinese Han Empire employed roughly twenty times as many state functionaries: Garnsey and Saller (2014) 35; Scheidel (2009) and (2015) for comparative research on the Roman and Chinese Empires.
[53] Garnsey and Saller (2014) 35–54; Millar (1977) is the classic modern study of Roman imperial government.

difficulties of transport typical of any pre-modern society, and the fact that the empire managed to maintain (with some minor interruptions) peace and unity for over two centuries becomes something of a historical curiosity.

One possible explanation is symbolic communication. Unlike the Hellenistic kingdoms, the Roman Empire grew out of a city, a *civitas*. This allowed Roman emperors, as 'first citizens' (*principes*), to act out, on a super-large scale, the typical public roles which had been expected from elite citizens in the former Republic and were still expected from civic elites in the cities throughout the empire. Thus, for instance, Richard Gordon has argued that the linked public roles, displayed on many reliefs and coins throughout the empire, of the *princeps* as priest (*pontifex maximus*) performing sacrifice on behalf of the community and of the *princeps* as (supreme) benefactor (*euergetes*) provided a template that could be adopted by local elites throughout the empire.[54] In this way, some coherence of ritual and sociopolitical practice was instituted throughout the empire by means of the dissemination of symbols and images rather than through bureaucratic imperative, but more crucially, their roles as priests and public benefactors allowed elite citizens to earn prestige and honours that served to legitimate their positions of authority.[55] Moreover, by imitating the imperial *exemplum*, the elites' own local civic authority came to be perceived as directly linked to, and was symbolically reinforced by, the authority of the *princeps*.

Simon Price similarly stressed the importance of symbolic communication between ruler and local civic communities in his study of emperor worship in Roman Asia Minor.[56] In an attempt to explain why Hellenistic ruler cults and the worship of Roman emperors or other members of the imperial family often arose on the initiative of cities themselves, Price argued that ruler worship was, in essence, a *modus operandi* developed by the poleis to deal with royal power that was neither wholly foreign (as the Persian kings had been) nor limited to the confines of the polis itself (as the power of Greek tyrants had been). Given the absence of a tradition of institutionalised monarchy among the polis-Greeks (Sparta excepted), the only available template for dealing with such mighty but not completely foreign powers was divine worship, given that the gods, too, were Greek (or Greco-Roman), yet possessed a power no polis could ever match. Under the empire, emperor worship developed into a 'system of exchange'

---

[54] Gordon (1990). [55] On civic munificence in the Roman Empire, see Zuiderhoek (2009a).
[56] Price (1984).

between provincial cities and the imperial centre; although the imperial cult was not explicitly created for this purpose, it did provide both the emperors and the cities with a discourse and a range of expected behaviours that served to ease communications and negotiations between them. Cities offered cult to emperors, and emperors offered honorific titles and privileges in return, yet the sheer flexibility of the system, typical of gift-exchange, allowed both parties crucial room for manoeuvre. Emperors could politely refuse but then accept divine honours on a later occasion or accept only through the Senate; cities could also vary what they offered, i.e. cult of the living emperor, of his genius, of his wife or children, of his predecessors and so on.

Again, as in the case of Ma's model of Hellenistic city-monarch relationships, we might argue that the respective roles played by cities and rulers suggested to both a broad but essentially limited set of behaviours and a sense of duties and entitlements that smoothed interaction and lessened the potential for conflicts. More recently, Clifford Ando has argued that the continued, everyday interaction between rulers and the ruled via a whole range of administrative processes (e.g. the census, the swearing of oaths of loyalty, the payment of taxes and the assises of the proconsul), rituals (imperial cult and Roman religious forms and practices) and communicative media (state documents, inscriptions, imperial portraits on coins and artwork, statues of the emperor and imperial artwork containing Roman imperialist themes) over time created an ideological consensus among the provincial (urban) populations concerning the legitimacy of Roman rule.[57] Other scholars have stressed the importance of patronage networks for tying imperial and provincial elites and populations together in a network of favours granted and favours owed that allowed the empire to function even in the absence of an institutionalised bureaucracy and generated cooperation without force.[58] In the unsettled political and military conditions of the Mediterranean region during the late Republic, the patron-client model was extended to the relationship between powerful Romans (generals, senators) and individual cities.[59] Significantly, under the empire, this type of patronage of cities disappeared during the first century CE, as civic attention became increasingly focussed on the person of the emperor alone. Yet individual cities retained their

---

[57] Ando (2000). See also Madsen (2009) on the keenness of Greek provincial urban elites to identify themselves as Roman.
[58] Saller (1982); MacMullen (1988); Lendon (1997); Garnsey (2010); Lavan (2013) 176–210.
[59] Eilers (2002); but see now Nicols (2014).

spokesmen, often deriving from the local civic elites. These were men who had connections at court, through a career in the imperial service and/or through repeated membership of the many civic embassies which, in a seemingly perpetual and almost ritual motion, were travelling back and forth between the court and their hometowns, delivering praise to the emperor and returning with honorific titles, favours and benefactions for their cities, weaving the invisible threads of reciprocity that helped to hold the empire together.

None of the above, of course, should serve to deny the very real misery and exploitation that kings and emperors could and occasionally did inflict on city populations, from the stationing of garrisons to forced labour (for instance on local roads), to the requisitioning of transport, to heavy tax burdens, to expropriation of city territories or local funds as and when required, to bloody interventions in local disputes and so on. Cities were ultimately defenceless against the rent-seeking and predation of rulers and their imperial elite agents.[60] A strong focus on rent-seeking, however, has its costs as well as its benefits for elites and rulers, especially in the longer term. For one thing, it requires constant vigilance and the transformation of society into an armed camp and might easily trigger resistance costly to suppress. Therefore, the predation should at least be clothed, or veiled, in terms of legality and legitimacy. Better still, however, if cooperation is unenforced, voluntary and apparently spontaneous. If achieving this imposes some costs on the ruler, in that he has to restrain predation to some extent and has to adopt the role of benefactor, which implies acknowledging some entitlement claims of the ruled, it at least limits or slows down the exhaustion of the imperial resource base (a danger of excessive predation) and lessens the risk of societal breakdown.

---

[60] Bang (2008) and (2012) for a model of the Roman economy with a strong emphasis on elite and imperial rent-seeking. We should note in this context, as Lavan (2013) has demonstrated, that in the Latin literature written by and for the Roman imperial elite, the metaphor most commonly used to conceptualise the relationship between Romans and provincials is that of master and slave. The language of benefaction and patronage, so common in provincial conceptualisations of relations with the emperor and his agents (in speeches, inscriptions), and in letters by the emperor and his officials to provincial cities, finds its place in Latin literature as well, but the master/slave-metaphor predominates.

CHAPTER 10

The End of the Ancient City?

Historians have a problem with endings (as well as with beginnings – see Chapter 2).[1] After all, can historical phenomena ever actually be said 'to have ended' at some specific point in time, or do they merely morph into something else? And if the latter is the case, at which moment can the transformation be said to have been so thorough that we are presented with a reality radically different from the one which existed before? Did the ancient city come to an end (it clearly did, because Greco-Roman cities no longer exist, except in ruins), and if so, when and how did this happen? What kind of 'ending' was it: an abrupt halt, a slow decline or a profound transformation?

There are no easy answers, partly because the terms are so unclear. Much of the debate over the history of the late antique city, and on the later Roman world more generally, during the past half century or so has turned precisely on the perceived opposition between a vision of 'decline', i.e. the slow unravelling of Roman economic, political and administrative structures and the deterioration of Greco-Roman culture during the centuries after Diocletian (itself a powerful motif in Western culture ever since the publication of Edward Gibbon's *History of the Decline and Fall of the Roman Empire*), and a more recent vision of creative transformation, of the making of a new world, Late Antiquity, starting with Diocletian, but especially with Constantine's embrace of Christianity.

Greek culture arose and developed in tandem with the polis, Roman culture and the *imperium Romanum* originated in the civitas, and the cities (poleis and civitates) constituted the essential administrative cogs in the wheel that allowed the Hellenistic kingdoms and the early Roman Empire to function at all. Given the essentially 'civic' or 'urban' character of Greco-Roman civilisation, the fate of the city in the late antique period

---

[1] The title of the current chapter is consciously copied from Liebeschuetz (1992) but with a question mark added.

is of course crucial to any definition of 'decline' or 'transformation' of the ancient world.

Decline or Transformation?

Ubi tantae splendidissimae civitates? – 'where are the great and most splendid cities?' Thus wrote Quodvultdeus, bishop of Carthage, lamenting the devastation and chaos apparently caused by the Vandal conquest of Roman North Africa during 429–439 CE (*Sermo II de tempore barbarico* 5.4).[2] Contemporary literary sources paint a bleak picture of conditions in the African provinces after the conquest, leading to modern scholarly notions of a flourishing urban civilisation overwhelmed by barbarian hordes. Recent archaeological research suggests a somewhat different reality, however. There was some destruction at urban sites, certainly at Carthage, where some public buildings (e.g. the Odeon, the circular monument and the theatre) were destroyed. On the whole, however, the material evidence does not suggest widespread economic or demographic decline; the distribution of African Red Slip ware pottery and African amphorae around the Mediterranean shows no diminution of exports, suggesting that overall economic performance remained intact. Many urban sites show dense suburban settlement and evidence of fairly intense economic activity in and around civic centres, signified by the abundant presence of lime kilns and olive presses.[3]

Yet there were some important changes, particularly in the urban topography. Fora seem to have lost their function as the focus of urban life in many African cities from the late fourth century CE onwards. Church buildings took their place, sometimes quite literally. Often, traditional public buildings, such as temples and bath houses, were no longer kept up or converted to other uses. Shops and booths crowded along the old colonnaded avenues and encroached on street frontages; Christian basilicas proliferated. Most significantly, however, after the Vandal conquest, the tradition of civic euergetism, of public benefactions by the political elite of the cities that had provided much of the stimulus for the provisioning and upkeep of civic buildings, amenities, games and festivals, and which had still flourished in fourth-century Africa, seems more or less to disappear, suggesting a profound change in civic-political culture.[4]

---

[2] Cited by Lepelley (1992) 52.
[3] Mattingly and Hitchner (1995) 209–11; Merrills (2004) 9–11; see in general Sears (2007), to be read with the review by Hitchner (2009).
[4] Lepelley (1992) 67–8; Mattingly and Hitchner (1995) 209–12; Ward-Perkins (1998) 379–80. Gifts by governors and emperors show a greater continuity.

The African case neatly encapsulates the dilemma faced by anyone wishing to write the history of late antique urbanism. The evidence from accross the Roman world, mostly archaeological, generally does not suggest a straightforward decline of the cities of the empire in economic or demographic terms (whatever might be said about individual sites), at least not before c. 400 CE in some regions of the West and c. 600 CE in some parts of the East. At the same time, in many regions, we seem to witness the disappearance, earlier and more pronounced in some areas, later and more diffuse in others, of a certain way of urban living, a certain model of urban society, a certain form of urban politics and a certain type of urban landscape, and with it, undeniably, some of the associated amenities and advantages, material and immaterial. Many of the characteristics of this form of urban life, that is, the ancient Greco-Roman city, have been discussed in the preceding chapters of this book. In this final chapter, I shall now discuss what happened to some of the most important of these characteristics from the third century CE onwards to come to an assessment of what the phrase 'the end of the ancient city' might actually mean. Where possible I shall try to pay attention to the regional and chronological differentiation within the processes of change during the later empire, which the vast amount of recent scholarship on late antique urbanism has brought so prominently to the fore.[5]

Politics and Administration

Ancient cities, as we saw in earlier chapters, were self-governing communities of citizens. Citizens ruled themselves by means of councils, popular assemblies and elected magistrates. This specific type of constitutional, formalised civic politics, characteristic of ancient cities since the beginnings of the Archaic period in Greece and the earliest days of the Roman Republic and the Latin civitates in Italy, eventually disappeared from Mediterranean lands and the other areas that (formerly) belonged to the Roman Empire. When, how and why it disappeared exactly, in different regions of the ancient world, continues to be the subject of intense debate. An earlier generation of scholars viewed the demise of civic institutions as part of an empire-wide trend of civic decline, and they saw the first symptoms manifesting themselves early on. 'Of the three basic elements in the [city] constitution, the people, the council and the magistrates, the first had by now long ceased to function', A. H. M. Jones wrote in the

---

[5] See Lavan (2001b) for a bibliographical overview.

'Cities' chapter of his monumental *Later Roman Empire*.[6] Several decades earlier, Frank Abbott and Allan Johnson, in their famous survey of civic administration under the Roman Empire, had already ascribed 'the atrophy of municipal institutions' to the discouragement of 'democratic government in the cities' by Rome, which led to the establishment of self-serving civic oligarchies, and in due course prompted the central administration to appoint bureaucratic officials (*curatores, defensores*) to oversee civic administration and to grant greater powers of intervention to provincial governors.[7] As we saw in Chapter 5, recent research has stressed the continued vitality of popular politics during the first two centuries CE, particularly in the Greek East, where assemblies remained a political force to be reckoned with, but also to a lesser extent in the West. During the third century, evidence for assemblies occurs sporadically, but from the early fourth century onwards, official public assemblies do not figure anymore in our sources, yet the people remained an important factor, manifesting itself primarily via informal acclamations at impromptu public meetings and during shows and games in the theatres and circuses.[8] Such acclamations, though often taking place at ostensibly 'non-political' occasions, e.g. during the games, at the dedication of a building, the welcoming of a new governor and so forth, acquired political significance precisely because they were taken seriously by the civic, provincial and even imperial authorities, as Charlotte Roueché has argued.[9] In this much diluted form, an element of informal popular 'politics' survived into the Byzantine period.

The main traditional argument for the decline of civic constitutional politics does not focus on assemblies, however, but on the city councils and the fate of the 'curial class' that constituted their membership (*decuriones, curiales, bouleutai*). The Roman Empire crucially depended on the local civic elites, that is, the city councillors, to carry out many vital tasks, including tax gathering, local administration and to some extent, jurisdiction. It also encouraged members of the local elites to use part of their private wealth to finance civic public buildings and amenities when public funds proved insufficient, through civic euergetism and liturgies.

This way of doing things seems to have served the needs of the empire well for some two hundred years but began to become seriously problematic from the early third century onwards. Various factors, such as the protracted civil wars of the third century CE, the need, at the same

---

[6] Jones (1964) 722.   [7] Abbott and Johnson (1926) 229–30.
[8] Jones (1940) 177–8, (1964) 722–4.   [9] Roueché (1984).

time, for constant defensive wars on the borders in both the East and West, against Persians and Germanic tribes, the increased tax burden caused by all this war-making, which placed enormous pressure on the *decuriones*, the inflationary policies of successive emperors and, some historians would now add, the demographic shockwave caused by the series of (probably) smallpox epidemics during the late second century CE known as the Antonine Plague (endangering the security of elite and state incomes by reducing the number of rent and tax payers at the start of the third century), all arguably served to undermine, in one way or another, the prosperity of the cities and particularly of the local urban elites.[10]

Arguably, we can see this change reflected very well in the stark reduction in the number of surviving public inscriptions from cities across the empire, from Spain to Italy to Asia Minor, and more particularly in the marked decrease in the number of honorific inscriptions for rich citizens listing the offices they held and the benefactions they made to their communities.[11] Such a significant decrease in the number of honorific inscriptions points to a far lower level of sociopolitical activity, if not to a qualitative change in political culture. The city of Aphrodisias offers an interesting example. It continued to produce inscriptions until very late antiquity, yet whereas 1,500 of the extant Aphrodisian inscriptions date to the three hundred years before the mid-third century CE, only 250 or so can be dated to the period 250–550 CE. Among these later texts are very few honorific inscriptions for benefactors from the local civic elite; most commemorate emperors or imperial officials. Acclamations increasingly replace decrees debated and voted on by the council and assembly.[12]

All of this suggests a slow change in political culture and practice in Aphrodisias from the mid-third century onwards. Paradoxically, the impact of the third-century crisis on civic social and political life can be well illustrated with reference to an area of the empire that was little affected by the crisis, safely ensconced as it was on the opposite side of the Mediterranean: Roman North Africa. Here, as we saw, civic constitutional politics and the tradition of local elite munificence continued in

---

[10] The bibliography on the so-called Third-Century Crisis is enormous. For a classic account, see Rostovtzeff (1957) chapters 9–11. A more recent overview can be found in Potter (2004). On the impact of the Antonine Plague, see Duncan-Jones (1996); Scheidel (2002), also (2012c); Jongman (2007b); and Lo Cascio (2012). For a possible effect on state and elite tax and rent incomes, see Zuiderhoek (2009b).
[11] Liebeschuetz (1992) 4–6.   [12] Roueché (1989) xx and *passim*; Liebeschuetz (1992) 4–6.

an unbroken sequence until the Vandal conquest.[13] The contrast with most other provinces of the empire is marked.

The scale of the changes should however not be exaggerated, even in those parts of the empire that *did* truly suffer during the third century. As recent research shows, the fourth and early fifth centuries CE saw an essential continuity, in most parts of the empire, of civic constitutional politics based on the rule of decurions (or *curiales* as they were now mostly called) and of the local administrative role of the poleis and civitates, even in areas where previous scholarship had considered the decline pronounced, such as Spain.[14] The local city councils remained the essential cogs in the wheels of the imperial administration, just as they had been in earlier centuries. They were perhaps even more important now than before, given the central government's greatly increased demand for taxes to finance a considerably enlarged army and imperial bureaucracy, taxes which the *curiales* were meant to gather and for which they stood surety with their own property. In addition, the city councillors were expected to keep financing local civic amenities from their own resources. Such contributions (*munera*) had now become a duty, instead of the (semi-) voluntary benefactions they had been in previous centuries, an obligation from which little status could be gained. The contributions had probably also become more onerous, given the confiscation of civic lands and civic public revenues by the emperors in the early fourth century CE (though later a partial restitution was made to the cities).[15]

The most important factor undermining the social and political power of the city councillors, however, was increased imperial centralisation. Diocletian's reform of the empire's administrative structure created many more and much smaller provinces, led by imperially appointed governors who exercised a far stricter control over the cities. Other semi-imperial officials also increasingly restricted the councillors' room for manoeuvre. From the early second century CE onwards, emperors had occasionally appointed so-called *curatores rei publicae* from among the senatorial or equestrian orders. These officials were sent to cities whose finances were in disarray. During the third century, *curatores*, who now often were drawn from the local civic elites, became increasingly common, until, under Diocletian, curators became elected officials within the cities. Nonetheless, they continued to be formally appointed by the emperor, and, as the chief

[13] Lepelley (1979–1981), (1992).   [14] Reece (1992) on Britain; Kulikowski (2004) on Spain.
[15] Jones (1964) 732–3.

financial overseers of the cities, acted as go-betweens between the cities and the imperial government.[16]

From the early fourth century onwards, another such semi-imperial, semi-civic official rose to prominence alongside the curator, namely the *defensor civitatis*. Originally a judicial officer, responsible for bringing local needs to the attention of the imperial administration, the *defensor* acquired increasing fiscal and administrative powers throughout the fourth century, until he eventually came to overshadow the curator. In general, provincial governors, curators and *defensores* gathered more and more power, at the expense of the city councillors. It is of course to some extent a matter of perspective whether one chooses to describe these developments as a 'decline'. From the vantage point of the central administration, they can also perhaps be seen as a rational administrative response to the military and political challenges facing the later empire. Also, the picture can be drawn too bleakly. Clearly, being a city councillor still brought some prestige at the local level, and the heavy involvement of *curiales* in taxation also undoubtedly created opportunities for enrichment.[17]

During the fifth and sixth centuries and later, city councils as a form of constitutional government increasingly came to be replaced by a more informal oligarchy composed of various powerful individuals and groups.[18] This was a long drawn-out development, with much regional divergence. The councils certainly did not disappear overnight, and in some regions in the West, councillors are attested alongside other powerful groups into the eighth century CE.[19] Already in the fourth century, however, if not earlier, many of the wealthiest among the civic elites had left the councils, seeking more remunerative and prestigious offices in the expanding imperial bureaucracy of the post-Diocletianic empire, or they had tried to gain membership of professional or status groups that were legally exempt from curial duties, e.g. senatorial or equestrian officials, doctors and teachers of grammar and rhetoric.[20]

At the same time, large local landowners who did not belong to the council, often ex-imperial officials of senatorial status, (former) staff members of the provincial administration, ex-military officials of higher rank or even wealthy traders (groups collectively referred to as *possessores* in case of those of senatorial rank or *habitatores* in case of those of lower rank)

---

[16] Liebeschuetz (2001) 110; Kulikowski (2004) 44–5 on *curatores* in Spain. See Burton (1979) for a nuanced account.

[17] Kulikowski (2004) 45–9.   [18] Liebeschuetz (2001); Laniado (2002); Wickham (2005) 596–602.

[19] Liebeschuetz (1992) 22.   [20] Jones (1940) 188–207 is the classic account.

increasingly gained political power in the cities.[21] Meanwhile, the traditional elective magistracies of the city were increasingly replaced by semi-imperial functionaries, such as the curator, the *defensor*, the *sitones* (corn-buyer) and the *pater tes poleos* (father of the city, an office attested in the East). Even though they were sometimes elected locally, these officials, who generally did not derive from the curial class, were formally appointed by the imperial government and were answerable to the provincial governor, not the council.[22] Another powerful group within the now Christian cities of the empire was the bishop and the clergy, who increasingly assumed a political and administrative role.

Together, this informal coalition of wealthy non-curial landowners, semi-imperial functionaries and bishop and clergy, often collectively termed 'notables' by modern scholars, increasingly took over the rule of cities from the councillors during the course of the fifth and sixth centuries CE, at least, in the East.[23] In the West, the situation was somewhat more complex. Regional divergence in development was greater due to the fragmentation of the post-Roman West into the Germanic successor kingdoms. Curial government also held out longer in places, into the seventh or eight centuries sometimes. The eventual outcome, however, was the same. Everywhere, the councils were more and more pushed to the sideline by groups called *honorati* or *possessores* (large non-curial landowners), the *defensor*, the curator, the bishop and, notably, in Italy and France for instance, by the local representative of the king, the *comes civitatis*.[24]

Again, whether this development should be termed a decline is a matter of debate. After all, the disappearance of traditional municipal institutions does not necessarily imply a decline of the city in broader (economic) terms. Scholars critical of the traditional narrative in which the 'flight of the *curiales*' is linked to a loss of civic 'initiative and vitality' and general urban decline[25] have pointed to the mainly archaeological evidence for urban economic prosperity in various regions of the (former) empire during the fifth and sixth centuries, arguing that a change in political and administrative institutions and practices need not necessarily reflect profound changes in the underlying society.[26] As Mark Whittow writes,

---

[21] Liebeschuetz (2001) 110–20; Wickham (2005) 597.   [22] Liebeschuetz (2001) 110.

[23] Jones (1964) 757–63; Liebeschuetz (2001) 108; Laniado (2002); Wickham (2005) 596–602; Cameron (2012) 160–1.

[24] Liebeschuetz (2001) 124–36; Wickham (2005) 597–8.

[25] Jones (1964) is the classic statement, for the quote see p. 757.

[26] See the contributions in Lavan (2001a); Whittow (1990).

with reference to the East: 'The disappearance of the *curiales* . . . was part of the process whereby [the cities'] landowning elites . . . adapted to changing circumstances' and 'embraced the new Christian world'.[27] One type of elite and one model of government slowly replaced another, but civic life continued.[28]

Wolfgang Liebeschuetz has nonetheless pointed to some evident long-term drawbacks of the end of urban government by classical city councils. It meant that there now no longer was a constitutionally appointed or elected body in the city that bore continuous and collective responsibility for the welfare of the civic community and the city's material infrastructure. Neglect of public buildings and public spaces (agora/forum), abandonment of municipal responsibilities (keeping the roads clear, sewage removal) and infringement of public property rights, all often attested in cities of the fifth century CE and later, were obvious consequences. From the point of view of the imperial (or, in the West, royal) government, moreover, the new, mixed and partly informal elite of 'notables' was much harder to control. Unlike the *curiales*, the notables were under no hereditary obligation to perform civic duties and pay for civic amenities, and they could not be coerced (the bishop and clergy least of all). In the East, the decline of curial government meant that the uniform Diocletianic system of tax gathering, to which the *curiales* had been instrumental, broke down in the sixth century and was replaced by a variety of *ad hoc* arrangements.[29] At the level of the individual city, we might add, the decline of curial government also meant that there was less legal and constitutional restraint on the behaviour of elites. Eventually, there were no longer present a constitutional body and associated elected magistrates (e.g. *aediles*, *agoranomoi*) with the legitimate authority to regulate economic transactions according to uniform legal procedures, to guarantee property rights and to help citizens enforce contracts. Greater economic insecurity, higher transaction costs and increased elite predation and free-riding behaviour were a likely result.

In due course, as stated above, the clergy and bishops partly came to fill the official power vacuum left by the disappearance of curial government, especially in the successor kingdoms in the West, but also in many cities of

---

[27] Whittow (1990) 29.
[28] Laniado (2002) is in this vein; Kulikowski (2004) stresses urban continuity in Spain; see in general Cameron (2012) 157–62.
[29] Liebeschuetz (2001) 121–4; also Wickham (2005) 68–70 (on civic elites' loss of responsibility for taxation) and 598–9 (on the shift to informal civic government by notables and neglect of public duties).

the East, assuming 'responsibility not only for civic leadership but also for social welfare in their communities'.[30] While such 'desecularization' or Christianisation of civic politics and society need not necessarily be viewed in terms of decline, it certainly helped to create a civic social order fundamentally different from that prevailing in the Greco-Roman city of earlier centuries.[31]

Economy and Society

From politics and governmental structures we now move to other aspects of civic life. In earlier chapters, we saw that some typical features of the ancient Greek and Roman city were the integration of town and country within the single civic unit of the polis/civitas, the highly specialised and commercialised nature of the cities' internal economies and the prevalence of a social, political and ideological model based on the notion of the citizen-community. When, how and why did these features cease to be characteristic of cities in the areas that belonged, or had formerly belonged, to the Roman Empire?

Poleis and civitates, as we saw, remained the basic units of imperial administration in most regions of the empire during the fourth and early fifth centuries CE, with responsibility for local law and order still being allocated to the city councils, if in a somewhat reduced form, given the introduction, by the emperor Diocletian, of an administrative system with many more and smaller provinces and more hands-on provincial governors. This suggests that the age-old model of the ancient city as a combination of urban centre and surrounding countryside was still the basic template of territorial organisation well into 'late late antiquity', particularly in the East. When and how did it cease to be this? This is a question that is difficult to answer, given the murky evidence, but we can point to some developments.

For instance, in the East, particularly in parts of Asia Minor and the Near East, cities' control over their rural territories was slowly eroded by the increasing prominence, prosperity and autonomy of villages, who looked to the rural monasteries and their leading 'holy men' for leadership and patronage rather than to the cities. Rural monastic patrons in the form of holy men such as Theodore of Sykeon in north-eastern Galatia during

---

[30] Cameron (2012) 157–60 (quote from p. 159); also Mitchell (1993) 2: 73–84; Liebeschuetz (2001) chapter 4; Whitby (2006).
[31] See Liebeschuetz (2001) 137–9, who coins the term 'desecularization'.

the later sixth and early seventh century CE were increasingly successful in defending rural communities against demands from civic potentates or provincial governors.[32]

Taxation was another factor: throughout imperial history, the city councillors had borne the responsibility for gathering the taxes owed by the inhabitants of their city and its territory to the imperial government. This city-based form of collecting taxes, which had for centuries guaranteed close administrative ties between cities and their territories, slowly unravelled with the decline of curial government in the East. Sixth-century laws show the imperial government trying to devolve responsibility for taxation onto various powerful groups or individuals within or outside the city: local landowners, (semi-)imperial officials, such as *exactores* (who formerly had often been *curiales*), *vindices* and *canonicarii* or even the provincial governor. Ultimately, such *ad hoc* measures undermined the fiscal and administrative role of the cities in the empire, and by implication also the administrative hold of cities over their territories. In the Byzantine Empire after the seventh century CE, taxation was no longer city-based.[33]

In the West, the picture is more mixed. In Britain, cities seem virtually to have disappeared by the end of the fourth century CE, whereas in southern Spain, Italy and North Africa, civic life along late Roman lines continued for far longer.[34] In northern Gaul and in the former German and Balkan provinces, however, during the fifth and sixth centuries many cities (with the exception of provincial or royal capitals) shrank to fortified sites, under the impact, partly, of barbarian invasions, with a defensive wall enclosing a few military and ecclesiastical structures.[35]

One factor traditionally thought to have undermined cities' control of their territories in parts of the West (Gaul, Spain) was what we might call the 'ruralisation of social power', that is, the wealthiest and most powerful individuals from the cities withdrew to often fortified country estates (villas), which became new local power centres (largely) independent of civic control, though this development is much discussed and should certainly not be interpreted as a wholesale 'feudalisation' of the West, as it has been by some scholars in the past.[36]

---

[32] Brown (1971); Mitchell (1993) 2: 122–50; Liebeschuetz (2001) 63–74; Wickham (2005) 406–11 .
[33] Liebeschuetz (2001) 122–4; Wickham (2005) 68–70.
[34] Lepelley (1979–1981), (1992) on North Africa; Reece (1992) on Britain; Liebeschuetz (2001) 74–103 for the West in general; Kulikowski (2004) on Spain.
[35] Liebeschuetz (2001) 74–86.
[36] Whittaker and Garnsey (1998) 299–304 and 307–11 for nuanced discussion.

In Merovingian Gaul and Visigothic Spain, the responsibility for collecting taxes eventually came to rest with royal officials.[37] As in the East, this undoubtedly loosened the traditional ties between cities and their territories. In Italy, the old heartland of the former Roman Empire, some aspects of curial government may have lasted longest, with *curiales* still playing some role in tax collection, and thus retaining some form of administrative control over their territories, well into the Ostrogothic period and later still. With a few debated exceptions, however, *curiales* disappear from view in Italy during the seventh century CE, and with them, presumably, the last vestiges of the ancient civic model in which town and country were integrated within a single social, political and administrative unit.[38]

None of the above of course necessarily implies that the cities of the fourth, fifth and sixth centuries and beyond did not flourish economically during some parts of this long period, particularly in the East, but also here and there in the West. Though, especially in some parts of the West (e.g. Britain), cities did shrink or even disappear, what we are discussing, once again, is primarily the disappearance of a certain model of urban life and organisation, i.e. that of the ancient city. So how did cities fare economically, during late antiquity, and did the patterns of their economic life still resemble those of earlier periods?

Archaeological evidence has in recent decades radically altered the almost uniformly pessimistic interpretation of the later Roman economy traditionally espoused by historians. Especially cities in (parts of) the East seem to have continued to flourish and indeed experienced a remarkable efflorescence in the fifth and sixth centuries CE, even despite the onslaught of bubonic plague during the reign of Justinian, as is attested in the Near East (Jordan, Palestine, Syria) and parts of Asia Minor and Macedon by major building works in cities even after 550 CE, the possession of considerable treasure in church and elite hands and the continued presence in cities of relatively abundant quantities of low denomination copper coinage.[39] In the West, North African cities flourished and even expanded during the fourth and early fifth centuries, and in Italy too, urban economic life on the Roman model seems to have continued for a long time.[40]

As recently argued forcefully by Bryan Ward-Perkins, however, from the fifth century onwards, with the unravelling of the western Roman Empire,

[37] Liebeschuetz (2001) 130 and 134; Wickham (2005) 69–70, 96–115.
[38] Liebeschuetz (2001) 127 with references.   [39] Whittow (1990) 13–20, (1996) 59–68, (2001).
[40] Lepelley (1979), (1992); Ward-Perkins (1984).

urban and overall economic decline in many parts of the West was
pronounced, eventually plunging the inhabitants of some regions back to
a standard of living well below immediate pre-Roman conquest levels.[41]
This suggests, as Ward-Perkins also argues, that Roman economic structures were sufficiently complex to be vulnerable to a systemic collapse. So
what did the urban economies of late antique cities look like?

To begin with, there is no clear evidence for a large-scale and permanent
retreat to the countryside by civic grandees from the later third century
onwards (as presupposed in earlier scholarship), despite the scattered indications from some areas of the West (e.g. northern Spain, northern Gaul).
This suggests that by and large, as in earlier periods of Greco-Roman
history, civic elites during late antiquity continued to be composed chiefly
of large landowners, who spent a significant part of their agrarian rent-
incomes in the cities.[42] Economically, it does not of course matter whether
these large landowners were *decuriones/curiales* or senatorial (ex-)imperial
officials and clergymen, i.e. the notables who came to dominate late Roman
and post-Roman cities. In Chapters 3 and 8, we saw that as a spin-off from
the expenditure of agrarian rent-based elite incomes there developed in
Greek and Roman cities highly specialised and diversified commercial
economies, generating also, in time, many commercial links between cities.
Given that landowning civic elites remained a prominent feature of late
antique cities, this urban economic model most likely continued to exist.

Indeed, there is good evidence for the continuation of a highly specialised artisanal and service economy in late antique cities, including the
Diocletianic price edict, the fifth- and sixth-century CE funerary epigraphy
from Korykos (referred to in Chapter 8) and the numerous categories of
tradesmen mentioned in the *Codex Theodosianus*.[43] This picture is further
reinforced, for parts of the East, by archaeological evidence for a continued
flourishing of urban commerce and manufacture.[44] In times of crisis, such
specialisation and economic complexity might come at a cost, however, as
a sufficiently large external shock may trigger a 'systems collapse', leaving
the survivors, who suddenly have to become 'economic generalists' again,
in considerable confusion.[45] In the West, the barbarian invasions and the

---

[41] Ward-Perkins (2005), esp. 117–21, 136–7.
[42] Garnsey and Whittaker (1998); Wickham (2005) 602–9 documents the continued urban residence
of local landowning elites throughout large parts of the late Roman and post-Roman world during
the period 400–800 CE. He convincingly argues (594–5, 706–8) that 'aristocratic spending-power'
(594) was and remained the primary economic basis of urbanism during these centuries.
[43] Garnsey and Whittaker (1998) 325 for references.   [44] See the survey in Wickham (2005) 609–26.
[45] On 'systems collapse', see Renfrew (1979), cited by Ward-Perkins (2005) 136–7, 210n25.

collapse of the western empire during the fifth century CE were such an external shock, according to Ward-Perkins.[46] In the East, the Persian wars and the Islamic conquests of the seventh century CE might have triggered similar shockwaves and consequent decline of economic systems, though perhaps not everywhere as pronounced or long-lasting as in the West.[47]

In sociocultural terms, the changes in civic society from the high empire to late antiquity were profound, even if they manifested themselves only slowly at first. The primary cause here, more perhaps than in other spheres, save maybe in the urban landscape, was the Christianisation of the empire. Of course, there were many elements of continuity as well – to name but one, the bishop and the higher clergy were mostly drawn from the same civic and imperial elites that traditionally provided (and continued to provide) the civic magistrates and imperial officials, and thus they shared with the latter the traditional elite background of training in pagan literature and rhetoric (*paideia*) – but in other respects the changes were fundamental.[48] They comprised what Peter Brown has called 'a revolution in the social imagination that accompanied the rise and establishment of the Christian Church in the Roman empire' between 300 and 600 CE.[49]

Though Greek and Roman urban societies consisted of a number of socioeconomic and status groups, with the citizen body (adult male citizens) being just one among them, politically and ideologically, the citizen-community had always been central to the ancient urban social vision. The figure who best exemplified this vision, which Brown terms 'the civic model of society', was that of the civic benefactor, the rich citizen who uses his private wealth for the benefit of his community. Civic benefactors gave, first and foremost, to their fellow-citizens, not to the poor *per se*: they did not practise charity.[50] Care for the poor, a focus on the poor as a specific social group in need of gifts (alms), was mostly a Judeo-Christian concern. This was not, as Brown writes, because classical civic benefactors were more 'hard-hearted'. Rather, social models, as idealised visions of society which people hold on to, necessarily generate 'invisible boundaries beyond which contemporaries [are] little inclined to think about their world'.[51]

[46] Ward-Perkins (2005), esp. 136–7.
[47] Loseby (2012) for general discussion; Foss (1975) on Asia Minor. Note that in Syrian and Palestinian cities, artisanal activity continued well into the Arab period, even while city centres and public areas were 'demonumentalized', see Wickham (2005) 616–18.
[48] Brown (1992).   [49] Brown (2002) 1 and *passim*, (2012) 53–90.
[50] Veyne (1976); Zuiderhoek (2009a).
[51] Brown (2002) 6–9 (quote from p. 9). The basic notion of a transition in late antique cities from a Greco-Roman civic model of society towards a Near Eastern or Judeo-Christian-inspired model focussed on the rich and the poor goes back to the works of Bolkestein (1939) and Patlagean (1977),

Brown links the rise, and ultimate success, of a novel vision of urban society as divided primarily between rich and poor, with an unceasing obligation on the rich to care for the poor, to the growing social and political power of the Christian bishops as urban leaders from the reign of Constantine onwards. Bishops were inveterate fundraisers, tirelessly promoting almsgiving to the poor.[52] They came to control the flows of money that resulted from the charity towards the poor that Judeo-Christian tradition demanded of the (wealthy) faithful. Bishops became stewards (*oikonomoi*) of the wealth of their church, which was spent on the poor and weak within the Christian communities, for the poor, of course, were made of the same human flesh as the rich, the same flesh which Christ himself had shared when he walked among men, and often, among the poor.[53] Among Christians, humanity as such, not citizenship, was thought to be the common denominator uniting society.

After Constantine, those members of the civic elites who were Christians extended their traditional euergetism increasingly towards the urban poor as well as to the church and its clergy, while the increasing wealth of the church and the social, political and, crucially, judicial power of the bishops (backed by the emperors) drew the traditional 'middling groups' of urban society towards the church, where they came to be included among those worthy of Christian charity alongside the truly poor.[54] One way in which this new inclusiveness was achieved and legitimated, as Richard Finn has shown, was through a deliberate vagueness concerning who qualified as 'the poor' (*pauperes*) that characterised the discourse of the chief promoters of the new social model, the bishops and clergy. In their sermons and homilies, bishops often spoke of the poor simply as those in need of charity from the rich, thus carefully avoiding any differentiation between the conjunctural poor and the structural poor or the truly destitute (i.e. beggars). Rich and poor formed an organic community, in which there was no place for the contempt that Greco-Roman urban elites had traditionally expressed towards their social inferiors and the destitute: anyone who was in need was worthy of charity.[55]

---

as Brown acknowledges. Brown, however, puts particular stress on 'the bishops and their helpers – lay and clerical alike' as the 'agents of change' (p. 8).

[52] See Finn (2006a) 34–89. I have borrowed the image of the bishop as a fundraiser from Serfass's (2007) review of Finn's book. On the realities of late antique poverty and the organisation of almsgiving, see also Neri (1998) 33–132.

[53] Brown (2002) 19–26.   [54] Brown (2002) 5–6, (2012) 79–81.

[55] Finn (2006b). Such Patristic discourse was, of course, primarily aimed at the wealthy, the greatest potential source of charitable donations, see MacMullen (1989); Grig (2006) 159: 'Eminent preachers like John Chrysostom and Augustine told their wealthy congregation how they should use their property correctly'.

The thesis of the shift in the civic social imagination fits well with, and provides a broad interpretative context for, the decline of curial government described above, and its replacement with rule by 'notables', among whom bishop and clergy were prominent. Still, it should not be overstated (as Brown himself acknowledges). For one thing, charity to the poor was not a Christian invention: almsgiving is already attested in the pagan Greco-Roman world, albeit sporadically.[56] Moreover, some phenomena associated with the 'civic model of society' proved remarkably tenacious, among them 'classical munificence', i.e. gifts towards games, shows and traditional public buildings. Though much reduced in frequency when compared to its heyday in the second century CE, such munificence did remain an abiding element of late antique civic culture and it was vigorously preached against by bishops in need of a convenient rhetorical scapegoat with wide societal resonance.[57]

On the whole, however, far more elite gifts now went to the church and clergy. The enduring social exclusion of slaves, who were not entitled to the bishop's charity, was another inheritance from the classical city.[58] Yet those free persons for whom there had formerly hardly been any place in the civic vision of society, the poorest, the social outcasts, the widows and orphans, the sick and elderly infirm, now came within the scope of the powers-that-be.[59] Not only were they entitled to charity (even if one may doubt whether what they received truly made much difference to their overall standard of living[60]), but also, as fellow-Christians, to burial in the consecrated ground of a church cemetery[61], sometimes within the city walls. This brings us to the built environment of the late antique city, the element of urban life where the new, Christian vision of society had the most clearly visible material impact.

Urban Landscape

The historian Procopius, detailing the emperor Justinian's embellishment of a city in Bithynia originally founded by Constantine (on the site of the

---

[56] Parkin (2006).

[57] Civic munificence, of course, absorbed elite wealth that might otherwise have been available to the church for charity, see Brown (2002) 28–9, (2012) 62–71; also Harries (2003); Lepelley (1979–1981).

[58] On late antique slavery, see Harper (2011).

[59] Finn (2006a) 74–6 on the recipients of episcopal charity. There appears to have been some sort of hierarchy of entitlement, with widows, orphans and poor virgins enrolled on the church's list (*matricula*) having first claim. After them came sick and elderly Christian beggars, i.e. those unable to work, then a range of people with 'competing claims' (p. 76), among them captives and the suddenly impoverished, both Christians and non-Christians. See also Neri (1998) 97–102.

[60] Note Finn (2006a) 88: 'The recipients [of episcopal almsgiving] were not lifted out of poverty, but kept from starvation'.

[61] Even if only anonymously, in communal graves, see Brown (2002) 109–10 on sixth-century Antioch.

village where the latter's mother Helena was born, therefore suitably named Helenopolis), describes in glowing terms the result of Justinian's intervention. After securing the city's water supply by means of a 'marvellous' new aqueduct, the emperor 'made for them a public bath which had not existed before, and he rebuilt another which was damaged and lay abandoned'. And as if that was not enough, Justinian also 'built here churches and a palace and stoas and lodgings for the magistrates, and in other respects he gave it the appearance of a prosperous city' (*Aed.* 5.2.1–5).[62]

Such depictions of cities, of which more can be found in Procopius' panegyric on Justinian's building programme in the eastern empire, strongly recall the classical, Greco-Roman ideal of the urban landscape (though note the churches). However, while cities of this type seemed to many late antique observers 'to be the embodiment of culture', the classical urban model 'was already coming under strain when Procopius wrote', in the mid-sixth century CE, as Averil Cameron has noted.[63] Partly, this was the result of decline, particularly in various regions of the West during the fifth and sixth centuries, but mostly of profound transformation. For instance, walls, which cities of the early and high Roman Empire had often lacked (unless they were Roman colonies or had them as a leftover of their Republican or Hellenistic past) were starting to reappear or were rebuilt from the third century CE onwards, and became a distinctive feature of late antique cities.[64] Often, late antique circuit walls already betray a reordering of priorities with regard to the shape of the urban landscape: construction material might be derived from traditional public buildings, which were used as quarries, and sometimes the new wall would by-pass vital elements of the classical urban landscape, as at Ephesus, where the agoras where left outside the new late antique city wall.[65]

The changes in political culture outlined above made themselves felt in the urban landscape. As government by city councils gave way to more informal rule by notables and the growing power of bishop and clergy, traditional public buildings, such as the council house (*curia/bouleuterion*), *prytaneion* or civic basilica, fell into disrepair, were quarried for construction material or were adapted to a different purpose. Churches now often housed civic archives.[66] Except for a while in imperial and provincial

[62] Tr. H. B. Dewing, Loeb Classical Library.   [63] Cameron (2012) 152.
[64] Christie (2001); Provost (2001); Ratté (2001) 125–7 on Aphrodisias.
[65] Liebeschuetz (2001) 32–4; Loseby (2009) 151; Whittow (2001) 140–2 on Hierapolis.
[66] Liebeschuetz (2001) 29–32 and *passim*.

capitals, where imperial funding might be more easily forthcoming, classical civic structures (theatres, gymnasia, bath houses) and temples similarly were allowed to decay, were looted for material or re-used for residential or commercial purposes. To the chagrin of Christian critics, circus games (chariot racing) nevertheless enjoyed a remarkable popularity in late antique cities, and financial support for the associated structures as well as the games themselves was for a long time available from urban elites.[67]

A change in the perception of urban public space is nonetheless clearly visible: the wide colonnaded streets typical of the ancient Greco-Roman city 'were invaded and divided up by intrusive structures, both houses and shops, and became more like narrow winding lanes', especially in the East, as stoas developed into souks.[68] Agoras and fora remained in use for a long time, given that they continued to be eminently suited to commerce and the representation, through statues and monuments, of aristocratic and imperial power. Yet from the later fifth century onwards, repair works became more haphazard, and fora and agoras were increasingly built over. Significantly, churches might be built on or near them, or existing public buildings near the agora might be converted into churches.[69] It was indeed Christianity which perhaps most profoundly changed the ancient urban landscapes. Every city needed a number of churches, which, by the fifth and sixth centuries, came to dot the cityscape.[70] Shrines were erected at the tombs of saints, and imperial and civic elite munificence poured not just into churches but also into other new building types associated with Christianity, such as hostels, monasteries and hospitals.[71] Churches even came to assume civic functions, as imperial letters were read out there, and decrees and ordinances were posted in the church, while church atria served as locations for judicial audiences before bishops, and as common meeting places.[72]

In general, the continuing but reduced role of cities as adminstrative centres in many parts of the post-Roman world was reflected in a reduced, or at least thoroughly restructured, urban landscape, as, for instance, in the 'institutional model' of post-Roman urban continuity sketched by Simon Loseby for cities in sixth-century CE Gaul. A building to house the count

[67] Liebeschuetz (2001) 203–20; Whitby (2006).
[68] Kennedy (1985) 4–5 for the quote; Ward-Perkins (1998) 381–3; Wickham (2005) 615–20.
[69] Lavan (2006).
[70] On the late antique church-building boom, see Jäggi and Meier (1997); also Jacobs (2013) on Asia Minor.
[71] Loseby (2009) 149; on hospitals see Horden (2005).   [72] Lavan (2003) 324–5.

and his staff (*palatium*), an archive, an open space for markets and gatherings, a cathedral complex and some space, outside the city, for military musters: this might suffice to accommodate a city's enduring administrative, economic, military and religious role in the post-Roman West.[73] Here, of course, we are in a world far removed from the heavily monumentalised city centres of the high Roman Empire.

So when, and how, did the ancient city come to its end? In this chapter, we have surveyed several profound transformations that occurred in cities during the late antique and post-Roman periods, in civic politics and administration, in urban economy and society and in the built environment. Without doubt there was a decline of cities in some areas, in parts of the West from the fifth century CE onwards, and in parts of the East during the sixth and seventh centuries CE. For the cities that remained, however, the end result of the complex processes of change and transformation discussed in this chapter need not necessarily be viewed in terms of a generalised decline of urban culture. These cities often retained their functions as commercial, religious, cultural and political centres, and some still boasted impressive urban landscapes. Structurally, however, they had changed so profoundly that we can no longer call them ancient cities.

---

[73] Loseby (2006) 94, though Loseby notes that such a model is to some extent 'forced upon us' by the poor state of the evidence for other aspects of contemporary urbanism, i.e. the role of cities in economic networks and the composition of the urban populations. For 'demonumentalization' in the East see Wickham (2005) 614–26.

Bibliographical Essay

The scholarly literature on ancient urbanism, both archaeological and historical, is immense. In this essay, therefore, I follow the same strategy that I have employed throughout this book. I focus on those aspects, debates and theories that seem to me most important and interesting given the needs and requirements of comparative urban history. The selection is biased towards works in English published during the last forty years.

COMPARATIVE APPROACHES

Comparative urban studies are a venerable tradition within archaeology. Childe (1950) on the 'Urban Revolution' is classic; Smith (2009) discusses the impact of Childe's theory on subsequent scholarship. Cowgill (2004) presents a bibliographical overview of mainly archaeological work on early cities across the globe, including Greece and Rome. Smith (2003a), Storey (2006b) and Marcus and Sabloff (2008a) contain a plethora of studies of (aspects of) urbanism in many premodern societies, including Classical Antiquity; note also Adams (1966). See Hansen (2000) and (2002a) for a wide range of studies of so-called city-state cultures around the world, again including Greco-Roman antiquity. Abrams and Wrigley (1978) is a classic collection of socioeconomic studies on cities in many historical periods and parts of the world, including Keith Hopkins' famous essay on towns and economic growth in Classical Antiquity, see Hopkins (1978). Clark (2009) offers an up-to-date historical survey of cities and towns in Europe between 400–2000 CE while Clark (2013) now provides the best starting point for anyone attempting to engage in research on comparative urban history. Jansen (1996) offers an interesting and wide-ranging reflection on the problems of definition in urban history, with many references to long-standing debates and schools of thought.

GENERAL STUDIES, OVERVIEWS AND COLLECTIONS

This book has mainly been about debates and theories. For readers of German, Kolb (1984) offers a thorough and comprehensive introduction to the city in Greece, Rome and the Near East. Beard (2008) is a splendidly evocative introduction to life in one particularly famous ancient town. Gates (2011) provides a broad overview of the archaeology of urban life in the Near East, Egypt, Greece and Rome. See also Owens (1992). Finley (1982) discusses nineteenth- and early twentieth-century debates on Greek and Roman urbanism and offers a strongly Weberian model of the ancient city; see also Finley (1999). The post-Finley debate produced a number of collections on various aspects of Greek and Roman urbanism, see Rich and Wallace-Hadrill (1991); Cornell and Lomas (1995); Parkins (1997); and Parkins and Smith (1998). On the alleged unimportance of cities in the wider ecological scheme of things see the challenging discussion in Horden and Purcell (2000, 89–122). The (supposedly) Eurocentric nature of modern studies of the Greek polis is argued by Vlassopoulos (2007). On the Archaic and Classical Greek polis, see Murray and Price (1990), an important collection of papers, but above all the prodigious output of the Copenhagen Polis Centre (*floruit* 1993–2005) and its former director Mogens Herman Hansen. See Hansen (2003), (2006) for syntheses of the Centre's results, with overviews of all related publications, and Hansen and Heine Nielsen (2004), an inventory of all known Archaic and Classical poleis. On the post-Classical (i.e. Hellenistic and Roman-era) polis, Jones (1940) remains fundamental. The post-Classical polis currently enjoys a vogue, see for example Alston and Van Nijf (2008); Van Nijf, Alston and Williamson (2011); Alston, Van Nijf and Williamson (2013); Martzavou and Papazarkadas (2013); and Rapp and Drake (2014), all important collections of studies. See Parrish (2001) for a collection of archaeological contributions on eastern Greek cities. Laurence, Esmonde Cleary and Sears (2011) offer an insightful overview of urbanism in the Roman West; see also Stambaugh (1988). Fentress (2000) collects various mainly archaeological contributions on the transformation of cities under the influence of Roman rule. Dobbins and Foss (2007) provide a host of perspectives on Pompeii, and they offer a good complement to Beard (2008). On the city of Rome, now see Erdkamp (2013) as a first port of call.

BEGINNINGS AND ENDINGS

On Archaic Mediterranean urbanisation, see the contributions in Osborne and Cunliffe (2005); on the origins of the polis, see Mitchell and Rhodes (1997); Osborne (2009); Morris (1991), (2000), (2006), (2009); Snodgrass (1980), (1993); and Raaflaub (1993). On early Rome and the Latin civitates, see Cornell (1995), (2000) and Smith (1996), (1997), (2005). Malkin (2009), (2011) offers the best modern discussion of Greek 'colonisation'. See Morris (2006) for an overview of the growth and spread of Greek cities during the first millennium BCE; Jones (1940) and Cohen (1995), (2006), (2013) on the spread of poleis during the Hellenistic period. For early Roman colonisation, see Cornell (1995) chapters 14 and 15; see also Stek and Pelgrom (2014); on western Roman cities see Edmondson (2006) and Laurence, Esmonde Cleary and Sears (2011). Liebeschuetz (2001) offers a comprehensive account of the decline of the Greco-Roman city and its institutions during late antiquity; see Whittow (1990) for a different perspective. Rich (1992); Lavan (2001a) and Krause and Witschel (2006) collect many contributions from both historians and archaeologists on the 'decline vs. transformation' controversy. Wickham (2005) offers a detailed overview of the socioeconomic history of late antique and early medieval Europe and the Mediterranean, including a long section on cities. Brown (2002) and (2012) presents a masterly evocation of the profound changes in civic culture in the late antique city.

CITY-COUNTRY AND URBAN LANDSCAPE

Finley (1982) and (1999) provides the now classic analyses of Greek and Roman cities as consumer cities and explicitly links the prevalence of cities of this type in the ancient world to the *comparative* underdevelopment of trade and markets in antiquity (his implicit, sometimes explicit, comparison is always with cities in later medieval and early modern Europe). See also Jongman (1991) on Pompeii and Hopkins (1978); Whittaker (1990); and Morley (1996) on the city of Rome. For criticism, see many of the contributions in Rich and Wallace-Hadrill (1991); Cornell and Lomas (1995); Parkins (1997); Parkins and Smith (1998); and Mattingly and Salmon (2001a). Hansen (2004) and Vlassopoulos (2007) for criticism of the model as applied to the Greek polis. Erdkamp (2001) convincingly demonstrates that there is no *a priori* reason why city-country relations of the consumer city-type should imply an underdeveloped commercial economy, thus invalidating much existing criticism of the model; see also Erdkamp (2012). Patterson (2006) and Bintliff (2008) discuss the results of decades of survey archaeology in Italy and Greece. On urbanisation and urban networks, particularly for the Roman world, see Woolf (1997); Morley (1996), (1997) and the contributions in Bowman and Wilson (2011), particularly those by Marzano (2011) and Hanson (2011). On the urban landscape, see Gates (2011) and Wycherley (1949) on Greek cities. Camp (1986) summarises over half a century of research on and around the Athenian agora. See Cahill (2002) on Olynthus and Parrish (2001) on Greek cities in Asia Minor. Zanker (1990) is a classic analysis of the urban landscape of Augustan Rome. Much innovative work on ancient urban landscapes understandably concentrates on the Vesuvian cities, see for example Laurence (1994) and Laurence and Newsome (2011); but note Goodman (2007); Kaiser (2011); Laurence, Esmonde Cleary and Sears (2011); and Dickenson and Van Nijf (2013).

URBAN ECONOMY, STRATIFICATION ('MIDDLING GROUPS') AND CIVIC CULTURE ('COLLECTIVE ACTIVITIES')

Bresson (2007), (2008) and Migeotte (2009) survey Greek urban economies from the Archaic period until the end of the Hellenistic age/well into the early Roman Empire respectively. See Harris (2002) on crafts, trades and specialisation in Classical Athens. For Roman cities, see Jongman (1991) on Pompeii, and Jongman

(2000) on the urban textile industry in Roman Italy; MacMahon and Price (2005) on crafts, trades and workshops; Flohr (2013a) on fullers' workshops in Roman Italy; and Holleran (2012) on the retail trade in the city of Rome. On occupational specialisation, see Treggiari (1980); Joshel (1992); Ruffing (2008); and Holleran (2012). For Greek civic finances, see Migeotte (2014). On urban building, see Salmon (1999), (2001); Anderson (1997); and DeLaine (2000). On civic intervention in the urban food supply, see Garnsey (1988) for Greece and Rome; Moreno (2007) and Oliver (2007), both on Athens; Erdkamp (2005) chapters 5 and 6 and Zuiderhoek (2008b) on the Roman Empire. Kamen (2013) surveys status distinctions in Classical Athens. On *metoikoi*, see Whitehead (1977) and Wijma (2014) on the religious participation of Athenian metics. On cooperation between citizens and non-citizens, see Cohen (2000) and Vlassopoulos (2007b). See Davies (1971), (1981) on socioeconomic differentiation within the Athenian citizenry. On the 'middling ideology' and middling groups in Greek poleis, see Morris (1996), (2000) and Ober (2010); on associations in Classical Athens, see Jones (1999); Gabrielsen (2001) on Hellenistic Rhodes. On Roman middling groups and the *plebs media*, see Veyne (2000); Scheidel (2006) and also, with some reservations, Mouritsen (2015). See Van Nijf (1997); Verboven (2007); Zuiderhoek (2008a) on *plebs media* and professional associations (*collegia*). Research on Roman *collegia* proliferates, see for example Royden (1988); Van Nijf (1997); Tran (2006); Verboven (2007), (2011); Liu (2009); and Broekaert (2011). Mouritsen (2011) offers a comprehensive treatment of Roman freedmen (*liberti*). See Schmitt Pantel (1990), (1992) for the concept of civic collective activities. See Iddeng (2012) on Greek and Roman festivals; Marshall (2000) on hero cult at Cyrene; Chaniotis (1995) on Hellenistic civic festivals; Mitchell (1990) on civic festivals in the Roman period; Rogers (1991) for a close-reading of a festival at Roman Ephesus. See Van Nijf (1997) on *collegia*, banquets, processions and civic hierarchy; and Zuiderhoek (2009a) on euergetism, festivals, civic hierarchy and legitimation.

CIVIC POLITICS, CITY AND STATE

Finley (1983) and (1985) are essential reading on ancient city politics and democracy, putting both in a wider theoretical and intellectual context (i.e. the debate on R. Michels' 'Iron Law of Oligarchy'). Mitchell (2006) provides a succinct overview of political institutions in the Greek polis. Ehrenberg (1969) is a classic. On Athenian democracy, Ober (1989) and Hansen (1991) are important studies; see also Ober and Hedrick (1996). On democracy in other Archaic and Classical poleis, see Robinson (1997), (2011) and Ostwald (2000) on oligarchic poleis. On politics and the supposed decline of democracy in Hellenistic and Roman-era poleis, see for example Jones (1940) and Quass (1993), emphasising 'oligarchisation'. See Grieb (2008); Carlsson (2010) and Mann and Scholz (2012) for the Hellenistic period and Ma (2000) and Zuiderhoek (2008a), both for the Roman period, who stress continuation of popular politics. On political institutions in

Bibliography

Abbott, F. F. and A. C. Johnson (1926) *Municipal administration in the Roman empire*. Princeton.

Abramenko, A. (1993) *Die munizipale Mittelschicht im kaiserzeitlichen Italien: zu einem neuen Verständnis von Sevirat und Augustalität*. Frankfurt.

Abrams, P. and E. A. Wrigley eds. (1978) *Towns in societies: essays in economic history and historical sociology*. Cambridge.

Acemoglu, D. and J. A. Robinson (2012) *Why nations fail: the origins of power, prosperity and poverty*. New York.

Adams, R. McC. (1966) *The evolution of urban society: urban Mesopotamia and Prehispanic Mexico*. Chicago.

Ades, A. F. and E. L. Glaeser (1995), 'Trade and circuses: explaining urban giants', *The Quarterly Journal of Economics* 110(1): 195–227.

Adkins, A. W. H. (1972) *Moral values and political behaviour in Ancient Greece: from Homer to the end of the fifth century*. London.

Alcock, S. E. (1993) *Graecia capta: the landscapes of Roman Greece*. Cambridge.

Alcock, S. E. and R. Osborne eds. (2007) *Classical archaeology*. Blackwell Studies in Global Archaeology. Malden, Oxford & Carlton.

Alföldy, G. (1984) *Römische Sozialgeschichte*. Wiesbaden.

Alston, R. and O. M. van Nijf eds. (2008) *Feeding the Ancient Greek city*. Groningen-Royal Holloway Studies on the Greek City after the Classical Age 1. Leuven.

Alston, R., O. M. van Nijf and C. G. Williamson eds. (2013) *Cults, creeds and identities in the Greek city after the Classical Age*. Groningen-Royal Holloway Studies on the Greek City after the Classical Age 3. Leuven.

Anderson, B. (2006) *Imagined communities: reflections on the origins and spread of nationalism*. Rev. edn. London & New York.

Anderson, G. (2009) 'The personality of the Greek state', *JHS* 129: 1–22.

Anderson, J. C. (1997) *Roman architecture and society*. Baltimore & London.

Ando, C. (2000) *Imperial ideology and provincial loyalty in the Roman Empire*. Berkeley.

Andrewes, A. (1966) 'The government of Classical Sparta', in E. Badian ed. *Ancient society and institutions: studies presented to Victor Ehrenberg on his 75th birthday*. Oxford, 1–20.

Arnaoutoglou, I. (2011) "'Ils étaient dans la ville, mais tout à fait en dehors de la cité': status and identity in private religious associations in Hellenistic Athens', in van Nijf, Alston and Williamson eds. *Political culture in the Greek city after the classical age*. Groningen-Royal Holloway Studies on the Greek City after the Classical Age 2. Leuven, 27–48.

Atkins, M. and R. Osborne eds. (2006) *Poverty in the Roman world*. Cambridge.

Austin, M. M. and P. Vidal-Naquet (1977) *Economic and social history of Ancient Greece: an introduction*. London.

Bagnall, R. (1992) 'Landholding in late Roman Egypt', *JRS* 82: 128–49.

Bagnall, R. and P. Derow eds. (2004) *The Hellenistic period: historical sources in translation*. Oxford.

Bang, P. F. (2008) *The Roman bazaar: a comparative study of trade and markets in a tributary empire*. Cambridge.

(2012) 'Predation', in Scheidel ed. *The Cambridge companion to the Roman economy*. Cambridge, 197–217.

Beard, M. (2007) *The Roman triumph*. Cambridge, MA.

(2008) *Pompeii: the life of a Roman town*. London.

Beetham, D. (1991) *The legitimation of power*. Basingstoke.

Berent, M. (1998) 'Stasis, or the Greek invention of politics', *History of Political Thought* 19(3): 331–62.

(2000a) 'Anthropology and the classics: war, violence and the stateless polis', *CQ* 50: 257–89.

(2000b) 'Sovereignty: ancient and modern', *Polis* 17(1–2): 2–34.

(2004) 'In search of the Greek state: a rejoinder to M. H. Hansen', *Polis* 21(1–2): 107–46.

(2006) 'The stateless polis: a reply to critics', *Social Evolution & History* 5(1): 141–63.

Bert Lott, J. (2004) *The neighborhoods of Augustan Rome*. Cambridge.

Betts, E. (2011) 'Towards a multisensory experience of movement in the city of Rome', in Laurence and Newsome eds. *Rome, Ostia, Pompeii: movement and space*. Oxford, 118–32.

Billows, R. A. (1990) *Antigonos the One-Eyed and the creation of the Hellenistic state*. Berkeley & Los Angeles.

Bintliff, J. (2002) 'Going to market in antiquity', in E. Olshausen and H. Sonnabend eds., *Zu Wasser und zu Land: Verkehrswege in der antiken Welt. Stuttgarter Kolloquium zur historischen Geographie des Altertums 7, 1999*. Geographica Historica Bd. 17. Stuttgart, 209–50.

(2008) 'Considerations on agricultural scale-economies in the Greco-Roman world', in Alston and van Nijf, *Feeding the Ancient Greek city*. Groningen-Royal Holloway Studies on the Greek City after the Classical Age 1. Leuven, 17–31.

Bissa, E. (2009) *Governmental intervention in foreign trade in archaic and Classical Greece*. Leiden.

Blok, J. H. (2005) 'Becoming citizens: some notes on the semantics of "citizen" in Classical Athens', *Klio* 87(1): 7–40.

(2007) 'Fremde, Bürger und Baupolitik im klassischen Athen', *Historische Anthropologie* 15: 309–26.

(2014) 'A "covenant" between gods and men: *hiera kai hosia* and the Greek *polis*', in Rapp and Drake eds., *The city in the Classical and post-Classical world: changing contexts of power and identity*. Cambridge, 14–37.

Bodel, J. (2000) 'Dealing with the dead: undertakers, executioners and potters' fields in Ancient Rome', in Hope and Marshall eds. *Death and disease in the ancient city*. London, 128–51.

Bolkestein, H. (1939) *Wohltätigkeit und Armenpflege im vorchristlichen Altertum*. Utrecht.

Boone, M. (2013) 'Medieval Europe', in P. Clark ed. *The Oxford handbook of cities in world history*. Oxford, 221–39.

Bosker, M., E. Buringh and J. L. van Zanden (2008) 'From Baghdad to London: The dynamics of urban development in Europe and the Arab world, 800–1800', www2.econ.uu.nl/users/marrewijk/newgeo/pdf/bagdadnaarlondon-dec2008 .pdf.

(2013) 'From Baghdad to London: unravelling urban development in Europe, the Middle East, and North Africa, 800–1800', *The Review of Economics and Statistics* 95(4): 1418–37.

Bowden, H. (1993) 'Hoplites and Homer: warfare, hero cult and the ideology of the polis', in Rich and Shipley eds. *War and society in the Greek world*. London & New York, 45–63.

Bowman, A. K. and A. Wilson eds. (2011) *Settlement, urbanization, and population*. Oxford Studies on the Roman Economy. Oxford.

Boyd, T. D. and M. H. Jameson (1981) 'Urban and rural land division in Ancient Greece', *Hesperia* 50(4): 327–42.

Braudel, F. (1981) *The structures of everyday life: the limits of the possible. Civilization and capitalism 15th–18th century vol. 1*. New York [French original 1979].

Brélaz, C. (2005) *La sécurité publique en Asie Mineure sous le Principat (Ier-IIIème s. ap. J.-C.)*. Basel.

Brenner, R. (1976) 'Agrarian class structure and economic development in pre-industrial Europe', *Past & Present* 70: 30–75.

Bresson, A. (2000) 'Prix officiels et commerce de gros à Athènes', in A. Bresson, *La cité marchande*. Paris, 182–210.

(2007) *L'économie de la Grèce des cités (fin VIe-Ier siècle a. C.) I: les structures et la production*. Paris.

(2008) *L'économie de la Grèce des cités (fin VIe-Ier siècle a. C.) II: les espaces de l'échange*. Paris.

Bringmann, K. (1993) 'The king as benefactor: some remarks on ideal kingship in the age of Hellenism', in A. Bulloch, E. S. Gruen, A. A. Long and A. Stewart eds., *Images and ideologies: self-definition in the Hellenistic world*. Berkeley, 7–24.

Broekaert, W. (2011) 'Partners in business: Roman merchants and the potential advantages of being a *collegiatus*', *Ancient Society* 41: 221–56.

(2012) 'Vertical integration in the Roman economy: a response to Morris Silver', *Ancient Society* 42: 109–25.

Broekaert, W. and A. Zuiderhoek (2013) 'Industries and services', in Erdkamp ed. *The Cambridge companion to Ancient Rome*. Cambridge, 317–35.

Brown, P. (1971) 'The rise and function of the holy man in Late Antiquity', *JRS* 61: 80–101.

(1992) *Power and persuasion in late antiquity: towards a Christian empire*. Madison, WI.

(2002) *Poverty and leadership in the later Roman Empire*. Hanover, NH.

(2012) *Through the eye of a needle: wealth, the fall of Rome, and the making of Christianity in the West, 350–550 AD*. Princeton.

Brunt, P. A. (1971) *Social conflicts in the Roman Republic*. London.

(1982) 'Nobilitas and novitas', *JRS* 72: 1–17.

(1987) *Italian manpower, 225 B.C.–A.D. 14*. Rev. edn. Oxford.

(1988) *The fall of the Roman Republic and related essays*. Oxford.

Burford, A. (1969) *The Greek temple builders at Epidauros: a social and economic study of building in the Asklepian sanctuary during the fourth and early third centuries B.C.* Liverpool.

Burkert. W. (1985) *Greek religion: archaic and classical*. Oxford [German original 1977].

Burton, G. P. (1979) 'The curator rei publicae: towards a reappraisal', *Chiron* 9: 465–79.

Busolt, G. (1920–1926) *Griechische Staatskunde*. 2 vols. Munich.

Butzer, K. W. (2008) 'Other perspectives on urbanism: beyond the disciplinary boundaries', in Marcus and Sabloff eds. *The ancient city: new perspectives on urbanism in the Old and New World*. Santa Fe, 77–92.

Cahill, N. (2002) *Household and city organization at Olynthus*. New Haven.

Cameron, A. (2012) *The Mediterranean world in late antiquity, 395–700 AD*. 2nd edn. Abingdon.

Cammack, D. (2012) 'Deliberation in Classical Athens: not talking, but thinking (and voting)' (October 7, 2012). Available at SSRN (Social Science Research Network): http://ssrn.com/abstract=2161074 or http://dx.doi.org/10.2139/ssrn.2161074.

Camp, J. M. (1986) *The Athenian Agora*. London.

Carl, P. et al. (2000) 'Were cities built as images?', *Cambridge Archaeological Journal* 10(2): 327–65.

Carlsson, S. (2010) *Hellenistic democracies: freedom, independence and political procedure in some east Greek city-states*. Stuttgart.

Cartledge, P. (1993) 'Classical Greek agriculture: recent work and alternative views', *Journal of Peasant Studies* 21: 127–36.

(1995) 'Classical Greek agriculture II: two more alternative views', *Journal of Peasant Studies* 23: 131–9.

(1999) 'Laying down polis law', *CR* 49: 465–9.

(2001) 'Spartan kingship: doubly odd?', in P. Cartledge, *Spartan reflections*. London, 55–67.

(2002a) *The Greeks: a portrait of self and others.* 2nd edn. Oxford.

(2002b) 'The economy (economies) of Ancient Greece', in Scheidel and Von Reden eds. *The ancient economy.* New York, 11–32.

(2009) *Ancient Greek political thought in practice.* Cambridge.

Cartledge, P., E. E. Cohen and L. Foxhall eds. (2002) *Money, labour and land: approaches to the economies of Ancient Greece.* London & New York.

Chaniotis, A. (1995) 'Sich selbst feiern? Städtische Feste des Hellenismus im Spannungsfeld von Religion und Politik', in M. Wörrle and P. Zanker eds., *Stadtbild und Bürgerbild im Hellenismus.* Munich, 147–72.

Childe, V. G. (1950) 'The urban revolution', *Town Planning Review* 21: 3–17.

Christie, N. J. (2001) 'War and order: urban remodelling and defensive strategy in Late Roman Italy', in Lavan ed. *Recent research in late-antique urbanism. JRA* Suppl. 42. Portsmouth, 106–22.

Cipolla, C. M. (1994) *Before the Industrial Revolution: European society and economy 1000–1700.* 3rd edn. New York & London.

Clark, P. (2009) *European cities and towns 400–2000.* Oxford.

ed. (2013) *The Oxford handbook of cities in world history.* Oxford.

Cohen, E. E. (1992) *Athenian economy and society: a banking perspective.* Princeton.

(2000) *The Athenian nation.* Princeton.

Cohen, G. M. (1978) *The Seleucid colonies: studies in founding, administration and organization.* Wiesbaden.

(1995) *The Hellenistic settlements in Europe, the islands and Asia Minor.* Berkeley.

(2006) *The Hellenistic settlements in Syria, the Red Sea Basin, and North Africa.* Berkeley.

(2013) *The Hellenistic settlements in the East from Armenia and Mesopotamia to Bactria and India.* Berkeley.

Corbier, M. (1991) 'City, territory and taxation', in Rich and Wallace-Hadrill eds. *City and country in the ancient world.* New York & London, 211–39.

Cornell, T. J. (1995) *The beginnings of Rome: Italy and Rome from the Bronze Age to the Punic Wars (c. 1000–264 BC).* London & New York.

(2000) 'The city-states in Latium', in Hansen ed. *A comparative study of thirty city-state cultures.* Copenhagen, 209–28.

Cornell, T. J. and K. Lomas eds. (1995) *Urban society in Roman Italy.* London.

Cowgill, G. L. (2003a) 'Some recent data and concepts about ancient urbanism', in W. T. Sanders, A. Guadalupe Mastache and R. H. Cobean eds., *El urbanismo en mesoamerica/Urbanism in Mesoamerica* Vol. I. Instituto Nacional de Antropología e Historia and Pennsylvania State University, 1–19.

(2003b) 'Teotihuacan: cosmic glories and mundane needs', in Smith ed. *The social construction of ancient cities.* Washington DC & London, 37–55.

(2004) 'Origins and development of urbanism: archaeological perspectives', *Annual Review of Anthropology* 33: 525–49.

Cox, C. A. (1998) *Household interests: property, marriage strategies, and family dynamics in Ancient Athens.* Princeton.

Crielaard, J. P. (2009) 'Cities', in Raaflaub and van Wees eds. *A companion to Archaic Greece.* Malden & Oxford, 349–72.

D'Agostino, B. (1990) 'Military organisation and social structure in archaic Etruria', in Murray and Price eds. *The Greek city from Homer to Alexander.* Oxford, 59–82.

Das, R. J. and A. K. Dutt (1993) 'Rank-size distribution and primate city characteristics in India – a temporal analysis', *GeoJournal* 29(2): 125–37.

Davies, J. K. (1971) *Athenian propertied families, 600–300 B.C.* Oxford.

(1981) *Wealth and the power of wealth in Classical Athens.* Salem.

(1997) 'The "origins of the Greek polis": where should we be looking?', in Mitchell and Rhodes eds. *The development of the polis in Archaic Greece.* London & New York, 24–38.

Deene, M. (2011) 'Naturalized citizens and social mobility in Classical Athens: the case of Apollodorus', *G&R* 58.2: 159–75.

(2013) *Aspects of social mobility in Classical Athens.* Unpub. PhD thesis, Ghent.

(2014) 'Let's work together! Economic cooperation, social capital, and chances of social mobility in Classical Athens', *G&R* 61.2: 152–73.

De Giorgi, A. U. (2008) 'Town and country in Roman Antioch', in Alston and van Nijf eds. *Feeding the Ancient Greek city.* Groningen-Royal Holloway Studies on the Greek City after the Classical Age 1. Leuven, 63–83.

Delaine, J. (1997) *The Baths of Caracalla: a study in the design, construction, and economics of large-scale building projects in imperial Rome. JRA* Suppl. 25. Portsmouth.

(2000) 'Building the Eternal City: the building industry of imperial Rome' in J. Coulston and H. Dodge eds., *Ancient Rome: the archaeology of the Eternal City.* Oxford, 119–41.

De Laix, R. A. (1973) *Probouleusis at Athens: a study of political decision-making.* Berkeley.

De Ligt, L. (1993) *Fairs and markets in the Roman empire: economic and social aspects of periodic trade in a pre-industrial society.* Amsterdam.

De Ligt, L. and P. Garnsey (2012) 'The Album of Herculaneum and a model of the town's demography', *JRA* 25: 69–94.

De Ligt, L. and S. J. Northwood eds. (2008) *People, land, and politics: demographic developments and the transformation of Roman Italy, 300 BC–AD 14.* Leiden & Boston.

De Polignac, F. (1995) *Cults, territory, and the origins of the Greek city-state.* Chicago & London [French original 1984].

De Ste. Croix, G. E. M. (1972) *The origins of the Peloponnesian War.* Ithaca.

(1975) 'Political pay outside Athens', *CQ* 25: 48–52.

(1981) *The class struggle in the Ancient Greek world: from the Archaic age to the Arab conquest.* London [corrected impression 1983].

De Vries, J. (1984) *European urbanization 1500–1800.* London.

Díaz Del Castillo, B. (1956) *The discovery and conquest of Mexico 1517–1521.* New York.

Dickenson, C. P. (2012) *On the agora: power and public space in Hellenistic and Roman Greece.* Unpub. PhD thesis, Groningen.

Dickenson, C. P. and O. M. van Nijf eds. (2013) *Public space in the post-Classical city.* Leuven.

Dmitriev, S. (2005) *City government in Hellenistic and Roman Asia Minor*. Oxford.

Dobbins, J. J. and P. W. Foss eds. (2007) *The world of Pompeii*. New York & London.

Donahue, J. F. (2004) *The Roman community at table during the Principate*. Ann Arbor.

Donlan, W. (1980) *The aristocratic ideal in Ancient Greece*. Lawrence.

(1985) 'The social groups of Dark Age Greece', *CP* 80: 293–308.

(1989) 'The pre-state community in Greece', *Symbolae Osloenses* 64: 5–29.

(1997) 'The relations of power in the pre-state and early state polities', in Mitchell and Rhodes eds. *The development of the polis in Archaic Greece*. London & New York, 39–48.

Duff, A. M. (1958) *Freedmen in the early Roman Empire*. Cambridge.

Duncan, J. S. (1990) *The city as text: the politics of landscape interpretation in the Kandyan kingdom*. Cambridge.

Duncan-Jones, R. (1982) *The economy of the Roman empire: quantitative studies*. 2nd edn. Cambridge.

(1990) *Structure and scale in the Roman economy*. Cambridge.

(1996) 'The impact of the Antonine Plague', *JRA* 9: 108–36.

Duthoy, R. (1978) 'Les *Augustales', in *ANRW* 16(2): 1254–309.

Edmondson, J. (2006) 'Cities and urban life in the western provinces of the Roman Empire, 30 BCE–250 CE', in Potter ed. *A companion to the Roman Empire*. Malden, Oxford & Carlton, 250–80.

Edwards, C. and G. Woolf eds. (2003) *Rome the cosmopolis*. Cambridge.

Ehrenberg, V. (1962) *The people of Aristophanes: a sociology of old Attic comedy*. 3rd edn. New York.

(1969) *The Greek state*. 2nd edn. London.

Eilers, C. (2002) *Roman patrons of Greek cities*. Oxford.

Emberling, G. (2003) 'Urban social transformations and the problem of the "first city"', in M. L. Smith ed. *The social construction of ancient cities*. Washington DC & London, 254–68.

Engels, D. (1990) *Roman Corinth: an alternative model for the classical city*. Chicago.

Epstein, S. R. and M. Prak eds. (2008) *Guilds, innovation, and the European economy, 1400–1800*. Cambridge.

Erdkamp, P. (2001) 'Beyond the limits of the "consumer city": a model of the urban and rural economy in the Roman world', *Historia* 50: 332–56.

(2005) *The grain market in the Roman Empire: a social, political and economic study*. Cambridge.

(2012) 'Urbanism', in Scheidel ed. *The Cambridge companion to the Roman economy*. Cambridge, 241–65.

ed. (2013) *The Cambridge companion to Ancient Rome*. Cambridge.

Erskine, A. (2001) 'Antiochus the Great', *CR* 51(2): 320–2.

Fentress, E. (2000) *Romanization and the city: creation, transformations, and failures*. *JRA* Suppl. 38. Portsmouth.

Ferguson, W. S. (1928) 'The leading ideas of the new world', in S. A. Cook, F. E. Adcock and M. P. Charlesworth eds., *The Cambridge ancient history. Vol. 7. The Hellenistic monarchies and the rise of Rome*. Cambridge, 1–40.

Finley, M. I. (1963) *The Ancient Greeks: an introduction to their life and thought.* London.

(1978) *The world of Odysseus.* 2nd rev. edn., London.

(1981a) 'The ancient city: from Fustel de Coulanges to Max Weber and beyond', in Finley, *Economy and society in Ancient Greece.* Ed. with an introduction by B. D. Shaw and R. P. Saller. London, 3–23.

(1981b) 'Was Greek civilization based on slave labour?', in Finley, *Economy and society in Ancient Greece.* Ed. with an introduction by B. D. Shaw and R. P. Saller. London, 97–115.

(1981c) 'The servile statuses of Ancient Greece', in Finley, *Economy and society in Ancient Greece.* Ed. with an introduction by B. D. Shaw and R. P. Saller. London, 133–49.

(1981d) *Economy and society in Ancient Greece.* Ed. with an introduction by B. D. Shaw and R. P. Saller. London.

(1983) *Politics in the ancient world.* Cambridge.

(1985) *Democracy ancient and modern.* 2nd edn. New Brunswick & London.

(1998) *Ancient slavery and modern ideology.* Expanded edn. by B. D. Shaw. Princeton.

(1999) *The ancient economy.* Updated edn. by I. Morris. Berkeley.

Finn, R. (2006a) *Almsgiving in the later Roman empire: Christian promotion and practice 313–450.* Oxford.

(2006b) 'Portraying the poor: descriptions of poverty in Christian texts from the late Roman Empire', in Atkins and Osborne eds. *Poverty in the Roman world.* Cambridge, 130–44.

Fleming, D. (2002) 'The streets of Thurii: discourse, democracy, and design in the Classical polis', *Rhetoric Society Quarterly* 32: 5–32.

Flohr, M. (2013a) *The world of the fullo: work, economy, and society in Roman Italy.* Oxford.

(2013b) Review of Mayer (2012), *JRS* 103: 308–9.

Foss, C. (1975) 'The Persians in Asia Minor and the end of Antiquity', *English Historical Review* 90: 721–47.

Fox, R. G. (1977) *Urban anthropology: cities in their cultural settings.* Englewood Cliffs.

Foxhall, L. (1992) 'The control of the Attic landscape', in Wells ed. *Agriculture in Ancient Greece.* Stockholm, 155–9.

(2002) 'Access to resources in Classical Greece: the egalitarianism of the polis in practice', in Cartledge, Cohen and Foxhall eds. *Money, labour and land: approaches to the economies of Ancient Greece.* London & New York, 209–20.

(2007) *Olive cultivation in Ancient Greece: seeking the ancient economy.* Oxford.

Frank, T. (1940) *Rome and Italy of the Empire.* An economic survey of Ancient Rome V. Baltimore.

Franklin, J. L. (1980) *Pompeii: the electoral programmata, campaigns and politics, AD 71–79.* Rome.

Fraser, P. M. (1996) *Cities of Alexander the Great.* Oxford.

Fuhrmann C. J. (2012) *Policing the Roman Empire: soldiers, administration, and public order*. Oxford & New York.

Fustel de Coulanges, N. D. (2001) *The ancient city*. Kitchener [French original 1864].

Gabrielsen, V. (2001) 'The Rhodian associations and economic activity', in Z. H. Archibald, J. Davies, G. J. Oliver and V. Gabrielsen eds., *Hellenistic Economies*. London & New York, 215–44.

(2009) 'Brotherhoods of faith and provident planning: the non-public associations of the Greek world', in I. Malkin, C. Constantakopoulou and K. Panagopoulou eds., *Greek and Roman networks in the Mediterranean*. London & New York, 176–203.

Gallant, T. W. (1991) *Risk and survival in Ancient Greece: reconstructing the rural domestic economy*. Cambridge.

Galley, C. (1995) 'A model of early modern urban demography', *Economic History Review* 48(3): 448–69.

Garlan, Y. (1988) *Slavery in Ancient Greece*. Ithaca.

Garland, R. (2009) *Daily life of the Ancient Greeks*. 2nd edn. Westport.

Garnsey, P. (1970) *Social status and legal privilege in the Roman Empire*. Oxford.

(1975) 'Descendants of freedmen in local politics: some criteria', in B. Levick ed., *The ancient historian and his materials: essays in honour of C. E. Stevens on his seventieth birthday*. Farnborough, 167–80.

(1988) *Famine and food supply in the Graeco-Roman world: responses to risk and crisis*. Cambridge.

(1998a) *Cities, peasants and food in Classical Antiquity: essays in social and economic history*. Ed. W. Scheidel. Cambridge.

(1998b) 'Urban property investment in Roman society', in Garnsey, *Cities, peasants and food in Classical Antiquity*. Cambridge, 63–76.

(1998c) 'Independent freedmen and the economy of Roman Italy under the Principate', in Garnsey, *Cities, peasants and food in Classical Antiquity*. Cambridge, 28–44.

(2010) 'Roman patronage', in S. McGill, C. Sogno and E. Watts eds., *From the Tetrarchs to the Theodosians: later Roman history and culture, 284–450 CE*. Cambridge, 33–54.

Garnsey, P. and R. Saller (2014) *The Roman Empire: economy, society and culture*. 2nd edn. London.

Garnsey, P. and C. R. Whittaker (1998) 'Trade, industry and the urban economy', in A. Cameron and P. Garnsey eds., *The Cambridge Ancient History. Vol. 13. The Late Empire, A.D. 337–425*. 2nd edn. Cambridge, 312–37.

Gates, C. (2011) *Ancient cities: the archaeology of urban life in the Ancient Near East and Egypt, Greece, and Rome*. 2nd edn. London & New York.

Gauthier, Ph. (1981) 'La citoyenneté en Grèce et à Rome: participation et intégration', *Ktèma* 6: 167–79.

(1993) 'Les cités hellénistiques', in Hansen ed. *The Ancient Greek city-state*. Copenhagen, 211–31.

Geertz, C. (1978) 'The bazaar economy: information and search in peasant marketing', *The American Economic Review* 68(2): 28–32.

Gehrke, H.-J. (2009) 'States', in Raaflaub and van Wees eds. *A companion to Archaic Greece*. Malden & Oxford, 395–410.

Gelzer, M. (1969) *The Roman nobility*. Oxford [German original 1912].

Gleason, M. W. (2006) 'Greek cities under Roman rule', in Potter ed. *A companion to the Roman Empire*. Malden, Oxford & Carlton, 228–49.

Gonzáles, J. and M. H. Crawford (1986) 'The *Lex Irnitana*: a new copy of the Flavian municipal law', *JRS* 76: 147–243.

Goodman, P. J. (2007) *The Roman city and its periphery: from Rome to Gaul*. London & New York.

Gordon, R. (1990) 'The veil of power: emperors, sacrificers and benefactors', in M. Beard and J. North eds. *Pagan priests*. London, 199–231.

Gowland, R. and P. Garnsey (2010) 'Skeletal evidence for health, nutritional status and malaria in Rome and the empire', in H. Eckhardt ed., *Roman diasporas: archaeological approaches to mobility and diversity in the Roman empire. JRA* Suppl. 78. Portsmouth, 131–56.

Green, P. (1990) *Alexander to Actium: the historical evolution of the Hellenistic age*. Berkeley.

Grieb, V. (2008) *Hellenistische Demokratie: politische Organisation und Struktur in freien griechischen Poleis nach Alexander dem Grossen*. Stuttgart.

Grig, L. (2006) 'Throwing parties for the poor: poverty and splendour in the late antique church', in Atkins and Osborne eds. *Poverty in the Roman world*. Cambridge, 145–61.

Grinin, L. (2004) 'Democracy and early state', *Social Evolution & History* 3(2): 93–149.

Gruen, E. (1974) *The last generation of the Roman Republic*. Berkeley.

Hall, J. M. (2002) *Hellenicity: between ethnicity and culture*. Chicago.

(2007) *A history of the Archaic Greek world, ca. 1200–479 BCE*. Malden, Oxford & Carlton [2nd edn. 2013].

Halstead, P. (1987) 'Traditional and ancient rural economy in Mediterranean Europe: plus ça change?', *JHS* 107: 77–87

Hansen, M. H. (1991) *The Athenian democracy in the age of Demosthenes: structure, principles, and ideology*. Oxford [Rev. edn. Bristol 1999].

ed. (1993) *The Ancient Greek city-state*. Copenhagen.

(1997) 'The polis as an urban centre: the literary and epigraphic evidence', in M. H. Hansen ed., *The polis as an urban centre and as a political community*. Copenhagen, 9–86.

(1998) *Polis and city-state: an ancient concept and its modern equivalent*. Copenhagen.

ed. (2000) *A comparative study of thirty city-state cultures*. Copenhagen.

(2002a) *A comparative study of six city-state cultures*. Copenhagen.

(2002b) 'Was the polis a state or a stateless society?', in T. Heine-Nielsen ed., *Even more studies in the Ancient Greek polis*. Stuttgart, 17–47.

(2003) '95 theses about the Greek polis in the Archaic and Classical periods: a report on the results obtained by the Copenhagen Polis Centre in the period 1993–2003', *Historia* 52(3): 257–82.

(2004) 'The concept of the consumption city applied to the Greek polis', in T. Heine-Nielsen ed., *Once again: studies in the Ancient Greek polis*. Stuttgart 9–47.

(2006) *Polis: an introduction to the Ancient Greek city-state*. Oxford.

(2008) 'Analyzing cities', in Marcus and Sabloff eds.*The ancient city: new perspectives on urbanism in the Old and New World*. Santa Fe, 67–76.

Hansen, M. H. and T. H. Nielsen (2004) *An inventory of archaic and classical poleis*. Oxford.

Hanson, J. W. (2011) 'The urban system of Roman Asia Minor and wider urban connectivity', in Bowman and Wilson eds. *Settlement, urbanization, and population*. Oxford Studies on the Roman Economy. Oxford, 229–75.

Hanson, V. D. (1995) *The other Greeks: the family farm and the agrarian roots of Western civilization*. New York.

(1996) 'Hoplites into democrats: the changing ideology of Athenian infantry', in Ober and Hedrick eds. *Demokratia: a conversation on democracies, ancient and modern*. Princeton, 289–312.

Harland, Ph. (2003) *Associations, synagogues, and congregations: claiming a place in Ancient Mediterranean society*. Minneapolis.

Harper, K. (2011) *Slavery in the late Roman world, AD 275–425*. Cambridge.

Harris, E. M. (2002) 'Workshop, marketplace and household: the nature of technical specialization in Classical Athens and its influence on economy and society', in Cartledge, Cohen and Foxhall eds. *Money, labour and land: approaches to the economies of Ancient Greece*. London & New York, 67–99.

Harries, J. (2003) '*Favor populi*: pagans, Christians and public entertainment in late antique Italy', in T. J. Cornell and K. Lomas eds. *'Bread and circuses': euergetism and municipal patronage in Roman Italy*. London & New York, 125–41.

Hawkins, C. (2012) 'Manufacturing', in Scheidel ed. *The Cambridge companion to the Roman economy*. Cambridge, 175–94.

Hedrick, C. W. (1994) 'The zero degree of society: Aristotle and the Athenian citizen', in J. P. Euben, J. R. Wallach and J. Ober eds., *Athenian political thought and the reconstruction of American democracy*. Ithaca, 289–318.

Heller, A. (2009) 'La cité grecque d'époque impériale: vers une société d'ordres?', *Annales. Histoire, Sciences Sociales* 64: 341–73.

Herman, G. (1997) 'The court society of the Hellenistic age', in P. Cartledge, P. Garnsey and E. S. Gruen eds., *Hellenistic constructs: essays in culture, history, and historiography*. Berkeley, 199–224.

Hill, H. (1952) *The Roman middle class in the Republican period*. Oxford.

Hin, S. (2013) *The demography of Roman Italy: population dynamics in an ancient conquest society*. Cambridge.

Hitchner, R. B. (2009) Review of Sears (2007), *JRS* 99: 299–301.

Hodkinson, S. (1988), 'Animal husbandry in the Greek polis', in C. R. Whittaker ed., *Pastoral economies in Classical Antiquity*. Cambridge, 35–74.

(1992) 'Imperialist democracy and market-oriented pastoral production in Classical Athens', *Anthropozoologica* 16: 53–60.

(2000) *Property and wealth in Classical Sparta*. London.

Hölkeskamp, K.-J. (2010) *Reconstructing the Roman Republic: an ancient political culture and modern research*. Princeton.

Holleran, C. (2011) 'The street life of Ancient Rome', in Laurence and Newsome eds. *Rome, Ostia, Pompeii: movement and space*. Oxford, 245–61.

(2012) *Shopping in Ancient Rome: the retail trade in the Late Republic and the Principate*. Oxford.

Holleran, C. and A. Pudsey eds. (2011) *Demography and the Graeco-Roman world: new insights and approaches*. Cambridge.

Hölscher, T. (1998) *Öffentliche Räume in frühen griechischen Städten*. Heidelberg.

(2007) 'Urban spaces and central places: the Greek world', in Alcock and Osborne eds. *Classical archaeology*. Blackwell Studies in Global Archaeology. Malden, Oxford & Carlton, 164–81.

Holton, R. J. (1986) *Cities, capitalism and civilization*. London.

Hope, V. M. and E. Marshall eds. (2000) *Death and disease in the ancient city*. London.

Hopkins, K. (1978) 'Economic growth and towns in classical antiquity', in Abrams and Wrigley eds. *Towns in societies: essays in economic history and historical sociology*. Cambridge, 35–77.

(1983) *Death and renewal*. Sociological studies in Roman History 2. Cambridge.

(2002) 'Rome, taxes, rents and trade', in Scheidel and Von Reden eds. *The ancient economy*. New York, 190–230.

Horden, P. (2005) 'The earliest hospitals in Byzantium, Western Europe, and Islam', *Journal of Interdisciplinary History* 35(3): 361–89.

Horden, P. and N. Purcell (2000) *The corrupting sea: a study of Mediterranean history*. Oxford.

Hunter, V. J. (1994) *Policing Athens: social control in the Attic lawsuits 420–320 B.C.* Princeton.

Iddeng, J. W. (2012) 'What is a Graeco-Roman festival? A polythetic approach', in J. Rasmus Brandt and J. W. Iddeng eds. *Greek and Roman festivals: content, meaning, and practice*. Oxford, 11–37.

Jacobs, I. (2013) *Aesthetic maintenance of civic space: the 'classical' city from the 4th to the 7th c. AD*. Leuven.

Jacobsen, T. (1943) 'Primitive democracy in Ancient Mesopotamia', *Journal of Near Eastern Studies* 2: 159–72.

Jäggi, C. and H.-R. Meier (1997) '"... this great appetite for church building still needs adequate explanation": zum Kirchenbauboom am Ende der Spätantike', in M. J. Gill, R. L. Colella, A. L. Jenkens and P. Lamers eds. *Pratum Romanum: Richard Krautheimer zum 100. Geburtstag*. Wiesbaden, 181–98.

Jameson, M. H. (1977–1978) 'Agriculture and slavery in Classical Athens', *CJ* 73(2): 122–45.

Jansen, H. S. J. (1996) 'Wrestling with the angel: on problems of definition in urban historiography', *Urban History* 23(3): 277–99.

Jashemski, W. (2007) 'Gardens', in Dobbins and Foss eds. *The world of Pompeii*. New York & London, 487–98.

Joffe, A. H. (1998) 'Disembedded capitals in western Asian perspective', *Comparative Studies in Society and History* 40(3): 549–80.

Johnson, G. A. (1980) 'Rank-size convexity and system integration: a view from archaeology', *Economic Geography* 56: 234–47.

Jones, A. H. M. (1940) *The Greek city from Alexander to Justinian*. Oxford.

(1957) *Athenian democracy*. Oxford.

(1964) *The later Roman Empire, 284–602: a social, economic and administrative survey*. 3 vols. Oxford.

Jones, C. P. (1978) *The Roman world of Dio Chrysostom*. Cambridge, MA.

Jones, N. F. (1999) *The associations of Classical Athens: the response to democracy*. Oxford.

(2004) *Rural Athens under the democracy*. Philadelphia.

Jongman, W. M. (1991) *The economy and society of Pompeii*. Amsterdam.

(2000a) 'Wool and the textile industry of Roman Italy: a working hypothesis', in E. Lo Cascio ed., *Mercati permanenti e mercati periodici nel mondo romano: atti degli Incontri capresi di storia dell'economia antica (Capri, 13–15 ottobre 1997)*. Bari, 187–97.

(2000b) 'Hunger and power: theories, models and methods in Roman economic history', in H. Bongenaar ed., *Interdependency of institutions and private entrepreneurs: proceedings of the second MOS Symposium, Leiden 1998*. Istanbul, 259–84.

(2002) 'The Roman economy: from cities to Empire', in L. De Blois and J. Rich eds., *The transformation of economic life under the Roman Empire: proceedings of the second workshop of the international network Impact of Empire (Roman Empire, c. 200 B.C.–A.D. 476), Nottingham, July 4–7, 2001*. Amsterdam, 28–47.

(2003) 'Slavery and the growth of Rome: the transformation of Italy in the first and second century BCE', in Edwards and Woolf eds. *Rome the cosmopolis*. Cambridge, 100–22.

(2007a) 'The early Roman empire: consumption', in Scheidel, Morris and Saller eds. *The Cambridge Economic History of the Greco-Roman World*. Cambridge, 592–618.

(2007b) 'The rise and fall of the Roman economy: population, rents and entitlement', in P. F. Bang, M. Ikeguchi and H. G. Ziche eds., *Ancient economies and modern methodologies: archaeology, comparative history, models and institutions*. Bari, 237–54.

Joshel, S. R. (1992) *Work, identity, and legal status at Rome: a study of the occupational inscriptions*. Norman.

Kaiser, A. (2011a) *Roman urban street networks*. Routledge Studies in Archaeology 2. New York.

(2011b) 'Cart traffic flow in Pompeii and Rome', in Laurence and Newsome eds. *Rome, Ostia, Pompeii: movement and space*. Oxford, 174–93.

Kamen, D. (2013) *Status in Classical Athens*. Princeton.

Kennedy, H. (1985) 'From *polis* to madina: urban change in late antique and early Islamic Syria', *Past & Present* 106: 3–27.

Kindt, J. (2012) *Rethinking Greek religion.* Cambridge.

Kirsten, E. (1956) *Die griechische Polis als historisch-geographisches Problem des Mittelmeerraumes.* Bonn.

Kloft, H. (1992) *Die Wirtschaft der griechisch-römischen Welt.* Darmstadt.

Kolb, F. (1984) *Die Stadt im Altertum.* Munich.

Kolendo, J. (1981), 'La répartition des places aux spectacles et la stratification sociale dans l'Empire Romain', *Ktèma* 6: 301–15.

Kostof, S. (1991) *The city shaped: urban patterns and meanings through history.* Boston.

Krause, J.-U. and C. Witschel eds. (2006) *Die Stadt in der Spätantike – Niedergang oder Wandel?* Stuttgart.

Krentz, P. (2007) 'Warfare and hoplites', in Shapiro ed. *The Cambridge companion to Archaic Greece.* Cambridge, 61–84.

Kron, G. (2012) 'Food production', in Scheidel ed. *The Cambridge companion to the Roman economy.* Cambridge, 156–74.

   (2014) 'Comparative evidence and the reconstruction of the ancient economy: Greco-Roman housing and the level and distribution of wealth and income', in F. De Callataÿ ed., *Quantifying the Greco-Roman economy and beyond.* Bari, 123–46.

Kulikowski, M. (2004) *Late Roman Spain and its cities.* Baltimore.

Kurke, L. (1992) 'The politics of *habrosune* in Archaic Greece', *Classical Antiquity* 11: 91–120.

Kusimba, C. M. (2008) 'Early African cities: their role in the shaping of urban and rural interaction spheres', in Marcus and Sabloff eds. *The ancient city: new perspectives on urbanism in the Old and New World.* Santa Fe, 229–46.

Kusimba, C. M., S. Barut Kusimba and B. Agbaje-Williams, 'Precolonial African cities: size and density', in Storey ed. *Urbanism in the preindustrial world: cross-cultural approaches.* Tuscaloosa, 145–58.

Lambert, S. D. (1993) *The phratries of Attica.* Ann Arbor.

Laniado, A. (2002) *Recherches sur les notables municipaux dans l'empire protobyzantin.* Paris.

Lassère, J.-M. (2007) *Manuel d'épigraphie romaine.* Paris.

Laurence, R. (1994) *Roman Pompeii: space and society.* London.

   (1997) 'Writing the Roman metropolis', in Parkins ed. *Roman urbanism: beyond the consumer city.* London & New York, 1–20.

Laurence, R., S. Esmonde Cleary and G. Sears (2011) *The city in the Roman West, c. 250 BC–c. AD 250.* Cambridge.

Laurence, R. and D. J. Newsome eds. (2011) *Rome, Ostia, Pompeii: movement and space.* Oxford.

Lavan, L. ed. (2001a) *Recent research in late-antique urbanism. JRA* Suppl. 42. Portsmouth.

   (2001b) 'The late-antique city: a bibliographical essay', in Lavan ed. *Recent research in late-antique urbanism. JRA* Suppl. 42. Portsmouth, 9–26.

   (2003) 'The political topography of the late antique city: activity spaces in practice', in L. Lavan and W. Bowden eds., *Theory and practice in late antique archaeology.* Leiden, 314–37.

(2006) 'Fora and agorai in Mediterranean cities during the 4th and 5th c. A.D.', in W. Bowden, C. Machado and A. Gutteridge eds., *Social and political life in Late Antiquity.* Leiden, 195–249.

Lavan, M. (2013) *Slaves to Rome: paradigms of empire in Roman culture.* Cambridge.

Lendon, J. E. (1997) *Empire of honour: the art of government in the Roman world.* Oxford.

Lepelley, C. (1979–1981) *Les cités de l'Afrique romaine au Bas-Empire.* 2 vols. Paris.

(1992) 'The survival and fall of the classical city in late Roman Africa', in Rich ed. *The city in late antiquity.* London, 85–104.

Leveau, Ph. (1983) 'La ville antique et l'organisation de l'espace rurale: villa, ville, village', *Annales ESC* 4: 920–42.

Levick, B. (1967) *Roman colonies in southern Asia Minor.* Oxford.

Liebeschuetz, J. H. W. G. (1992) 'The end of the ancient city', in Rich ed. *The city in late antiquity.* London, 1–49.

(2001) *The decline and fall of the Roman city.* Oxford.

Lindert, P. H. (2003) 'Voice and growth: was Churchill right?', *Journal of Economic History* 63(2): 315–50.

Lintott, A. (1982) *Violence, civil strife, and revolution in the classical city, 750–330 B.C.* London.

(1993) *Imperium Romanum: politics and administration.* London.

(1999) *The constitution of the Roman Republic.* Oxford.

Liu, J. (2009) *Collegia centonariorum: the guilds of textile dealers in the Roman West.* Leiden.

Lo Cascio, E. (2006) 'Did the population of imperial Rome reproduce itself?', in Storey ed. *Urbanism in the preindustrial world: cross-cultural approaches.* Tuscaloosa, 52–68.

(2009) 'Urbanization as a proxy of demographic and economic growth', in A. Bowman and A. Wilson eds., *Quantifying the Roman economy: methods and problems.* Oxford Studies on the Roman Economy. Oxford, 87–106.

ed. (2012) *L'impatto della "peste antonina".* Bari.

Lomas, K. (1996) *Roman Italy 338 BC–AD 250: a sourcebook.* London.

Loseby, S. T. (2006) 'Decline and change in the cities of late antique Gaul', in Krause and Witschel eds. *Die Stadt in der Spätantike – Niedergang oder Wandel?* Stuttgart, 67–104.

(2009) 'Mediterranean cities', in Rousseau and Raithel eds., *A companion to Late Antiquity.* Chichester & Malden, 139–55.

(2012) 'Post-Roman economies', in Scheidel ed. *The Cambridge companion to the Roman economy.* Cambridge, 334–60.

Love, J. R. (1991) *Antiquity and capitalism: Max Weber and the sociological foundations of Roman civilization.* London.

Ma, J. (1999) *Antiochos III and the cities of western Asia Minor.* Oxford.

(2000a) 'Public speech and community in the *Euboicus*', in S. Swain ed., *Dio Chrysostom: politics, letters, and philosophy.* Oxford, 108–24.

(2000b) 'Fighting poleis of the Hellenistic world', in H. van Wees ed., *War and violence in Ancient Greece.* London, 337–76.

Macaulay-Lewis, E. (2011) 'The city in motion: walking for transport and leisure in the city of Rome', in Laurence and Newsome eds. *Rome, Ostia, Pompeii: movement and space.* Oxford, 262–89.

Mackay, C. S. (2002) Review of Mouritsen (2001), *Phoenix* 56: 399–401.

Mackinnon, M. (2013) 'Pack animals, pets, pests and other non-human beings', in Erdkamp ed. *The Cambridge companion to Ancient Rome.* Cambridge, 110–28.

Mackil, E. (2013) *Creating a common polity: religion, economy, and politics in the making of the Greek koinon.* Berkeley, Los Angeles & London.

MacMahon, A. and J. Price eds. (2005) *Roman working lives and urban living.* Oxford.

MacMullen, R. (1974) *Roman social relations 50 B.C. to A.D. 284.* New Haven & London.

(1988) *Corruption and the decline of Rome.* New Haven.

(1989) 'The preacher's audience (AD 350–400)', *Journal of Theological Studies* n.s. 40: 503–11.

Madsen, J. M. (2009) *Eager to be Roman: Greek response to Roman rule in Pontus and Bithynia.* London.

Magie, D. (1950) *Roman rule in Asia Minor to the end of the third century after Christ.* 2 vols. Princeton.

Malkin, I. (2009) 'Foundations', in Raaflaub and van Wees eds. *A companion to Archaic Greece.* Malden & Oxford, 373–94.

(2011) *A small Greek world: networks in the Ancient Mediterranean.* Oxford.

Mann, C. and P. Scholz eds. (2012) *"Demokratie" im Hellenismus: von der Herrschaft des Volkes zur Herrschaft der Honoratioren?* Mainz.

Manning, S. W. (2013) 'The Roman world and climate: context, relevance of climate change, and some issues', in W. V. Harris ed. *The Ancient Mediterranean environment between science and history.* Leiden and Boston, 103–70.

Marcus, J. and Sabloff, J. A. eds. (2008a) *The ancient city: new perspectives on urbanism in the Old and New World.* Santa Fe.

(2008b) 'Introduction', in Marcus and Sabloff eds. *The ancient city: new perspectives on urbanism in the Old and New World.* Santa Fe, 3–26.

Marek, C. (2006) 'Stadt, Bund und Reich in der Zollorganisation des kaiserzeitlichen Lykien. Eine neue Interpretation der Zollinschrift von Kaunos', in H.-U. Wiemer ed., *Staatlichkeit und politisches Handeln in der römischen Kaiserzeit.* Berlin, 107–22.

Marshall, E. (2000) 'Death and disease in Cyrene: a case study', in Hope and Marshall eds. *Death and disease in the ancient city.* London, 8–23.

Martin, J. (1994) 'Der Verlust der Stadt', in Ch. Meier ed., *Die Okzidentale Stadt nach Max Weber: zum Problem der Zugehörigkeit in Antike und Mittelalter. Historische Zeitschrift* Beihefte n.s. vol. 17. Munich, 95–114.

Martin, R. (1951) *Recherches sur l'agora grecque. Études d'histoire et d'architecture urbaines.* Paris.

Martzavou, P. and N. Papazarkadas eds. (2013) *Epigraphical approaches to the post-Classical polis.* Oxford.

Marx, K. (1976–81) *Capital.* Tr. B. Fowkes. 3 vols. Harmondsworth [German original 1867–1894].

Marzano, A. (2011) 'Rank-size analysis and the Roman cities of the Iberian Peninsula and Britain: some considerations', in Bowman and Wilson eds. *Settlement, urbanization, and population.* Oxford Studies on the Roman Economy. Oxford, 196–228.

Matthews, J. F. (1984) 'The tax law of Palmyra: evidence for economic history in a city of the Roman east', *JRS* 74: 157–80.

Mattingly, D. J and R. B. Hitchner (1995) 'Roman Africa: an archaeological review', *JRS* 85: 165–213.

Mattingly, D. J. and Salmon, J. eds. (2001a) *Economies beyond agriculture in the classical world.* London & New York.

(2001b) 'The productive past: economies beyond agriculture', in Mattingly and Salmon eds. *Economies beyond agriculture in the classical world.* London & New York, 3–14.

Mattingly, D. J., D. Stone, L. Stirling and N. Ben Lazreg (2001) 'Leptiminus (Tunisia): a "producer" city?', in Mattingly and Salmon eds. *Economies beyond agriculture in the classical world.* London & New York, 66–89.

Maurizio, L. (1998) 'The Panathenaic procession: Athens' participatory democracy on display?', in D. Boedeker and K. A. Raaflaub eds., *Democracy, empire, and the arts in fifth-century Athens.* Cambridge, MA & London, 297–317.

Mayer, E. (2012) *The ancient middle classes: urban life and aesthetics in the Roman empire, 100 BCE–250 CE.* Cambridge, MA & London.

Merkelbach, R. (1983) 'Ehrenbeschluss der Kymäer für den prytanis Kleanax', *Epigraphica Anatolica* 1: 33–37.

Merrills, A. H. (2004) 'Vandals, Romans and Berbers: understanding late antique North Africa', in A. H. Merrills ed., *Vandals, Romans and Berbers: new perspectives on late antique North Africa.* Aldershot, 3–30.

Michels, R. (1959) *Political parties: a sociological study of the oligarchical tendencies of modern democracy.* New York [German original 1911].

Migeotte, L. (1992) *Les souscriptions publiques dans les cités grecques.* Genève.

(2009) *The economy of the Greek cities: from the Archaic period to the early Roman Empire.* Berkeley, Los Angeles & London.

(2014) *Les finances des cités grecques: aux périodes classique et hellénistique.* *Epigraphica* 8. Paris.

Millar, F. (1967) 'Emperors at work', *JRS* 57: 9–19.

(1977) *The emperor in the Roman world (31 BC–AD 337).* London.

(1998) *The crowd in Rome in the late Republic.* Ann Arbor.

Millender, E. (2009) 'The Spartan dyarchy: a comparative perspective', in S. Hodkinson ed., *Sparta: comparative approaches.* Swansea, 1–67.

Millett, M. (1991) 'Roman towns and their territories: an archaeological perspective', in Rich and Wallace-Hadrill eds. *City and country in the ancient world.* New York & London, 173–93.

Millett, P. (1998) 'Encounters in the agora', in P. Cartledge, P. Millett and S. Von Reden eds. *Kosmos: essays in order, conflict and community in Classical Athens.* Cambridge, 203–28.

Mills, C. Wright (1956) *The power elite.* Oxford.

Mitchell, L. G. (2006) 'Greek government', in K. H. Kinzl ed. *A companion to the Classical Greek world.* Malden, Oxford & Carlton, 367–86.

Mitchell, L. G. and P. J. Rhodes, eds. (1997) *The development of the polis in Archaic Greece.* London & New York.

Mitchell, S. (1990) 'Festivals, games, and civic life in Roman Asia Minor', *JRS* 80: 183–93.

(1993) *Anatolia: land, men, and gods in Asia Minor.* 2 vols. Oxford.

Momigliano, A. (1994) 'The Ancient City of Fustel de Coulanges', in A.D. Momigliano, *Studies on modern scholarship.* Eds. G. W. Bowersock and T. J. Cornell. Berkeley & London, 162–78.

Mommsen, T. (1887–1888) *Römisches Staatsrecht.* 3rd edn. 3 vols. Leipzig.

Moore, T. J. (1994) 'Seats and social status in the Plautine theatre', *CJ* 90: 113–23

Moore, J. D. (2003) 'Life behind walls: patterns in the urban landscape on the prehistoric north coast of Peru', in M. L. Smith ed. *The social construction of ancient cities.* Washington DC & London, 81–102.

Moreno, A. (2007) *Feeding the democracy: the Athenian grain supply in the fifth and fourth centuries B.C.* Oxford.

Morgan, C. (2003) *Early Greek states beyond the polis.* London & New York.

Morley, N. (1996) *Metropolis and hinterland: the city of Rome and the Italian economy, 200 B.C.–A.D. 200.* Cambridge.

(1997) 'Cities in context: urban systems in Roman Italy', in Parkins ed. *Roman urbanism: beyond the consumer city.* London & New York, 42–58.

(2011) 'Cities and economic development in the Roman empire', in Bowman and Wilson eds. *Settlement, urbanization, and population.* Oxford Studies on the Roman Economy. Oxford, 143–60.

Morris, I. (1987) *Burial and ancient society.* Cambridge.

(1991) 'The early polis as city and state', in Rich and Wallace-Hadrill eds. *City and country in the ancient world.* New York & London, 24–57.

(1994) 'The Athenian economy twenty years after *The Ancient Economy*', *CP* 89: 351–66.

(1996) 'The Strong Principle of Equality and the archaic origins of Greek democracy', in Ober and Hedrick eds. *Demokratia: a conversation on democracies, ancient and modern.* Princeton, 19–48.

(1998a) 'Beyond democracy and empire: Athenian art in context', in D. Boedeker and K. Raaflaub eds., *Democracy, empire, and the arts in fifth-century Athens.* Cambridge, MA, 59–86.

(1998b) 'Archaeology as a kind of anthropology (a response to David Small)', in I. Morris and K. Raaflaub (eds.) *Democracy 2500? Questions and challenges.* Dubuque, 229–39.

(1999) 'Foreword', in Finley, *The ancient economy.* Berkeley, ix–xxxvi.

(2000) *Archaeology as cultural history: words and things in Iron Age Greece.* Malden & Oxford.

(2004) 'Economic growth in Ancient Greece', *Journal of Institutional and Theoretical Economics* 160: 709–42.

(2006) 'The growth of Greek cities in the first millennium BC', in Storey ed. *Urbanism in the preindustrial world: cross-cultural approaches.* Tuscaloosa, 26–51.

(2009) 'The eighth-century revolution', in Raaflaub and van Wees eds. *A companion to Archaic Greece.* Malden & Oxford, 64–80.

Morris, I. and B. Powell eds. (1997) *A new companion to Homer.* Leiden.

Morstein-Marx, R. (2004) *Mass oratory and political power in the late Roman Republic.* Cambridge.

Mosca, G. (1980) *The ruling class.* Westport [Italian original 1896].

Mouritsen, H. (1988) *Elections, magistrates and municipal elite: studies in Pompeian epigraphy.* Rome.

(1990) 'A note on Pompeian epigraphy and social structure', *Classica et Mediaevalia* 41: 131–49.

(1997) 'Mobility and social change in Italian towns during the Principate', in Parkins ed. *Roman urbanism: beyond the consumer city.* London & New York, 57–80.

(2001) *Plebs and politics in the late Roman Republic.* Cambridge.

(2011) *The freedman in the Roman world.* Cambridge.

(2012) Review of Mayer (2012), *BMCR* 2012.09.40.

(2015) 'Status and social hierarchies: the case of Pompeii', in A. Kuhn ed., *Sozialer Status und Prestige in der römischen Welt.* Stuttgart, 87–114.

Mrozek, S. (1987) *Les distributions d'argent et de nourriture dans les villes du Haut-Empire romain.* Collection Latomus 198. Brussels.

(1992) 'Caractère hiérarchique des repas officiels dans les villes romaines du Haut Empire', in M. Aurell, O. Dumoulin and F. Thélamon eds., *La sociabilité à table: commensalité à travers les âges. Actes du Colloque de Rouen (14–17 novembre 1990).* Rouen, 181–6.

Mueller, K. (2006) *Settlements of the Ptolemies: city foundations and new settlements in the Hellenistic world.* Leuven, Paris and Dudley.

Muir, E. (1981) *Civic ritual in renaissance Venice.* Princeton.

Mumford, L. (1961) *The city in history: its origins, its transformation, and its prospects.* London.

Münzer, F. (1920) *Römische Adelsparteien und Adelsfamilien.* Stuttgart.

Murray, O. and S. Price eds. (1990) *The Greek city from Homer to Alexander.* Oxford.

Neri, V. (1998) *I marginali nell'occidente tardoantico: poveri, 'infames' e criminali nella nascente società cristiana.* Bari.

Nicolet, C. (1980) *The world of the citizen in Republican Rome.* Berkeley & Los Angeles.

Nicols, J. (2014) *Civic patronage in the Roman Empire.* Leiden & Boston.

Nippel, W. (1995) *Public order in Ancient Rome.* Cambridge.

North, J. (1990) 'Democratic politics in Republican Rome', *Past and Present* 126: 3–21.

(2006) 'The constitution of the Roman Republic', in N. Rosenstein and R. Morstein-Marx eds., *A companion to the Roman Republic*. Malden, Oxford & Carlton, 256–77.

Ober, J. (1989) *Mass and elite in democratic Athens: rhetoric, ideology, and the power of the people*. Princeton.

(2000) 'Quasi-rights: participatory citizenship and negative liberties in democratic Athens', *Social Philosophy and Policy* 17: 27–61.

(2001) *Political dissent in democratic Athens: intellectual critics of popular rule*. Princeton.

(2008) *Democracy and knowledge: innovation and learning in Classical Athens*. Princeton & Oxford.

(2010) 'Wealthy Hellas', *TAPA* 140: 231–86.

(2015) *The rise and fall of Classical Greece*. Princeton.

Ober, J. and C. Hedrick eds. (1996) *Demokratia: a conversation on democracies, ancient and modern*. Princeton.

O'Connor, A. M. (1983) *The African city*. London.

Oliver, G. J. (2007) *War, food, and politics in early Hellenistic Athens*. Oxford.

Osborne, M. J. (1981–1983) *Naturalization in Athens*. 4 vols. Verhandelingen van de Koninklijke Academie voor Wetenschappen, Letteren en Schone Kunsten van België. Klasse der Letteren. Brussels.

Osborne, R. (1985) *Demos: the discovery of Classical Attika*. Cambridge.

(1992) '"Is it a farm?" The definition of agricultural sites and settlements in Ancient Greece', in Wells ed. *Agriculture in Ancient Greece*. Stockholm, 21–8.

(1997) 'Law and laws: how do we join up the dots?', in Mitchell and Rhodes eds. *The development of the polis in Archaic Greece*. London & New York, 74–82.

(2002) Review of Cohen (2000), *CP* 97: 93–98.

(2005) 'Urban sprawl: what is urbanization and why does it matter?', in Osborne and Cunliffe eds. *Mediterranean urbanization 800–600 BC*. Proceedings of the British Academy 126. Oxford, 1–16.

(2009) *Greece in the making, 1200–479 BC*. 2nd edn., London & New York.

Osborne, R. and B. Cunliffe eds. (2005) *Mediterranean urbanization 800–600 BC*. Proceedings of the British Academy 126. Oxford.

Ostwald, M. (1986) *From popular sovereignty to the sovereignty of law: law, society, and politics in fifth-century Athens*. Berkeley.

(2000) *Oligarchia: the development of a constitutional form in Ancient Greece*. Stuttgart.

Owens, E. J. (1992) *The city in the Greek and Roman world*. London & New York.

Pareto, V. (1963) *The mind and society*. 4 vols. New York.

Parker, R. (1996) *Athenian religion: a history*. Oxford.

Parkin, A. (2006) '"You do him no service": an exploration of pagan almsgiving', in Atkins and Osborne eds. *Poverty in the Roman world*. Cambridge, 60–82.

Parkins, H. M. ed. (1997) *Roman urbanism: beyond the consumer city*. London & New York.

Parkins, H. M. and C. J. Smith eds. (1998) *Trade, traders and the ancient city.* London.

Parrish, D. ed. (2001) *Urbanism in western Asia Minor: new studies on Aphrodisias, Ephesos, Hierapolis, Pergamon, Perge and Xanthos. JRA* Suppl. 45. Portsmouth.

Patlagean, E. (1977) *Pauvreté économique et pauvreté sociale à Byzance, 4e–7e siècles.* Paris.

Patterson, J. R. (1991) 'Settlement, city and elite in Samnium and Lycia', in Rich and Wallace-Hadrill eds. *City and country in the ancient world.* New York & London, 150–72.

(2006) *Landscapes and cities: rural settlement and civic transformation in early imperial Italy.* Oxford.

Pearson, L. (1937) 'Party politics and free speech in Classical Athens', *G&R* 7: 41–50.

Pirenne, H. (1939) *Les villes et les institutions urbaines.* 2 vols. Paris.

Pleket, H. W. (1984) 'Urban elites and the economy in the Greek cities of the Roman empire', *Münstersche Beiträge zur antiken Handelsgeschichte* 3(1): 3–36.

(1990) 'Wirtschaft', in F. Vittinghoff ed., *Europäische Wirtschafts- und Sozialgeschichte in der römischen Kaiserzeit. Handbuch der europäischen Wirtschafts- und Sozialgeschichte.* Stuttgart, 25–160.

(1998) 'Political culture and political practice in the cities of Asia Minor in the Roman Empire', in W. Schuller ed., *Politische Theorie und Praxis im Altertum.* Darmstadt, 204–16

(2003) 'Economy and urbanization: was there an impact of empire in Asia Minor?', in E. Schwertheim and E. Winter eds., *Stadt und Stadtentwicklung in Kleinasien.* Asia Minor Studien Bd. 50. Bonn, 85–95.

Poehler, E. E. (2011) 'Where to park? Carts, stables, and the economics of transport in Pompeii', in Laurence and Newsome eds. *Rome, Ostia, Pompeii: movement and space.* Oxford, 194–214.

Polignac, F. de (1984) *La naissance de la cité grecque.* Paris.

Pomeranz, K. (2000) *The Great Divergence: China, Europe and the making of the modern world economy.* Princeton.

Postan, M. M. (1975) *The medieval economy and society.* Harmondsworth.

Potter, D. S. (2004) *The Roman empire at bay, AD 180–395.* London.

ed. (2006) *A companion to the Roman Empire.* Malden, Oxford & Carlton.

Potter, T. W. (1979) *The changing landscape of South Etruria.* London.

(1991) 'Towns and territories in southern Etruria', in Rich and Wallace-Hadrill eds. *City and country in the ancient world.* New York & London, 194–213.

Prak, M. (2010) 'The Dutch Republic as a bourgeois society', *BMGN - Low Countries Historical Review* 125(2–3): 107–39.

Price, S. R. F. (1984) *Rituals and power: the Roman imperial cult in Asia Minor.* Cambridge.

Provost, S. (2001) 'City walls and urban area in late-antique Macedonia: the case of Philippi', in Lavan ed. *Recent research in late-antique urbanism. JRA* Suppl. 42. Portsmouth, 123–35.

Purcell, N. (2010) 'Urbanism', in A. Barchiesi and W. Scheidel eds., *The Oxford Handbook of Roman Studies*. Oxford, 579–92.

Putnam, R. D. (1993) *Making democracy work: civic traditions in modern Italy*. Princeton.

(2000) *Bowling alone: the collapse and revival of American community*. New York.

Quass, F. (1993), *Die Honoratiorenschicht in den Städten des griechischen Ostens: Untersuchungen zur politischen und sozialen Entwicklung in hellenistischer und römischer Zeit*. Stuttgart.

Raaflaub, K. A. (1983) 'Democracy, oligarchy and the concept of the "free citizen" in late fifth-century Athens', *Political Theory* 11: 517–44.

(1993) 'Homer to Solon: the rise of the polis (the written sources)', in Hansen ed. *The Ancient Greek city-state*. Copenhagen, 41–105.

(1997) 'Homeric society', in Morris and Powell eds. *A new companion to Homer*. Leiden, 624–48.

(2000) 'Poets, lawgivers, and the beginnings of political reflection in Archaic Greece', in Rowe and Schofield eds. *The Cambridge History of Greek and Roman political thought*. Cambridge, 23–59.

Raaflaub, K. A., J. Ober and R. W. Wallace eds. (2007) *Origins of democracy in Ancient Greece*. Berkeley & Los Angeles.

Raaflaub, K. A. and H. van Wees eds. (2009) *A companion to Archaic Greece*. Malden & Oxford.

Raaflaub, K. A. and R. W. Wallace (2007) '"People's power" and egalitarian trends in Archaic Greece', in Raaflaub, Ober and Wallace eds. *Origins of democracy in Ancient Greece*. Berkeley & Los Angeles, 22–48.

Rapoport, A. (1988) 'Levels of meaning in the built environment', in F. Poyatos ed., *Cross-cultural perspectives in nonverbal communication*. Toronto, 317–36.

(1990) *The meaning of the built environment: a nonverbal communications approach*. Tucson.

Rapp, C. and H. A. Drake eds. (2014) *The city in the classical and post-classical world: changing contexts of power and identity*. Cambridge.

Rathbone, D. (1993) 'The census qualifications of the *assidui* and the *prima classis*', in H. Sancisi-Weerdenburg, R. J. Van der Spek, W. C. Teitler and H. T. Wallinga eds., *De Agricultura: in memoriam Pieter Willem de Neeve (1945–1990)*. Amsterdam, 121–52.

Ratté, C. (2001) 'New research on the urban development of Aphrodisias in late antiquity', in Parrish ed. *Urbanism in western Asia Minor: new studies on Aphrodisias, Ephesos, Hierapolis, Pergamon, Perge and Xanthos. JRA* Suppl. 45. Portsmouth , 117–47.

Reece, R. (1992) 'The end of the city in Roman Britain', in Rich ed. *The city in late antiquity*. London, 136–44.

Reinhold, M. (2002) 'Historian of the classical world: a critique of Rostovtzeff', in M. Reinhold, *Studies in classical history and society.* Oxford, 82–100 [orig. publ. in *Science & Society* 10(4) 1946: 361–91].

Renfrew, C. (1979) 'Systems collapse as social transformation: catastrophe and anastrophe in Early State Societies', in C. Renfrew and K. L. Cooke eds., *Transformations: mathematical approaches to culture change.* New York, San Francisco & London, 481–506.

  (2008) 'The city through time and space: transformations of centrality', in Marcus and Sabloff eds. *The ancient city: new perspectives on urbanism in the Old and New World.* Santa Fe, 29–51.

Rhodes, P. J. (1995) 'The "acephalous" polis?', *Historia* 44: 153–67.

Rich, J. ed. (1992) *The city in late antiquity.* London.

Rich, J. and G. Shipley eds. (1993) *War and society in the Greek world.* London & New York.

Rich, J. and A. Wallace-Hadrill eds. (1991) *City and country in the ancient world.* Leicester-Nottingham Studies in Ancient Society 2. London & New York.

Rickman, G. (1980) *The corn supply of Ancient Rome.* Oxford.

Robinson, E. W. (1997) *The first democracies: early popular government outside Athens.* Stuttgart.

  (2011) *Democracy beyond Athens: popular government in the Greek classical age.* Cambridge.

Rogers, G. M. (1991) *The sacred identity of Ephesos: foundation myths of a Roman city.* London & New York.

  (1992) 'The assembly of imperial Ephesos', *ZPE* 94: 224–8.

Rostovtzeff, M. (1941) *The social and economic history of the Hellenistic world.* 3 vols. Oxford.

  (1957) *The social and economic history of the Roman empire.* 2 vols., 2nd edn. Oxford.

Roueché, C. (1984) 'Acclamations in the later Roman empire: new evidence from Aphrodisias', *JRS* 74: 181–99.

  (1989) *Aphrodisias in late antiquity: the late Roman and Byzantine inscriptions including texts from the excavations at Aphrodisias conducted by Kenan T. Erim* (with contributions from J. M. Reynolds). London.

Rowe, C. and M. Schofield eds. (2000) *The Cambridge History of Greek and Roman political thought.* Cambridge.

Royden, H. L. (1988) *The magistrates of the Roman professional collegia in Italy from the first to the third century A.D.* Pisa.

Rozman, G. (1978) 'Urban networks and historical stages', *Journal of Interdisciplinary History* 9(1): 65–91.

Ruffing, K. (2008) *Die berufliche Spezialisierung in Handel und Handwerk: Untersuchungen zu ihrer Entwicklung und zu ihren Bedingungen in der römischen Kaiserzeit im östlichen Mittelmeerraum auf der Grundlage griechischer Inschriften und Papyri.* Rahden.

Runciman, W. G. (1990) 'Doomed to extinction: the *polis* as an evolutionary dead-end', in Murray and Price eds. *The Greek city from Homer to Alexander.* Oxford, 347–67.

Ruschenbusch, E. (1985) 'Die Zahl der griechischen Staaten und Arealgrösse und Bürgerzahl der "Normalpolis"', *ZPE* 59: 253–63.

Rykwert, J. (1976) *The idea of a town: the anthropology of urban form in Rome, Italy and the ancient world.* London.

Sallares, R. (1991) *The ecology of the Ancient Greek world.* London.

(2002) *Malaria and Rome: a history of malaria in Ancient Italy.* Oxford.

Saller, R. (1982) *Personal patronage under the early Empire.* Cambridge.

(1994) *Patriarchy, property and death in the Roman family.* Cambridge.

(2002) 'Framing the debate over growth in the ancient economy', in Scheidel and Von Reden eds. *The ancient economy.* New York, 251–69.

Salmon, J. (1999) 'The economic role of the Greek city', *G&R* 46(2): 147–67.

(2001) 'Temples the measures of men: public building in the Greek economy', in Mattingly and Salmon eds. *Economies beyond agriculture in the classical world.* London & New York, 195–208.

Scheid, J. (1985), 'Sacrifice et banquet à Rome: quelques problèmes', *Mélanges de l'École française de Rome – Antiquité* 97(1): 193–206.

Scheidel, W. (1994) 'Libitina's bitter gains: seasonal mortality and endemic disease in the ancient city of Rome', *Ancient Society* 25: 151–75.

(1999) 'Emperors, aristocrats and the Grim Reaper: towards a demographic profile of the Roman élite', *CQ* 49: 245–81.

(2001) *Death on the Nile: disease and the demography of Roman Egypt.* Leiden, Boston & Cologne.

(2002) 'A model of demographic and economic change in Roman Egypt after the Antonine plague', *JRA* 15: 97–114.

(2003a) 'Germs for Rome', in Edwards and Woolf eds. *Rome the cosmopolis.* Cambridge, 158–76.

(2003b) 'The Greek demographic expansion: models and comparisons', *JHS* 123: 120–40.

(2006) 'Stratification, deprivation and quality of life', in Atkins and Osborne eds. *Poverty in the Roman world.* Cambridge, 40–59.

(2007) 'Demography', in Scheidel, Morris and Saller eds. *The Cambridge Economic History of the Greco-Roman World.* Cambridge, 38–86.

(2008) 'Roman population size: the logic of the debate', in De Ligt and Northwood eds. *People, land, and politics: demographic developments and the transformation of Roman Italy, 300 BC–AD 14.* Leiden & Boston, 17–70.

ed. (2009) *Rome and China: comparative perspectives on ancient world empires.* Oxford.

ed. (2012a) *The Cambridge companion to the Roman economy.* Cambridge.

(2012b) 'Physical well-being', in Scheidel ed. *The Cambridge companion to the Roman economy.* Cambridge, 321–33.

(2012c) 'Roman wellbeing and the economic consequences of the Antonine Plague', in Lo Cascio ed. *L'impatto della "peste antonina".* Bari, 265–95.

ed. (2015) *State power in Ancient China and Rome*. Oxford.

Scheidel, W., I. Morris and R. Saller eds. (2007) *The Cambridge Economic History of the Greco-Roman World*. Cambridge.

Scheidel, W. and S. J. Friesen (2009) 'The size of the economy and the distribution of income in the Roman empire', *JRS* 99: 61–91.

Scheidel, W. and S. Von Reden eds. (2002) *The ancient economy*. New York.

Schmitt Pantel, P. (1990) 'Collective activities and the political in the Greek city', in Murray and Price eds. *The Greek city from Homer to Alexander*. Oxford, 199–213.

(1992) *La cité au banquet: histoire des repas publics dans les cités grecques*. Rome.

Schuler, Ch. (1998) *Ländliche Siedlungen und Gemeinden im hellenistischen und römischen Kleinasien*. Munich.

Schuller, W., W. Hoepfner and E. L. Schwandner eds. (1989) *Demokratie und Architektur: der hippodamische Städtebau und die Entstehung der Demokratie*. Munich.

Schwarz, H. (2001) *Soll oder Haben? Die Finanzwirtschaft kleinasiatischer Städte in der römischen Kaiserzeit am Beispiel von Bithynien, Lykien und Ephesos (29 v. Chr. - 284 n. Chr.)*. Bonn.

Scott, M. (2012) *Space and society in the Greek and Roman worlds*. Cambridge.

Scobie, A. (1986) 'Slums, sanitation, and mortality in the Roman world', *Klio* 68: 399–433.

Scully, S. (1981) 'The polis in Homer', *Ramus* 10: 1–34.

(1990) *Homer and the sacred city*. Ithaca.

Sears, G. (2007) *Late Roman African urbanism: continuity and transformation in the city* (BAR International Series 1693). Oxford.

Serfass, A. (2007) Review of Finn (2006a), *BMCR* 2007.07.50.

Shapiro, H. A. ed. (2007) *The Cambridge companion to Archaic Greece*. Cambridge.

Sharlin, A. (1978) 'Natural decrease in early modern cities: a reconsideration', *Past & Present* 79: 126–38.

Shaw, B. D. (1996) 'Seasons of death: aspects of mortality in imperial Rome', *JRS* 86: 100–38.

(2006) 'Seasonal mortality in imperial Rome and the Mediterranean: three problem cases', in Storey ed. *Urbanism in the preindustrial world: cross-cultural approaches*. Tuscaloosa, 86–109.

Silver, M. (2009) 'Glimpses of vertical integration/disintegration in Ancient Rome', *Ancient Society* 39: 171–84.

Sjöberg, G. (1960), *The preindustrial city: past and present*. Glencoe.

Slater, W. (2013) 'The victor's return, and the categories of games', in Martzavou and Papazarkadas eds. *Epigraphical approaches to the post-Classical polis*. Oxford, 139–63.

Small, D. B. (1987) 'Social correlations to the Greek cavea in the Roman period', in S. Macready and F. H. Thompson eds. *Roman architecture in the Greek world*. London, 85–93.

Smith, C. J. (1996) *Early Rome and Latium: economy and society c. 1000–500 B.C.* Oxford.

(1997) 'Servius Tullius, Cleisthenes and the emergence of the polis in Central Italy', in Mitchell and Rhodes eds. *The development of the polis in Archaic Greece.* London & New York., 208–16.

(2005) 'The beginnings of urbanization in Rome', in Osborne and Cunliffe eds. *Mediterranean urbanization 800–600 BC.* Proceedings of the British Academy 126. Oxford , 91–111.

(2011) 'Thinking about kings', *BICS* 54(2): 21–42.

Smith, M. E. (2007) 'Form and meaning in the earliest cities: a new approach to ancient urban planning', *Journal of Planning History* 6: 3–47.

(2009) 'V. Gordon Childe and the Urban Revolution: a historical perspective on a revolution in urban studies', *Town Planning Review* 80: 3–29.

Smith, M. L., ed. (2003a) *The social construction of ancient cities.* Washington DC & London.

(2003b) 'Introduction: the social construction of ancient cities', in M. L. Smith, ed. *The social construction of ancient cities.* Washington DC & London, 1–36.

(2003c) 'Early walled cities of the Indian Subcontinent as "Small Worlds"', in M. L. Smith ed. *The social construction of ancient cities.* Washington DC & London, 269–89.

Snodgrass, A. M. (1974) 'An historical Homeric society?', *JHS* 94: 114–25.

(1977) *Archaeology and the rise of the Greek state.* Cambridge.

(1980) *Archaic Greece: the age of experiment.* Berkeley & Los Angeles.

(1991) 'Archaeology and the study of the Greek city', in Rich and Wallace-Hadrill eds. *City and country in the ancient world.* New York & London, 1–23.

(1993) 'The rise of the polis: the archaeological evidence', in Hansen ed. *The Ancient Greek city-state.* Copenhagen, 30–9.

Sourvinou-Inwood, C. (1990) 'What is *polis* religion?', in Murray and Price eds. *The Greek city from Homer to Alexander.* Oxford, 295–322.

Spitzl, T. (1984) *Lex municipii Malacitani.* Munich.

Stambaugh, J. E. (1988) *The Ancient Roman city.* Baltimore & London.

Stanier, R. S. (1953) 'The cost of the Parthenon', *JHS* 73: 68–76.

Starr, C. G. (1986) *Individual and community: the rise of the polis, 800–500 BC.* New York.

Stek, T. D. and J. Pelgrom eds. (2014) *Roman Republican colonization: new perspectives from archaeology and ancient history.* Rome.

Storey, R. (1992) *Life and death in the ancient city of Teotihuacan: a modern paleodemographic synthesis.* Tuscaloosa.

Storey, G. R. (2006a) 'Introduction: urban demography of the past', in Storey ed. *Urbanism in the preindustrial world: cross-cultural approaches.* Tuscaloosa, 1–23.

ed. (2006b) *Urbanism in the preindustrial world: cross-cultural approaches.* Tuscaloosa.

Strauss, B. S. (1986) *Athens after the Peloponnesian War: class, faction and policy 403–386 B.C.* Beckenham.

Strootman, R. (2011) 'Kings and cities in the Hellenistic age', in van Nijf, Alston and Williamson eds. *Political culture in the Greek city after the classical age.* Groningen-Royal Holloway Studies on the Greek City after the Classical Age 2. Leuven, 141–53.

Strubbe, J. H. M. (1987) 'The *sitonia* in the cities of Asia Minor under the Principate (I)', *Epigraphica Anatolica* 10: 45–82.

(1989) 'The *sitonia* in the cities of Asia Minor under the Principate (II)', *Epigraphica Anatolica* 13: 97–122.

Tacoma, L. E. (2006) *Fragile hierarchies: the urban elites of third-century Roman Egypt.* Leiden.

(2008) 'Graveyards for Rome: migration to the city of Rome in the first two centuries A.D.' Unpublished working paper, available at http://media.leidenuniv.nl/legacy/graveyards-for-rome.pdf.

Taylor, L. R. (1966) *Roman voting assemblies: from the Hannibalic War to the dictatorship of Caesar.* Ann Arbor.

Thommen, L. (1996) *Lakedaimonion politeia: die Entstehung der spartanischen Verfassung.* Stuttgart.

Tilly, C. (1990) *Coercion, capital, and European states, AD 990–1990.* Cambridge, MA.

Todd, S. C. (1993) *The shape of Athenian law.* Oxford.

Tomlinson, R. A. (1972) *Argos and the Argolid: from the end of the Bronze Age to the Roman occupation.* London.

Toner, J. P. (2002) *Rethinking Roman history.* Cambridge.

Tran, N. (2006) *Les membres des associations romaines: le rang social des collegiati en Italie et en Gaules, sous le Haut-Empire.* Rome.

Treggiari, S. (1969) *Roman freedmen during the late Republic.* Oxford.

(1980) 'Urban labour in Rome: *mercennarii* and *tabernarii*', in P. Garnsey ed., *Non-slave labour in the Greco-Roman world.* Cambridge, 48–64.

Trevett, J. (1992) *Apollodorus, the son of Pasion.* Oxford.

Trexler, R. C. (1980) *Public life in renaissance Florence.* New York.

Trigger, B. (1972) 'Determinants of urban growth in pre-industrial society', in Ucko, Tringham and Dimbleby eds. *Man, settlement and urbanism.* Cambridge, MA, 575–99.

(1990) 'Monumental architecture: a thermodynamic explanation of symbolic behaviour', *World Archaeology* 22: 119–32.

(2003) *Understanding early civilizations.* Cambridge.

Trümper, M. (2011) 'Where the non-Delians met in Delos: the meeting-places of foreign associations and ethnic communities in late Hellenistic Delos', in van Nijf, Alston and Williamson eds. *Political culture in the Greek city after the classical age.* Groningen-Royal Holloway Studies on the Greek City after the Classical Age 2. Leuven, 49–100.

Tscherikower, V. (1927) *Die hellenistischen Städtegründungen von Alexander dem Grossen bis auf die Römerzeit.* Leipzig.

Ucko, P. J., R. Tringham and G. W. Dimbleby eds. (1972) *Man, settlement and urbanism*. Cambridge, MA.

Valdés Guía, M. and J. Gallego (2010) 'Athenian *zeugitai* and the Solonian census classes: new reflections and perspectives', *Historia* 59(3): 257–81.

van Andel, T. H. and C. Runnels (1987) *Beyond the Acropolis: a rural Greek past*. Stanford.

Vandevoorde, L. (2013) 'Respectability on display: *alba* and *fasti* of the *Augustales in the context of collegial and magisterial hierarchy', *Revue Belge de Philologie et d'Histoire* 91(1): 127–52.

van Nes, A. (2011) 'Measuring spatial visibility, adjacency, permeability, and degrees of street life in Pompeii', in Laurence and Newsome eds. *Rome, Ostia, Pompeii: movement and space*. Oxford, 100–17.

van Nijf, O. M. (1997) *The civic world of professional associations in the Roman east*. Amsterdam.

(2000) 'Inscriptions and civic memory in the Roman East', in A. Cooley ed. *The afterlife of inscriptions: reusing, rediscovering, reinventing & revitalizing ancient inscriptions*. BICS 44 (Suppl. 75). London, 21–36.

(2011) 'Public space and the political culture of Roman Termessos', in van Nijf, Alston and Williamson eds. *Political culture in the Greek city after the classical age*. Groningen-Royal Holloway Studies on the Greek City after the Classical Age 2. Leuven, 215–42.

van Nijf, O. M., R. Alston and C. G. Williamson eds. (2011) *Political culture in the Greek city after the classical age*. Groningen-Royal Holloway Studies on the Greek City after the Classical Age 2. Leuven.

van Zanden, J. L. and M. Prak (2006) 'Towards an economic interpretation of citizenship: the Dutch Republic between medieval communes and modern nation-states', *European Review of Economic History* 10: 111–45.

Verboven, K. (2007) 'The associative order: status and ethos among Roman businessmen in Late Republic and Early Empire', *Athenaeum* 95: 861–93.

(2009) 'Magistrates, patrons and benefactors of *collegia*: status building and romanisation in the Spanish, Gallic and German provinces', in B. Antela-Bernárdez and T. Ñaco del Hoyo (eds.) *Transforming historical landscapes in the ancient empires*. BAR Int. Ser. 1986. Oxford, 159–67.

(2011) 'Professional *collegia*: guilds or social clubs?', *Ancient Society* 41: 187–95.

Veyne, P. (1976) *Le pain et le cirque: sociologie historique d'un pluralisme politique*. Paris.

(2000) 'La "plèbe moyenne" sous le Haut-Empire romain', *Annales. Histoire, Sciences Sociales* 55: 1169–99.

Vlassopoulos, K. (2007a) *Unthinking the Greek polis: Ancient Greek history beyond Eurocentrism*. Cambridge.

(2007b) 'Free spaces: identity, experience and democracy in Classical Athens', *CQ* 57(1): 33–52.

Von Reden, S. (2003) *Exchange in Ancient Greece*. London.

(2007) 'Classical Greece: consumption', in Scheidel, Morris and Saller eds. *The Cambridge Economic History of the Greco-Roman World*. Cambridge, 385–406.

Von Thünen, J. H. (1930) *Der isolierte Staat in Beziehung auf Landwirtschaft und Nationalökonomie*. Jena.

Wallace-Hadrill, A. (1990) 'The social spread of Roman luxury: sampling Pompeii and Herculaneum', *PBSR* 58: 145–92.

(1991) 'Elites and trade in the Roman town', in Rich and Wallace-Hadrill eds. *City and country in the ancient world*. New York & London, 244–77.

(1994) *Houses and society in Pompeii and Herculaneum*. Princeton.

(2013) 'Trying to define and identify the Roman "middle classes"', *JRA* 26: 605–9.

Ward-Perkins, J. B. (1984) *From Classical Antiquity to the Middle Ages: urban public building in Northern and Central Italy AD 300–850*. Oxford.

Ward-Perkins, B. (1998) 'The cities', in A. Cameron and P. Garnsey eds., *The Cambridge Ancient History. Vol. 13. The Late Empire, A.D. 337–425*. 2nd edn. Cambridge, 371–410.

(2005) *The fall of Rome and the end of civilization*. Oxford.

Weaver, P. R. C. (1972) *Familia Caesaris: a social study of the emperor's freedmen and slaves*. Cambridge.

Weber, M. (1958) *The city*. New York.

(1972) *Wirtschaft und Gesellschaft: Grundriss der verstehenden Soziologie*. 5. Auflage. Tübingen = (1978) *Economy and society*. Ed. G. Roth and C. Wittich. 2 vols. Berkeley, Los Angeles & London.

Wells, B. ed. (1992). *Agriculture in Ancient Greece*. Proceedings of the 7th International Symposium, Swedish Institute at Athens. Stockholm.

Whitby, M. (2006) 'Factions, bishops, violence and urban decline', in Krause and Witschel eds. *Die Stadt in der Spätantike – Niedergang oder Wandel?* Stuttgart, 441–61.

Whitehead, D. (1977) *The ideology of the Athenian metic. PCPhS* Suppl. 2. Cambridge.

(1986) *The demes of Attica, 508/7–ca. 250 B.C.: a political and social study*. Princeton.

Whittaker, C. R. (1990) 'The consumer city revisited: the *vicus* and the city', *JRA* 3: 110–8.

Whittaker, C. R. and P. Garnsey (1998) 'Rural life in the later Roman empire', in A. Cameron and P. Garnsey eds., *The Cambridge Ancient History. Vol. 13. The Late Empire, A.D. 337–425*. 2nd edn. Cambridge, 277–311.

Whittow, M. (1990) 'Ruling the late Roman and early Byzantine city: a continuous history', *Past & Present* 129: 3–29.

(1996) *The making of orthodox Byzantium, 600–1025*. Basingstoke.

(2001) 'Recent research on the late-antique city in Asia Minor: the second half of the 6th c. revisited', in Lavan ed. *Recent research in late-antique urbanism. JRA* Suppl. 42. Portsmouth, 137–53.

Wickham, C. (2005) *Framing the early Middle Ages: Europe and the Mediterranean, 400–800*. Oxford.

Wijma, S. (2010) *Joining the Athenian community: the participation of metics in Athenian polis religion in the fifth and fourth centuries B.C.* Unpub. PhD Thesis, Utrecht.

(2014) *Embracing the immigrant: the participation of metics in Athenian polis religion (5th–4th century BC)*. Stuttgart.

Wilson, A. (2011) 'City sizes and urbanization in the Roman empire', in Bowman and Wilson eds. *Settlement, urbanization, and population*. Oxford Studies on the Roman Economy. Oxford, 161–95.

'Raw materials and energy' in Scheidel ed. *The Cambridge companion to the Roman economy*. Cambridge, 133–55.

Wilson, P. (2000) *The Athenian institution of the Khoregia: the chorus, the city, and the stage*. Cambridge.

Wisseman Christie, J. (1991) 'States without cities: demographic trends in early Java', *Indonesia* 52: 23–40.

Witcher, R. (2008) 'Regional field survey and the demography of Roman Italy', in De Ligt and Northwood eds. *People, land, and politics: demographic developments and the transformation of Roman Italy, 300 BC–AD 14*. Leiden & Boston, 273–303.

Woolf, G. (1997) 'The Roman urbanization of the East', in S. E. Alcock ed., *The early Roman Empire in the East*. Oxbow Monographs 95. Oxford, 1–14.

Wrigley, E. A. (1967) 'A simple model of London's importance in changing English society and economy 1650–1750', *Past & Present* 37: 44–70.

(1990) *Continuity, chance and change: the character of the Industrial Revolution in England*. Cambridge.

Wycherley, R. E. (1949) *How the Greeks built cities*. London [2nd edn. 1962].

(1956) 'The market of Athens: topography and monuments', *G&R* 3(1): 2–23.

Yakobson, A. (1999) *Elections and electioneering in Rome: a study in the political system of the late Republic*. Stuttgart.

Yavetz, Z. (1958) 'The living conditions of the urban *plebs* in Republican Rome', *Latomus* 17: 500–17.

(1969) *Plebs and princeps*. Oxford.

Zanker, P. (1990) *The power of images in the age of Augustus*. Ann Arbor.

Zeder, M. A. (1991) *Feeding cities*. Washington.

Zuiderhoek, A. (2007) 'The ambiguity of munificence', *Historia* 56: 196–213.

(2008a) 'On the political sociology of the imperial Greek city', *GRBS* 48: 417–45.

(2008b) 'Feeding the citizens: municipal grain funds and civic benefactors in the Roman East', in Alston and van Nijf eds. *Feeding the Ancient Greek city*. Groningen-Royal Holloway Studies on the Greek City after the Classical Age 1. Leuven, 159–180.

(2009a) *The politics of munificence in the Roman empire: citizens, elites and benefactors in Asia Minor*. Cambridge.

(2009b) 'Government centralization in late second and third century A.D. Asia Minor: a working hypothesis', *CW* 103(1): 39–51.

(2011) 'Oligarchs and benefactors: elite demography and euergetism in the Greek east of the Roman empire', in van Nijf, Alston and Williamson eds. *Political culture in the Greek city after the classical age*. Groningen-Royal Holloway Studies on the Greek City after the Classical Age 2. Leuven, 185–95.

Index

aediles, 92, 138, 175
Aegina, 145
ager, 37, 67
agora, 29–30, 65, 67, 69, 86, 146
  and forum in late antique cities, 184
  Athenian, 69, 142, 188
agoranomoi, 92, 138, 175
agricultural productivity, 24
  in Classical Greece, 115
agriculture, 11–12, 20, 50, 55, 77, 106, 109, 113, 118,
  126, 134
  in city and suburban areas, 133
agro-towns, 45
Alba Fucens, 59
Alexandria, Egypt, 3, 22, 58, 145
amphitheatres, 65, 96
ancient city, concept of, 1, 8
ancient economy, Finley's model of, 11, 17
animals, in cities, 133
annona, 145
Antioch, Syria, 3, 51, 145
Aphrodisias, 171
aqueducts, 146
arboriculture, 40
archaeological surface surveys, results of, 38
Archaic polis, 3, 26
Archaic Rome, 26, 28–9
archons, 92
Areopagus, 88
Argos, 24, 29, 31, 89
associations, 13, 18, 138, 147, 189
  at Athens, 121
  in Hellenistic poleis, 122
  professional, 102, 140
  Roman professional, 126
  Roman professional, organisation of, 125
asty, 37
Athens, 24, 27, 29–30, 46, 49, 54, 58, 66, 68, 87,
  89, 96, 109, 133, 141–2, 144–5, 188–9
  grain supply of, 49
  magistrates at, 90

Augusta Praetoria, 61
augustales, 102, 124, 129
autonomy, as characteristic of the polis, 158

banquet, public, 94
basilica, 65
baths, 146
benefactors, public, 94, 180
bishop and clergy, role in late antique cities, 174–5,
  180–1
bourgeoisie, 13
  in medieval and early modern Europe, 106

capitalism, 10–12, 14, 43, 107, 130–1
Carthage, 7, 76, 145
Celaenae-Apamea, 38, 141
cemeteries, 30
censors
  at Rome, 92
  urban, 143
census classes, Roman, 110, 126
Central Place Theory, 51
charity, 181
chattel slaves, 111
children, 96, 102, 110
chora, 37–8, 41, 49, 51
churches, 184
circus, 97
cities and states, 149, 159
citizen community, 20
citizens, 110
  differentiation among citizens in poleis, 114
citizenship, 8, 11–12, 19, 28, 78, 146, 181
  Greek, 26
  origin of, 26
  Roman, 26, 28, 83
city and country, 37
  in late antiquity, 176
  literary representations of, 41
city council, 78, 86–7, 153
  at Sparta, 82, 88

city council (cont.)
  replacement by 'notables' in late antique cities,
    173
city councillors, 93, 102–3, 122, 129, 156
city plan, 3
  'organic', 57
  orthogonal ('Hippodamian'), 33, 57, 59
city walls, 1, 29, 40, 67, 183
city, definition of, 4
  density, 4
  Greek and Roman definition, 7
  legal and political criteria, 7
  population, 4
  population makeup, 5
  universal concept of urbanism, 7
city-state, 149, 159
  and macro-state, 150
city-state cultures, 150
civic identity, 94
civic ideology, Athenian, 112
civic model of society, 180, 182
civic munificence, 101, 103
  in late antiquity, 182
civic political institutions, 78
civic politics, 78, 189
  Christianization of, 176
  in late antiquity, 169
civic ritual, 94
civil society, 19
civitates peregrinae, 7, 84
cohesion, civic, 99
collective practices, 95–6
collegia. See associations
collegia magistrates, 129
colonia. See colonies
Colonia Agrippina, 61
colonies
  Greek, 21, 32
  Latin, 83
  Roman, 7, 22, 34, 84, 92, 187
colonisation, Archaic Greek, 25, 32, 187
concentration of wealth, in democratic Athens, 116
construction, 138
consuls, 91–2, 155
consumer city, 11, 13–14, 44, 132, 188
  criticism of the model, 44
  Erdkamp's model of, 46
cooperation, between citizens and non-citizens in
    the polis, 112
Corinth, 27, 31, 144–5
Cosa, 59
Council of 500, 79, 87
council of elders, 88
created cities, 21
cross-town traffic, 70

crystallisation of the polis, 23
cult rituals, 95
curatores rei publicae, 172
cursus honorum, 92
customs dues, 142
Cyrene, 30, 97, 189

dairy farming, 50, 133
decline
  of cities, 167, 188
  of the Roman Empire, 167
defensor civitatis, 173
Delos, 142
demand, seasonality of, 138
demes, 37, 121
democracy, 11, 82, 89, 189
  Athenian, 79
  in the Roman Republic, 84, 190
democracy, Athenian
  reality of, 80
democratic cities, 79
demographic volatility
  and social mobility, in Classical poleis, 119
  and social mobility, in Roman cities, 128
dispersed cities, 5
distributions, 95, 102
  of grain, 145
diversity, within status groups, 110
division of labour, 134
Dreros, 30
  archaic law, 27, 90
duoviri, 92

economic growth, 44
  in Archaic and Classical Greece, 116
elections
  Roman, 85
elitist school in political theory, 79, 157
emperors, Roman, 51
empire, Athenian, 33
Emporiae, 70
Ephesus, 68, 98, 102, 145, 183
ephors, 82, 92
Epidaurus, 143
equality, political, 12
  and economic growth, 117
Erythrai, 163
ethnos, 13, 16–17, 25, 160
Etruscan cities, 28, 83
European urban exceptionalism, 107

factories, 137–8
failed poleis, 29
farmers, 108, 115
Ferentinum, 102

fertility, 5, 74
festivals, 40, 94, 103, 189
  gifts towards, 104
  tax remissions during, 143
Finley, Moses
  model of ancient city, 9, 11, 44, 131
  spectrum of statuses model, 111
food supply, urban, 144, 189
formalisation of the polis, 23, 28
forum, 29–30, 65, 67, 86, 146
foundation of cities, 51
  Hellenistic, 34
  Roman, 34
founder, colonial, 33
free spaces, in the Greek polis, 120
freedmen, 11, 13, 44, 96, 102, 110, 189
  at Athens, 112
  economic role in the polis, 112
  Roman, 123
  Roman, differentiation among, 123
Fustel de Coulanges, 9, 68

games, 95–7, 104, 110, 184
grain, 139
  import of, 144
grain funds, municipal, 145
gymnasium, 65, 146

Hellenistic kings and cities, relationship
  between, 162
helots, 82
Hierapolis, 139
hinterland, 6, 49, 133
Hippodamus of Miletus, 59
Homeric *basileis*, 22
Homeric polis, 22
homoioi, 82
honestiores, 122
Honoratiorenschicht, 79, 81
horticulture, 40, 50, 133
humiliores, 122

identity, collective, 97
imperium, 91–2, 155
Industrial Revolution, 12, 14, 107, 131
insula, 61, 72, 137
Iron Law of Oligarchy, 79, 189
Ithaca, 7, 24

jury courts, 79

Kaunos, 142
kingdoms, Hellenistic, 162
kings
  at Sparta, 82

Hellenistic, 34, 51
  in Archaic Rome, 28, 82
kitchen gardens, 40, 133
koinon, 18, 158, 160
Korykos, 135, 179
Kyme, 94, 102
Kyzikos, 142

landownership, in Attica, 116
Laodicea, 139
Latium Vetus, 25
  cities in, 83
leisure class, at Athens, 114
liberti. *See* freedmen
liturgies, at Athens, 104
liturgy-class, at Athens, 114
livestock breeding, 50
Lydian kingdom, 159

Macedon, kingdom of, 54, 159
magistracies
  categorisation of, 92
  in Republican Rome, 83
magistrates, 78, 155
  election of, 91
  power of, 91
  rules and regulations concerning, 90
manufacture, 13, 48, 131–2, 188
  specialised, 134
manufacture and commerce, elite involvement
  in, 137
manufacturers, 108, 143
market dues, 142
Megara, 30, 145
Megara Hyblaea, 30, 33, 59
memory, civic, 97
Metapontum, 30
metoikion, 120, 142
metoikoi. *See* resident foreigners
middle class, 11, 129
  dominating the Athenian assembly, 80
  in medieval and early modern European cities, 106
  or bourgeoisie, absence in ancient cities, 107
middling groups, 31, 86, 108, 130, 189
  in the Classical polis, 118
  Roman, economic basis of, 126
  Roman, or *plebs media*, not a bourgeoisie/
    middle class, 127
  size at Athens, 115
  size of, in fourth century BCE Greek world, 115
  size of, in Roman Empire, 124
middling ideology, in Archaic Greece, 117
Miletus, 59, 139
mixed constitution, 82, 84
monarchy, 82

monopoly of violence, 152, 154
mortality, 5, 74
  seasonal, 76
municipal charters, Roman, 90
municipium, 7, 34, 83, 92
  Latin, 84
Myra, 142

naturalisation, in Greek poleis, 112, 120
nauarchs, 92
Nemausus, 38, 141
Nicaea, 144
non-citizens in the polis, social differentiation, 112

Oenoanda, 38, 40
oligarchic poleis, 80
oligarchy, 82, 89
  in the Roman Republic, 84
olive oil, 139
Olynthus, 59
Orcistus, 7
ordo decurionum, 103, 124
  decline of, in late antique cities, 170
ordo equester, 107, 122
ordo senatorius, 122
origins of the ancient city, 20, 187
Ostia, 70

Palmyra, 142
Parthenon, 68, 143
participation, 78
participation, political, 12
  economic effects, 19, 146
participatory ideal (of the polis), 79
pastoralism, 50
patronage, 78, 84
  civic, 165
Pergamon, 68
Pericles, citizenship law of, 120
perioikoi, 82
Persia, confrontation of the Greeks with, 160
philoi, 81, 162
Piraeus, 59, 145
plebs media, 125, 189
  as origin of *collegia* membership, 126
Pnyx, 66, 86
polis membership, concept of, 120
polis/civitas as a stateless society, 151–2, 190
  and collective practices, 100
political autonomy, 16
political systems, 79
Pompeii, 62, 69–70, 85, 90, 133, 136, 143, 186–8, 190
popular assembly, 78, 89
  at Athens, 89
  City of Rome, 28, 83, 89

Greek, 28, 42, 79, 153
  in Roman cities, 90
  Roman, 85, 155
  Sparta, 82
post-Classical polis, 187
  monumentalisation of, 65
  oligarchisation of, 81, 160, 189
  popular politics in, 81, 161
post-Roman urban continuity, model of, 184
praetors, 91–2, 155
predation, 147, 166, 175
price regulation, 145
Priene, 59
probouleusis, 88
processions, 95–6, 104
  at imperial Ephesus, 98
producer city, 11, 14, 43
property rights, 146
property, urban, 137
public banquet
  Greek, 101
  Roman, 101
public buildings, 57–8, 143
  gifts towards, 104
  in late antique cities, 183
public honours, 104
public slaves, 111

quaestors, 92
quattuorviri, 92

rank-size model, 52
resident foreigners, 11, 13, 44, 95, 102, 110, 142, 189
  at Athens, 112
  Athenian, integration of, 121
  economic role in the polis, 112
  participation in festivals, 96
  privileges of, in Classical poleis, 120
retailers, 108, 142
revenues, of cities, 141
Rhodes, 141
Roman emperors and cities, relationship between, 163
Roman provincial city, 3, 42
Roman Republic, 51, 66, 151
Rome, City of, 30, 46, 54, 68–9, 76, 133, 141, 144, 187–8
  food supply of, 50
  immigration into, 73
  material appearance after Augustus, 66
  public building, 144

Samos, 145
Scheria, 28
Selinous, 59
Selymbria, 145

Senate
  in Archaic Rome, 82
  in Republican Rome, 83–4, 87–8, 155
senatusconsulta, 88
service city, 13
service providers, 108, 143
service provision, 132
sewers, 72, 146
ship-building, 138
Silchester, 70
sitonai, 92
slavery, 11
slaves, 11, 13, 44, 96, 111, 113, 142, 182
  economic role in the polis, 112
social hierarchy, civic, 101
social mobility, 106, 108
  among non-citizens in Classical poleis, 119
  in Roman cities, 128
  in the Classical polis, 118
Solon, reforms of, 27–8, 110, 114, 145
Sparta, 8, 24, 27, 29, 33, 54, 82, 89, 109, 119, 151
specialisation, 134, 179, 188
  horizontal, 134, 139
  occupational, 5, 21, 135
  vertical, 134, 138
specialist cities, 139
spread of cities, 20, 32
stasis, 156
state and society, in the polis, 109
state formation, cities and, 20
state, definition of, 149, 157
status groups, at Athens, 111
strategoi, 92
stratification
  in Roman imperial cities, 122
  in the Classical polis, 111
streets, 58, 67, 70
suburban areas, 40, 133
synoecism, 24

Tarsus, 139
taxation
  civic control over, in late antiquity, 177
  direct, 141
  indirect, 142
temples, 29–30, 58, 65, 146
Teos, 142
Termessos, 68
territorium, 37, 41, 49, 51
textile manufacture, 139
Thasos, 141
theatres, 86, 96, 146
Thera, 97
Tifernum, 38
trade, 13, 48, 131–2, 188

interregional, 139
traders, 108, 143
trades and crafts, geographical clustering of, 140
transaction costs, 48, 138, 175
tribunes of the *plebs*, 92
Troy, 7, 23

urban disease environment, 18, 72, 76
urban ecology, 18
urban economy, 131, 188
  in late antiquity, 178
  intervention by civic authorities, 140
urban excess mortality, 17
'urban graveyard' theory, 5, 72–3
  criticism of, 74
urban landscape, 5, 7, 18, 20, 56–7, 86, 133, 188
  differences between Greek and Roman, 65
  in late antiquity, 183
  meaning of, 67
  origin of typical Greco-Roman, 28
urban living conditions, 71
urban network, 4, 50, 54, 188
  'top-heavy', 35, 52
Urban Revolution, Childe's model of, 6, 20, 57, 186
urban society, 106
  stratification, 106
urban space, 18
  innovative approaches to, 71
urban street networks, 70
urban systems, 14, 52
urbanisation, 3, 5, 35, 137, 187–8
  as proxy for agricultural productivity, 55
urbanism, comparative study of, 2
urbs, 37, 67

Veii, 141
villages, 1, 37–8, 41, 50, 149
  political institutions, 40
Von Thünen's model of agricultural location, 50
voting
  at Athens, 89
  in Sparta, 89

Weber, Max, model of ancient city, 9–10, 44
wholesale traders, 142
wine, 139
wives, of citizens, 110
women, 96, 102, 113, 142
wool production, 139
workshops, 62, 136, 138, 189
  location of, 136
  public, 141
  Roman, 127

CPSIA information can be obtained
at www.ICGtesting.com
Printed in the USA
FFHW02n2123050818
47668714-51286FF